TRADING

FOR A LIVING

HOW TO TRADE FOR BEGINNERS

4 BOOKS IN 1

Download the Audio Book Version of This Book for FREE

If you love listening to audio books on-the-go, I have great news for you. You can download the audio book version of this book for **FREE** just by signing up for a **FREE** 30-day audible trial!

See below for more details!

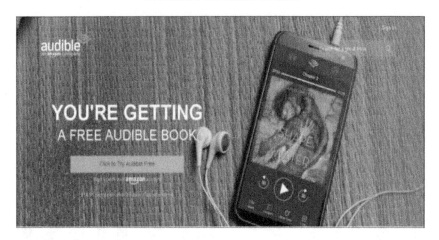

Audible Trial Benefits

As an audible customer, you will receive the below benefits with your 30-day free trial:

Chapter 1. FREE audible book copy of this book

Chapter 2. After the trial, you will get 1 credit each month to use on any audiobook

Chapter 3. Your credits automatically roll over to the next month if you don't use them

Chapter 4. Choose from Audible's 200,000 + titles

Chapter 5. Listen anywhere with the Audible app across multiple devices

Chapter 6. Make easy, no-hassle exchanges of any audiobook you don't love

Chapter 7. Keep your audiobooks forever, even if you cancel your membership

click the links below to get started!

For Audible US

For Audible UK

For Audible FR

For Audible DE

Table of Contents

BOOK 4 CRYPTO

STOCK MARKET

INVESTING

A Crash Course Guide to Trading from

Beginners to Expert:

How to Create Passive Income to Get

Fresh Money to Buy and Sell Options

Anthony Sinclair

Introduction

The fact is that for most young people, investing might not be the most important thing in their lives. Until they get older and established in a career, saving and investing for retirement may not be at the top of their priority list; there are other things that might seem more pressing and exciting at this stage in life.

When you're young, you have limited resources to invest. You're also still trying to figure out who you are — what kind of career or education you want to pursue, and how much risk you want to take with your money. For these reasons, it's not a good idea to jump into the stock market before you have a better handle on your financial circumstances and goals.

This doesn't mean you'll never be able to invest in the stock market, but it does mean that you're a long way off from making a decision that will have a major impact on your life. Until then, there are plenty of other ways to get started with investing and he stock market without getting ahead of yourself.

It is difficult to believe there was a time when the stock market didn't exist. The stock market is on the tip of nearly everyone's tongue. Even individuals who do not invest at least know it exists. It is largely understood that the New York Stock Exchange is the biggest market of them all, with any company listed on it that wants to be recognized globally. However, how did the stock market come to fruition? Is there more than the NYSE (New York Stock Exchange)? There are more exchanges and it started with the Real Merchants of Venice and British Coffeehouses.

Europe was filled with moneylenders that filled in the gaps of the larger banks. Moneylenders would trade between themselves. One lender might get rid of a high-risk, high-interest loan by trading it to another lender. Moneylenders also purchased government debt. In a natural evolution, lenders started selling debts to customers who were looking to invest.

Investors also put their money into ships and crews. Most of the time-limited liability companies would go on a single voyage to gain merchandise from Asia and the East Indies as a way to bring a profit to the investor. New companies were usually formed for the next voyage to reduce the risk of investing in ships that could end up in disaster. The East India companies worked with investors by providing dividends made from the goods that came in. Stocks were now in place, where the first joint-stock company was created. At the time, there were royal charters that made competition impossible and thus, investors gained huge profits.

It was not without its troubles. The stock market is based on economic stability. When instability reigns the stock market can crash because there is no liquidity, which is what happened during the Great Depression. Everyone saw the banks failing due to debts and little liquidity, which in turn caused others to suffer, businesses too close, and stock shares to plummet.

The stock market formed from a need to have a place to conduct the business of selling shares, which was already happening. Governments needed to regulate stock sales, and prevent issues like the SSC crash. Nevertheless, there was also greed on behalf of wealthy citizens. There was a clear way to earn money from someone else's labor, thus the stock exchanges were started.

Investors and traders sell stocks after the IPO based on the perceived value. A company's value can go up or down, which is where investors make their money. A company's stock price that rises can provide a profit. If an investor has purchased those shares and the price or company value decreases, then the investor will lose money. In addition, the investors and traders will push the price in an up or down direction.

Investors have one of two goals: investing in the short or the long term. A long-term investment is based on a stock continuing to rise in price. A short-term investment is to gain quick cash and pulling out before the stock price decreases.

Mature companies offer dividends to their shareholders. If you have stocks, then you are a shareholder in a company. If you hold the stocks long enough and have enough stock in a company, you can vote on new board members. Dividends are company profits that you get a cut of.

Investors will make money on the price fluctuations and the dividends. A seller is often trying to gain a profit by selling to a new buyer. The new buyer is also trying to buy as low as possible so that when the stock price continues to increase, they will make a profit.

The profit is calculated by taking the initial buy price and subtracting it from the closing or sale price. For example, if you buy into Google at $400 and wait for it to go up to $600, then the profit is $200 per share.

Sellers can push the price down due to supply and demand. This financial market works based on supply and demand.

You should already know that in economics when there is an oversupply of a product, the price is low. There is no demand for the product; therefore, a company or in this case a stock is not of interest.

When there is an undersupply of something like a stock, the demand is high. With more interested parties, the price will continue to increase.

If there is an even amount of supply and demand, then equality exists and there is no movement to see.

For the stock market, when too many people sell a stock, the price will decline. When too many people buy a stock, the price will continue to rise. If there is an equal number of shares and interest, then the price usually trades sideways because there is a balance.

As you learn about the stock market, you will hear the word volume, often. Volume is the number of shares that change hands on a daily basis. Millions of shares can be traded on the stock exchange in a day as investors attempt to make money from increasing or decreasing prices.

The stock market works based on the interest or volume of traders. If a stock does not have any volume or very little, then it is not being actively traded, thus the price is not moving. Traders such as market makers get into the market in order to buy or sell stocks for companies with low volume. They do not stop a stock from rising or falling. Instead, market makers just trying to garner interest in the company's stock.

When it comes to the stock market and traders, most individuals are looking for high-volume traders, with fluctuating prices. They get in, make a profit, and get out finding the next big profit.

BEGINNERS

Chapter 1. The Basics of Investing in Stocks

.0 6
27 1 | P1
11 6 | Water £

hare Price

Delayed gratification is a strong suit that few have and this is why investing has always been a challenge for many. You want to make money but not in a decade or a couple of years, but right now. Ponzi schemes aside, profitable investments that can actually build you wealth for a lifetime take time and lots of patience. These two things are probably the most important tools that any beginner in stock market investing needs to be aware of.

Our motivations for investing may differ but ultimately all investments have one goal in common; to make a return or profit on the investment. You may be eyeing early retirement, you may be in it for financial freedom or maybe you are just sick of having your money sitting in a savings account attracting point nothing interest. Regardless of what your goals are, the idea behind investing is that you use your money to make more money.

The stock market presents a unique opportunity for both retail and corporate investors because anyone can do it at any scale. You can invest as little as $1000 or as much as a million dollars. There are room and opportunity for everyone to get in and make a decent return on their investment. That said, the stock market is not the way to go if you want quick money. Stocks like most other investments have one thing in common; they depend on the power of time.

Time is your biggest ally when it comes to investing. If you have been waiting for a magical moment when you will have "enough" money to start investing, the bad news is that you will probably never have "enough" money and the other bad news is that the right time to start investing was yesterday.

A common misconception that most people have is that you need to have a lot of money to start investing. In actual fact, people who invest do not necessarily have more money than you, they simply make investing a priority. And because they make investing a priority, they end up having more money than you. See how that works?

Unlike consumption, investment takes money out of your pocket and puts it towards your future. When you can think of investment as an insurance policy to safeguard your financial future then the decision on when and if to invest becomes pretty much a no-brainer. Nobody wants to be cash-strapped forever or have to work themselves to the grave because they did not put their money to work when they had the chance.

The beauty of this golden age of technology that we live in is that anyone with the will and determination to do so can access all the tools they need to start investing in the stock market. This ease of accessibility coupled with its affordability has made the stock market increasingly popular with retail investors. With just a few a hundred dollars you can find an online brokerage at the click of a button and get started as an investor in the stock market. Yes, it is that easy. Before you jump on the bandwagon, however, it is important to understand what you are investing in. The natural starting point is, of course, understanding how the stock market works.

How Does the Stock Market Work?

It is no coincidence that most people who have wealth have a big part of this wealth invested in stocks. Stocks carry their fair share of risks for any investor but when done right, stock market investing can be one of the most efficient ways to build and retain wealth.

A stock market is an exchange where people trade by buying and selling shares on traded companies. Once you have bought shares in a company your stock gives you ownership of a small part of that company. With this ownership, the value of your investment will be determined by the movements of the price of the company's shares. If for instance, you bought Apple stocks and the price moves up while you are holding the stock then the value of your investment increases. On the other hand, if the price of the Apple stocks decreases while you are holding the stocks, the value of your investment decreases.

The price of a stock is driven by the forces of supply and demand. Naturally, when the demand for a particular stock is higher than the supply, the price of that stock will increase. In much the same way, when the supply is higher than the demand, then the price of that stock will decrease. In essence, the stock price is a reflection of the value as set by the market conditions. When you buy a stock as an investor, your general goal is to make money when the price of the stock increases. This is why a big part of investing in the stock market is knowing how to select the right stocks to buy.

When the price of the shares you have appreciates, you can sell your shares at a profit. This means that you will get a return on your investment and you can reinvest your capital back into the market or you can cash out. The beauty of stock market investing is that there is usually no limit to how long you can hold your investment. You can keep your shares for 20 years or you can choose to sell them when the share price appreciates. This will ultimately depend on what your end goal is.

Price appreciation is not the only way to make money in the stock market. Dividends are payments made out to shareholders when a company makes a profit. This means that depending on the type of shares you have, you will receive dividends from the company whose shares you hold.

For instance, if you bought Tesla stocks and the company pays out dividends quarterly to their shareholders, you will get a percentage of these dividends based on the value of your shares. You can choose to take these dividends as a cash payment or you can choose to reinvest them back into the company by buying more shares.

It is important to note that not all companies pay dividends. This means that if you want to make money in the stock market by earning regular dividends, you will need to understand the type of stocks to buy and which company's stocks will get you dividends.

Stock exchanges like the NYSE (New York Stock Exchange), NASDAQ, the Tokyo Stock Exchange are some of the largest exchanges. However, stocks are also sold in over-the-counter markets where they trade directly through brokers and not in open exchanges like the NYSE. These markets are referred to as secondary markets where investors trade stocks by buying and selling amongst themselves.

Basic Terms and Concepts

- **Stocks**

  A stock is a share of ownership in a company. Stocks are also referred to as shares. When you buy a stock you acquire a fraction of ownership of the company whose shares you have bought. When you buy stocks, you become a shareholder in a particular company and the percentage or size of your shares will determine the dividends you can earn.

Investors in the stock market can make money from their stocks in different ways. You can earn money in the form of dividends paid out on the shares you own. You can also earn money by selling your shares or stocks.

- **Common Stock**

Common stocks give you ownership of a company based on the number of shares you own. Common stocks are the most basic type of shares to own and they entitle you to dividends where applicable and voting rates proportionate to the shares you own.

- **Preferred Stock**

Preferred stocks entitle you to a fixed dividend rate for your shares. With this type of stock, you earn dividends before shareholders who have common stock but you do not get voting rights. Unlike shareholders of common stocks, preferred stocks give you a guarantee that you will receive dividends on your stock.

- **Penny Stocks**

A penny stock is a stock that trades for less than $5 per share. Penny stocks are typically short-term holdings where you want to take advantage of price movements in volatile markets. Penny stocks investing works for short-term investors who do not plan to hold the stocks for long periods.

- **Blue Chip Stocks**

Blue-chip stocks are shares of large established corporations that have solid reputations in the market. Blue-chip stocks are characterized by solid balance sheets and steady cash flows. Most blue-chip stocks have a history of earning increasing dividends for their shareholders. These types of stocks are ideal for long-term investors who want to hold stocks for long periods.

- **Primary Market**

In a primary market, companies sell their shares directly to investors. In most cases, companies in primary markets sell to corporations and institutions rather than to individual investors. Hedge funds, mutual funds, and similar investors are typically the kind of investors that buy shares directly from companies in primary markets.

- **Secondary Markets**

In a secondary market, investors buy and sell shares amongst themselves. Individual investors buy shares in secondary markets. In this type of market, you can choose to buy shares of a particular company or a mix of different companies' shares in exchange-traded funds or EFTs.

- **Over-the-Counter Markets**

OTC markets are where companies that are not listed in exchanges like NYSE trade their shares. In OTC markets there is no public price for the shares and the value of the transaction is dependent on the buyer and seller.

- **Bid**

A bid is a price at which you want to buy the share.

- **Ask**

The ask is the price at which the seller wants to sell the share at

- **Spread**

The spread is the difference between the bids and sell prices of a stock. If you want to buy a stock at $50 and the buyer wants to sell it at $45, the spread, in this case, is $5.

- **Volatility**

Volatility refers to the movement of share prices in the market. When the price fluctuates widely within short periods of time then it is said to be highly volatile. The higher the volatility of a particular share, the higher the risk associated with it and also the higher the profit potential.

- **Dividend**

A dividend is the percentage of a company's earnings that is paid out to shareholders. Dividends can be paid out annually or quarterly depending on the company. Not all companies pay dividends to the shareholders.

- **Broker**

A broker is a trader who buys and sells shares for an
investor for a fee or commission.

- **Bear Market**

A bear market refers to a downward trend in the market
where stock prices are falling

- **Bull Market**

A bull market refers to an upward trend in the market
where stock prices are rising.

- **Beta**

Beta is the measurement of the price of a stock relative
to the movement of the whole market. If a stock
moves 1.5 points for every 1-point move in the
market, then it has a beta of 1.5.

- **Index**

An index is a measure that is used as a benchmark to
gauge market performance. Some of the most
famous indices include the Dow Jones and the S&P
500.

Chapter 2.   Steps to Evaluate Your Financial Health, Setting, Goals (What to Consider Before Opening a New Account)

There are many ways to go about investing and knowing which path to take can be a daunting process. You can narrow down the possibilities to a strategy that works for you by evaluating your current financial situation. This should be done before you enter into your first trade. To be successful, an investor needs a clear picture of where they are going. Keep in mind this is not a one-time event. You should reevaluate your financial situation on an annual basis since it's going to be changing. When you find yourself in a different financial situation, your investment strategies will change over time.

Where

Establishing a starting point is the first step. You don't have to be a financial wizard, but you need to be aware of your present situation before jumping in and buying stocks. Consider the following scenario. An investor with a large personal debt that has an interest rate of 17% keeps putting money in the stock market, hoping to build wealth over time. That sounds reasonable, but most market returns are, going to be in the range of 5-10%. That means that someone in this situation is actually losing money.

Seek Liquidity

We are going to recommend that you look for assets you can sell.

The money can be used to pay debts, back taxes, or to seed investment capital. You'll want to list all of your assets by liquidity, which means how easily they can be converted into cash. You'll also want to consider how much cash you can raise by selling each item if you were to sell it. A house might have a lot more value than a television set, but you might sell the television set in 24 hours while you'd have to wait months to sell the house.

Dealing with Debts

Taking care of debts is one of the first things that a budding investor needs to do. While you might be anxious to get started with a large-scale investment plan if you have debts to take care of you might want to put it off. So, the first step in preparing your investment plan is to create a simple balance sheet. You don't have to be an accountant, and you're only doing this for yourself, but it needs to be honest and accurate.

You're going to want to put together a listing of all of your assets and liabilities. When compiling assets, include everything of value that you could possibly sell. This could be a computer that you're not using, a dusty TV in a room nobody goes into very often, or an old guitar. Selling things, you don't need can help you pay off debts faster and raise investment capital. You might object that you wouldn't raise much money but imagine having an extra $500 to $1,000 to start off with.

When listing your liabilities, you're going to want to know how much debt you have, what the interest rates are, and what your monthly payments are.

Monthly payments are less important than interest rates. Once you've listed all of your debts, you'll want to develop a plan to pay them off in a reasonable amount of time. There are many calculators available online, and you can also read many books on how to pay off debt. The series of books by debt guru Dave Ramsey is highly recommended. Here is an example of a good debt calculator:

https://www.creditkarma.com/calculators/
debt_repayment/

You can use this calculator to figure out how long it will take to pay off a debt for a given monthly payment. You can enter the interest rate, and the time frame you would like along with the monthly payment you're willing to make. Start off with the current minimum payment in order to determine the time required to pay off the debt and work up from there.

In this example, we considered a $21,000 debt with a high 11% interest rate. Paying $450 a month would take five years to pay off the debt.

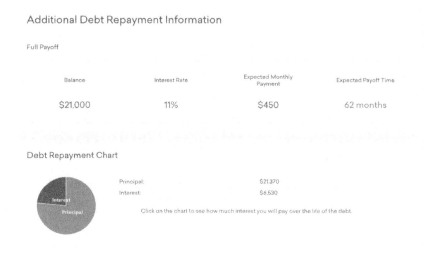

Additional Debt Repayment Information

Full Payoff

Balance	Interest Rate	Expected Monthly Payment	Expected Payoff Time
$21,000	11%	$450	62 months

Debt Repayment Chart

| Principal: | $21,370 |
| Interest: | $6,530 |

Click on the chart to see how much interest you will pay over the life of the debt.

That isn't a good situation to be in — do you want to saddle yourself with a $21,000 debt for five years?

When you have listed all of your debts, then you can prioritize them. In order to make the most progress in the shortest amount of time, it can be helpful to tackle the smallest debts first. This not only helps you get rid of your debt faster, but it will also have psychological benefits as you improve your financial situation.

If you have back taxes, you should make these a priority. The reason is that the government tacks on lots of fees and penalties, and if the tax debt is allowed to sit around, it can grow substantially in size. Get payment plans arranged to take care of these debts before they become unmanageable.

Take a look at your spending habits. Having material goods now isn't important if you plan to become a successful investor. You will be able to buy that BMW or Mercedes you want later when you can really afford it. For now, your focus should be on being able to direct your financial resources into your investments so that you can grow your wealth over time. Expensive toys, like a new car, can be a large financial drain. If you have car loans, consider getting out of the car and into a used car that is reliable but costs a lot less. From this point forward, don't use debt to finance purchases. Keep a credit card on hand for emergencies, but don't use it to buy things like books or groceries that should be paid for using cash. If you can't pay for something with cash, it can wait.

Having an Emergency Fund

Life is never fair, and we are all going to encounter emergencies.

Recent studies have shown that most Americans don't have enough cash on hand to pay a $500 bill. If you are in that situation, you need to rectify it before you jump in with a large-scale investment plan. Remember that paying off debt first is always the priority. Debt is a sink that sucks important financial resources down the drain that could be used for other purposes. However, it's important to start putting money away for an emergency fund to be prepared for the unexpected — and being able to pay for it without having to take on more debt. Or worse, getting into a situation where you can't get credit but still need to find money to pay emergency bills. Set aside a small amount of money that you can start depositing into a savings account that you won't touch unless there is an emergency. Over time, the goal should be to have enough cash on hand to take care of emergency bills ranging up to $5,000 and to have funds on hand to cover times when you might be unemployed.

Consider Additional Sources of Income

If you have a large amount of debt or find yourself in a situation where coming up with a significant amount of money to invest is difficult, you should consider taking action to increase your income. There are many paths to consider. You can start by looking for a higher-paying job.

Alternatively, you can look into taking a second job, at least until you are in a better financial situation. Another approach that can be used is to either take on "gigs" or short-term contract work.

This can be done online or by doing some side work with companies like Uber. You can even look into starting your own online business to generate more income.

This doesn't have to be a permanent situation, but you are going to want to get to a place where you are debt-free and can put $1,000 or more into the stock market every month.

Net Worth and Changes Over Time

When you've gathered everything together, you'll want to determine your net worth. You are doing this for yourself, so don't be embarrassed if it's in a bad position right now. Simply add up the total current value of your assets and liabilities and subtract the total value of the liabilities from the total value of your assets. This is your net worth. If you can compare the value of each asset now to the value it had at the beginning of the year; you can also calculate the change in your net worth in percentage terms.

Are You Ready to Invest?

If you are debt-free or have a plan in place to take care of your debts and to build an emergency fund, you are ready to begin investing. The first rule of investing is to never invest more than you can afford to lose. If you go about your investment plan carefully, the chances of losing everything are slim to none. That said it's a wise approach to invest as if that could really happen. So, you shouldn't be investing next month's house payment or your kid's college funds in the hopes of gaining returns. After you have taken care of your debts and emergency fund, add up all of your basic living expenses, so you know how much you actually need per month. Anything left over above that is the amount of money you can invest for now.

Determining Your Financial Goals

Once you are in a position to invest something — even if you can only put in $100 a month now because you're paying off large debts — it's time to sit down and figure out your financial goals. There are several things to keep in mind:

Age: Generally speaking, the older you are, the more conservative you should be in your investment approach. The reason for this is simple. When things go badly, it takes time to recover and get back on the road to profitability. The older you are, the less time you have to grow your wealth in the future. That means a market crash, or a bad investment has larger consequences than it would have if you had thirty years to recover. Financial advisors generally recommend that older investors put their money in safer investments, which means putting some money into bonds and safe investments like US

Treasuries that preserve capital. In the stock market, the older investor will seek out more stable companies that are larger, and while they may be growing, they have slow and steady growth with lower levels of risk. Of course, age can cut both ways. Many people reach their fifties with little to no savings or investment. If that describes your situation, you're going to want to invest more aggressively to seek rapid growth. Younger people also want to invest more aggressively, as they have a time horizon that permits taking on more risk. But time horizon isn't the only factor if you have no capital to protect; you definitely want to be more aggressive.

Chapter 3. Risks in Investing in Stocks

Understanding risk and volatility are two of the most important things to keep in mind with the stock market.

There are many different types of risk in the stock market. Some are direct, such as a small company that has the *potential* to make gains because of innovative products. Others are indirect and external. You can't manage all types of risks. Some come out of the blue, like the 9/11 terrorist attacks or the 2008 financial crash. So, if you think that you can control every form of risk, take a deep breath and realize you can't. In this chapter, we are going to try and describe every major category of risk investor's face, and if possible, we'll suggest ways to deal with them.

Emotional and Person Risk

First and foremost, you can control the risks to your investments that come from personal factors. These include fear, impatience, and greed. Emotions like these can be hard to control, but learning to take charge of them is essential if you are going to be a successful investor.

When real money is on the line, these emotions can become strong and overpowering. You must not let that happen.

The most common problem when it comes to emotions and personal risk is fear. When a stock market starts looking bearish, many investors immediately jump ship. They are making a huge mistake. A good investor is not getting in and out of the market at the slightest sign of a problem. In fact, selling off when everyone else is could be one of the biggest mistakes individual investors make. By the way, that doesn't exempt large investors. Many professional traders are subject to the same emotions and exhibit the same behavior during downturns. Massive selloffs are what cause bear markets to develop.

First of all, remember that you are looking to hold your investments over the long term. So, the ups and downs of the market and even recessions are not a reason to sell them. Over the past 50 years, by far the worst stock market contraction happened in the 2008 financial crisis. However, even that was short-lived. People that sold off their investments were either faced with being out of the markets altogether or having to get back in the markets when prices were appreciating. The lifetimes of other major bear markets were similar or even more short-lived. The first lesson in managing personal risk is to hold your investments through downturns.

The second lesson is that rather than giving into fear, you should start to see market downturns as opportunities. When prices are rapidly dropping due to a market sell-off, you should be buying shares. It's impossible to know where the bottom of a market is, and you shouldn't concern yourself with that.

At any time that share prices are declining, it's an opportunity, and so you should be making regular stock purchases. In one year, two years, or five years down the road, on average, the stocks that you purchased in a downturn are going to be worth quite a bit more.

The second problem that arises as a part of personal risk is greed. Many people start seeing dollar signs when they begin investing. Having a get-rich-quick mentality is not compatible with successful investing. Your approach should be centered on slowly and steadily accumulating wealth and not making a quick buck. As you invest, you're going to be coming across claims that certain trades or stocks are the next best thing, but you're better off ignoring such claims. More often than not, they turn out to be false. The stock market is not a gambling casino, even though many people treat it that way. You can avoid succumbing to greed by maintaining a regular investment program and not being taken in by the temptation that you can profit from short-term swings or "penny stocks" that are going to supposedly take off.

Finally, there is the related problem of impatience. After the Great Depression, people developed a more reasonable and cautious approach to the stock market. They realized that you're not going to get rich in six months or a year. The idea of long-term investing became dominant.

Unfortunately, in recent years, this lesson seems to be getting lost. More people are behaving like traders rather than as investors. Far too many investors are being taken in by the seduction of being able to beat market returns. Instead of being impatient, you should realize that you're in it for the long haul. Rather than trying to make a few extra bucks now, you're seeking to build wealth.

Risk of Loss of Capital

Obviously, financial risk is something you face when investing. Theoretically, there is a chance that you will lose all the money you invest in the stock market. This can happen if you tie your fate to a small number of companies. Several well-known companies like Lumber Liquidators, Bear-Stearns, and GM have either had major problems or gone completely under. Investors may have lost large sums in the process. The way to deal with this is to avoid investing in a small number of companies. Later in the chapter, we will investigate diversification as an investment strategy.

You'll also want to pay attention to the types of companies you invest in. Putting all of your money into small-cap stocks, for example, is probably a bad idea. So is putting all of your money into emerging markets, or into one sector of the stock market. Again, the key message is diversification. It's the way to protect you from financial risk.

Market and Economic Risk

Some factors are beyond your control, and the economy inevitably cycles through slowdowns and downturns. The market will cycle along with the economy, and also experience crashes when the economy may be doing fine overall. This happened in 1987, for example.

While these factors are not under your control, how you react to them is under your control. As we discussed in the section on emotional risk, you should not panic when there is a downturn. Remain level-headed, and use downturns as a buying opportunity. They are always followed by a brighter day; your job is to have the patience to wait for it to arrive.

Interest Rate Risk

Changing interest rates can impact the markets. Although this is a book about stock market investing, you should have some awareness of how bond markets work. You should also be aware that investor money can flow back and forth between bond and stock markets depending on conditions.

One thing that bond markets offer is the safety of capital, especially when we are talking about U.S. government bonds. When interest rates are high, U.S. government bonds (and other types of bonds, including corporate and municipal bonds) become very attractive.

Interest rate changes have risks for bond investors, however. Bonds are traded on secondary markets. When interest rates rise, bond prices fall because older bonds that offer lower interest rates become less attractive. Conversely, when interest rates fall, older bonds that pay higher interest rates have more value than new bonds being issued that pay relatively low rates.

This doesn't directly affect a stock market investor, but if demand for bonds rises, that can mean less capital flowing into the stock market. Less demand means lower prices, so the market may see declines.

Also, as we'll see, you can invest in bonds through the stock market using exchange-traded funds. If you are using this method, you'll want to keep close tabs on interest rates. That means paying closer attention to the Federal Reserve and its quarterly announcements. You should be doing so even if you are not going to invest in bonds in any way.

Announcements on interest rate changes can have a large impact on stock prices. But as always, keep your eye on the long ball. If the markets react negatively to an increase in interest rates that can be an opportunity to buy undervalued stocks.

Political Risk and Government

Government and politics can create big risks in the stock market. International events can cause market crashes, and these days even a tweet from the President can cause markets to rise and fall. Lately, some politicians have also been discussing breaking up the big tech companies. Others are talking about investigating them. Such talk — and worse actions— can have a negative impact on the markets. Part of your job as an investor is to keep a close eye on the news. You're going to want to know what's happening so that you can adjust if necessary.

Inflation Risk

Inflation hasn't been high in decades. However, in the late 1970s inflation rates were routinely in the double digits. Hopefully, that isn't going to be something that happens anytime soon, because high inflation rates can eat your returns alive. If the stock market is appreciating at 7% per year, but inflation is 14%, you can see that it's like having debt but investing in stocks — it's a losing proposition. Right now, inflation risk is very low, but you'll want to have some awareness of it and always keep tabs on it. High inflation rates also tend to go hand-in-hand with high interest rates, since the Federal Reserve will raise rates to try and slow down inflation. That means that bonds might become more attractive when inflation gets out of control.

Taxes and Commissions

Finally, we have the risk imposed by taxes. Of course, we are all going to be hit with taxes no matter where our money comes from. However, you need to take into account the taxes that you are going to pay when it comes to any gains you realize on the stock market. Part of being a successful investor is having an understanding of how much your taxes are cutting into your profits. If you are investing for the long-term, it will be less of an issue. But keep in mind that taxes can really eat into short-term trades. Frequent, short-term traders also face risk from commissions and fees. If you execute a lot of trades, the commissions can add up. This is not an issue for long-term investors.

Risk vs. Return

One of the fundamental trade-offs that an investor will make is risk vs. return. Generally speaking, the higher the risk, the greater the *possibility* of good returns. In 1998, Amazon was a pretty high-risk investment. While it had potential, major bookstores like Borders and Barnes & Noble dominated the space. Amazon was on shaky ground at the time, and another company could have come in and competed successfully for online book sales. That never happened, and Amazon ended up dominating book sales and expanding widely across retail and into cloud computing. That risk has translated into massive returns. A $10,000 investment in 1998 would be worth more than $1 million today.

But hindsight is 20/20. Today, there are similar opportunities all around us, but it's hard to know which ones will end up being successful over the long term. If you are an aggressive investor, part of your job will be estimating which companies are the best bets for the future.

Chapter 4.   How to Invest in Stocks

(How to Buy Your First Stock)

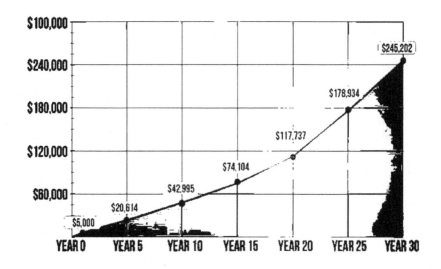

How to Get Start

Stock may seem incredibly intimidating for those starting in the investment world. It looks like a completely different world, and the hardest step for most is the beginning. However, it is quite simple to get started in stock investments. First, one must set goals for themselves and determine how they would like to invest in a stock. By writing down goals and ensuring that the investor's money is used in the best possible way, the investor is helping them yield the highest return on their investment. Once the individual's goals are made clear, they must plan on how to meet those goals. After this, they may choose the best investment method for achieving these goals. Then, it must be decided on where exactly the investor will go to invest their money. It is crucial, as this will be the platform by which the investor will trade their stocks. After this, the investor must open an account with whomever they choose. Before they start trading, the investor must make an initial investment using this account. While doing so, they may have to link their bank account to their stock trading account. The investor must then begin the process of buying and selling stocks using this account. Although this seems like a lengthy process, it is quite simple.

Planning and Meeting Goals

Investors must familiarize themselves with their goals. It is quite helpful to write down one's goals in each area and put them somewhere that is easily accessible. It is useful to have measurable goals to reach. This way, there may be a specific period and amount that may be assigned to the targets. It may help to come up with monthly goals. For instance, the investor may start with the purchase of 100 shares of stock in February. They may wish to increase that to 150 shares by March, 200 shares by April, and so on. This way, the investor may have a period to achieve their goals. It will allow them to measure their progress easily.

To set proper goals, one must reflect upon their past. How much will the investor be able to set aside for stock realistically? If one's goals are not realistic, it may become discouraging and set the investor back from their full potential. The investor must consider any past investments they have made. They must consider what worked and what did not. It is crucial to consider income and expenses when investing, and one must also consider any savings goals that one has. This will make it more apparent what may be invested in stocks.

Without a clear guide on how to invest, the investor will lack direction. It may lead to spur-of-the-moment decisions, and the investor may regret these choices. There may be some periods where one will not trade, as it won't be as profitable. Perhaps the market is down, and the trader does not wish to sell any stock. Perhaps the market is up, and the trader does not want to buy any stock. There will be events such as vacations, holidays, stressful events, or emergencies.

One must also consider how much money they have. Although it is possible to double one's money in a year, it is not likely for a beginner to do so. One may also choose to invest one time and hold it, or they may choose to invest more into their account often. This time and amount will depend on the investor and their financial situation.

The investor must also choose a strategy. They may wish to buy and sell stocks or to buy and hold stocks. They may even consider options trading. Whichever method that the investor chooses, there will be different goals to fit those strategies.

Long-term goals may be set to help the investor. Although planning for the following year may help the investor, longer periods may prove even more beneficial. Perhaps the investor wishes to acquire a million dollars worth of stock in the succeeding ten years. Perhaps the investor wishes to save a certain amount for retirement, which they wish to have by the next 25 years. Whatever the end goal is, the investor must make that clear so that they can begin working towards it immediately. Once a proper plan is created for meeting the investor's goals, they may move to the next step.

Choosing an Investment Method

After the investor has set goals and created a plan to meet them, it is time to decide on which investment method they wish to pursue. For those that wish to trade on their own completely, the DIY (do-it-yourself) method is the best fit. The investor may conduct all their trades online, making transfers from the bank manually or automatically. It will allow full control of one's investments. There will also be complete independence over what the investor wishes to buy and sell, how much they wish to trade, and how often they wish to trade.

They will, however, need to dedicate time to researching, making any transfers, trading, and other procedures. There is also a higher risk for this choice, as a beginning investor will not have the education that a financial advisor will. They also won't be under the control of a Robo-Advisor. However, all the profit that is made by the investor will be theirs to keep. They won't have to pay commission and fees outside of any required by the broker that they use.

The least independent approach to investing in stock is by hiring a financial advisor. It is for those who do not wish to touch their stock at all and to have it fully regulated for them. Hesitant beginners may benefit from this method. It is important to remember, however, that this method tends to be the costliest. It is most beneficial for those with higher assets and larger portfolios. It is also important to choose an investor that will work to meet the investor's goals, not just the goals of themselves. Therefore, the investor must set specific goals for themselves and how they wish to invest their money. They may more easily communicate with the advisor their desires, which may be carried out for them.

Choosing a Stockbroker

When investing for oneself, a proper stockbroker must be chosen. This will depend on the individual's needs and wants. For some, their bank that they already operate offers stock investments through their bank. This is a quick and simple option, as their money will already be linked through the bank, and they may already be familiar with their style. There may also be options for financial advisors in the bank that are free of charge. Otherwise, the investor must research their options before settling on a broker.

When choosing a stockbroker, the investor should research any fees (transaction fees, maintenance fees, etc.), minimum funds required to open an account, any commission collected by the stockbroker, and accessibility. The investor may prefer a specific type of formatting for their broker to have. There may also be free education, customer service, and other ways to make investing easier for the investor.

The investor must choose the option that will allow them to make the highest return on their investments. The investor should keep in mind which services they are likely to use most frequently, and they should choose the broker that charges the least to use those services. There may be transactional fees, which are costs for buying and selling stocks. Many beginning investors tend to forget this, so it is essential to take this into account.

Opening an Account

When opening an account, there are often a few steps that are required. This is typically not a lengthy process, but the investor should be aware of the potential actions associated with opening an account.

The first step when opening an online account is typically to create an account. This will consist of a username and password, as well as some personal information. This may include setting goals, determining which types of features the investor wishes to use, and the investor's experience level. This information will help to create the optimal experience for the investor.

There may also be an application for the account to ensure that the investor is qualified to hold the account. There may also be an agreement stating that the investor assumes all the risks of investing and understands that the money is not insured or guaranteed. Initial Investment and Linking Accounts

During the application process, the investor will most likely be prompted to fund the account. This can be done in several ways. The investor may transfer the funds electronically via an EFT (Electronic funds transfer). This is transferring the money from a linked bank account and will most likely only take one business day to transfer. The investor may also choose to make a wire transfer, which is a transfer directly from the bank. It is important to consider how much to invest in the account initially carefully. For those just starting, there may not be much money to invest at first. The minimum investment amounts for the broker should be looked over beforehand.

Chapter 5.   When to Buy

and Sell Stock

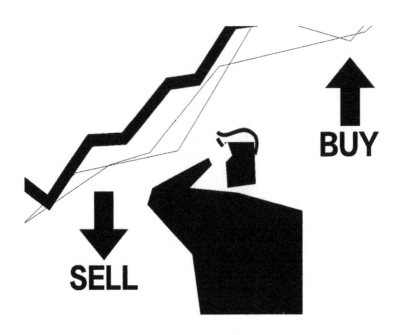

When to Sell a Stock

Determining when to sell a stock is a decision that even the world's best investors wrestle with. Warren Buffett has said that his holding period for a stock is forever. Does Buffett really hold every stock that he buys forever? Of course not! The point that he is making is that you should always purchase a stock with the intention of holding it forever; therefore, make sure your money has been put into your best investment ideas. An investor should leave his or her portfolio intact for at least five years, as long as the fundamentals for which a particular stock was purchased do not deteriorate. Investors should pay no attention to a stock's price volatility because it is a normal part of the investment cycle. As a long-term investor, there will be times when it makes sense to sell or reduce your position in stock earlier than you had planned. Next, we will talk about different circumstances in which you should consider selling a stock or reducing your position in a stock.

- **The Time Frame** — If you need the money within five years, it should not be invested in stocks. It would be best to invest your money in safe and stable short-term instruments. Money market accounts, money market funds, and short-term certificates of deposits would be better options. Since the Great Recession struck, some investment professionals now recommend that you not invest any money in stocks that will be needed within 10 years.

- **An Overvalued Stock** — When a stock is significantly overvalued, sell it. Take the proceeds from the sale and invest them into other undervalued stocks that you have researched. The P/E ratio is still one of the best indicators of value. For example, if a stock has traded at an average P/E of 15 for the last seven to 10 years and the business is thriving, but the stock currently trades at a P/E of 30 or more on consistent or increasing EPS, you should seriously consider selling the stock. The PEG ratio is also a very effective method for determining if a stock is now overvalued.

- **Too Much Debt** — Too much debt is dangerous for any business because there's always the chance that a business may be unable to pay its debt. Too much debt also puts a business at greater risk of failure if a downturn in the industry or economy were to occur. Upon entering the 2007 recession, thousands of businesses here in the United States literally disappeared overnight and that was before things really got bad.

- **Too Much Risk** — You have already learned the importance of staying away from investments that are too risky. Sometimes new management will come to a business and begin to implement new policies; along with that implementation, they will knowingly or unknowingly expose a business to greater risk. If you purchased the stock of a business that stayed away from very risky practices, but the business has now begun to display risky behaviors that make you uncomfortable, sell the stock and find yourself a better investment.

- **Loss of Competitive Advantage** — You have also learned that we should only be purchasing the stocks of businesses that have a durable competitive advantage. When a business changes its business model, resulting in it losing its competitive advantage, sell the stock.

- **The Portfolio Lacks Balance or Diversification** — It's very easy for your best performing stock to become the largest holding in your portfolio, and there's absolutely nothing wrong with that. The problem arises when the stock makes up more than 20-25% of your portfolio's total value. Legendary investor, Jim Slater suggests that individual investors limit the number of funds invested in a single stock within their portfolios to a maximum of 15%. When your portfolio becomes heavily weighted in one stock, consider reducing your position of that stock to bring more balance and better diversification into your portfolio.

- **Stock Reaches Its Fair Value** — Our goal as investors should always be to purchase a stock at a discount to its fair value and it is recommended at least a 25% discount to its fair value. By doing so, when you sell a stock that has reached its fair value, you are guaranteed a gain of at least 25% from the sale. This is a disciplined approach to selling a stock.

According to research, it was common for Benjamin Graham to sell a stock once it had a 50% gain in price. If the future prospects of a particular stock look good, you may decide to sell only a portion of the stock, such as half of its shares, and hold on to the rest when using this approach.

- **When Your Analysis is Found to Be Flawed**— There will be times when an investor will be very detailed and careful in his or her analysis of a particular company or its stock, only to find out later that his or her analysis is incorrect or flawed. Whether a stock should be sold at that time depends on the seriousness of the error and its impact on the long-term performance of the business. So, when you find that you have incorrectly analyzed a particular business, it is essential for you to take a serious look at all available information to determine whether or not to sell the stock or to continue holding it. One thing is certain, as an investor, you will not always be right when analyzing a company or its stock.

There is no clear-cut way to determine the optimal time to sell a stock. There will be times that you will sell a stock because it has not performed well, only to see it skyrocket and double or triple in price soon after you sell it. There will also be occasions when you have purchased what seems to be the perfect stock, only to watch it tumble in price and for no apparent reason. Learn what you can from these events and move on. Even Peter Lynch, Jim Slater, and other great investors have sold stocks too early or too late. It's going to happen sometimes.

When to Buy a Stock

After the investor funds their account, it is time to start trading the stocks. It must be decided what stock, how much of the stock, and how the investor wishes to buy. Once these factors are decided, the investor must buy the stock. It is usually as simple as searching the stock symbol and selecting "buy." It is best to wait until the stock is at a low, but the investor must also begin investing as early as possible in experiencing the benefits of investing. When the stock is bought, it will typically take a bit to process and for the broker to receive these funds. After that, it will show up in the online portfolio of the investor. When it is time to sell this stock, the investor may typically visit their portfolio and click "sell" on the desired stock.

Starting out as a stock investor is quite simple. The investor must follow a few steps to become a stock trader. They must choose an investment method, select a stockbroker, open an account, a fund that account, and they will be ready to go.

Your very first stock trade can be frightening - not to mention confounding. You've done your stock research, you believe you've found a winner, and now you're all set to put your brand-new brokerage account to excellent usage and begin trading — nevertheless, you're not quite sure how to "carry it out."

Trade "execution" is just an elegant technique for describing an exchange. To "trade" typically describes a particular kind of investing method, so certifying your use of the term "trade" with "carry out" lets other financiers understand that you're going over a particular exchange.

The real-time it takes to perform your trade can move from broker to broker and market to market. (The SEC requires that all brokerage companies supply documents quarterly to the basic population about the handling of their customer orders).

Your broker will unquestionably put your order through their complicated trading computer system network to get a hold of your shares when you do put in your order. In many cases, your order will never ever leave the broker — your brokerage company ought to clean out shares of the organization you're purchasing from its stock.

You have a couple of choices when it comes to trading stocks beyond merely selling and purchasing. Basically, you get shares of a particular stock and sell them, relying on that the stock will diminish in worth, leaving the distinction between the selling rate and ultimate repurchase rate in your pocket.

Stock Order Types

Naturally, buying stocks is similarly more complex than only one purchase. There are numerous different approaches for considering your purchase, all going concerning cost, the time point of confinement, which is simply the start.

Anyhow, what are your alternatives for purchasing stock? There are 5 various types of stock orders that your broker will likely let you utilize.

A market order is a demand to sell a stock or buy at the existing market value. Market orders are quite a great deal for the basic stock order, and because the capability is typically performed instantly.

Something to keep as a primary top priority with a market order is the way you do not manage the amount you pay for your stock purchase or sale; the marketplace does.

The speed with which online market orders have actually launched might have made this less of a danger than it used to be. The market still moves quicker.

Some individuals do not have problems with this, for those that do this, imperfection can be met with a breaking point order.

- **Point of Confinement Order**

A breaking point order can keep you from purchasing or selling your stock at a rate that you do not want, possibly assisting you in keeping a strategic range from a horrible choice. On the off possibility that the cost is a misdirected base and not in tune with the market, nevertheless, the order will never ever be made.

Keep in mind that some brokers charge more for point of confinement orders, as the trade might not go through.

- **Stop-loss Order**

Stop-loss orders, when that price is reached, transform into market orders. The target price is hit, and the trade is executed at market value.

- **Stop-Limit Order**

Stop-limit orders are also stopped orders based on hanging tight at a particular expense. Stop-limit orders end up being point of confinement orders when the target cost is reached as opposed to market orders.

Changing into a breaking point order can be something useful for a stop order, staying away from particular threats. On the occasion that the shares topple to

$20.00 at the very same time, then instantly shoot back up, your market order might go through in any case.

- **Tracking Stop**

Generally, this is a stop order based upon a portion modification in the market cost instead of setting a target cost.

You can pick to what degree the order stays open when you put an order into your broker. Naturally, orders are day orders, indicating that they are signed up until completion of the trading day. Outstanding till-canceled orders stay open until you really enter and cancel them.

Chapter 6.   How to Generate Passive Income from the Stock Market

Income investing is a little bit of a different ballgame than growth investing. In this case, we are seeking out companies that pay dividends. That means ignoring a lot of high growth stocks like Amazon and Netflix. It also means ignoring disruptive companies with potential like Tesla. When you are an income investor, you are looking to make a certain level of income from your stock holdings. That may be now, or it may be in the future. But your portfolio is going to look quite different from a growth investor, and even a value-oriented growth investor.

Yield

Start compiling a diverse list of companies that pay dividends that you find interesting. In each case, track the yield, which is the dividend divided by the share price. That will help you compare apples-to-apples when judging one dividend stock against another. Keep in mind that you are going to be seeking some kind of balance, so buying up stocks with the highest yields isn't the best philosophy. To see why to consider a company called consolidated communications. They pay a yield of 32%. The problem is, it's a penny stock. That means it's only $4 or so a share. Most analysts are rating it a SELL. A glance at the chart indicates it has dropped from a $29 share price over the past couple of years, and yet it's still rated as being overvalued. These are major red flags.

Dividend

You may also be interested in the actual dividend payment, and not just the yield. IBM pays $6 a share, but Apple only pays $1.55 a share. So, you'd have to own more than three Apple shares for every share of IBM you could buy in order to get the same annual income from your stocks. Since IBM is cheaper on a per-share basis, that is something to take into consideration.

Dividend Growth

For any stock that you invest in, you're going to want to look at the history of their dividend payments. The ideal dividend stock is one that pays higher dividends over time. IBM is a great example because they paid consistent dividends through the 2008 financial crisis, and they have been increasing their dividends since then. Dividend growth ensures that your dividend payments will keep up with or exceed inflation.

DRIPS and Reinvesting

If you have a large amount of capital available right now, you can buy up shares of stock and start living off the dividend payments. However, if you are looking at a long-term investment program, you are going to want to reinvest your dividends. In the future, you're going to want to have as many shares as possible, so taking cash out now simply doesn't make sense. Instead, the payments from dividends should be used to purchase additional shares. Some companies even allow you to purchase fractional shares with the money.

A DRIP is a Dividend Reinvestment Program. In this case, the company will automatically take any dividends you earn and use them to buy additional shares. This will help enforce discipline in case you get tempted to cash out your dividends and waste the money on a trip or new car. Instead, the company will force you to save for the future.

Exchange-Traded Funds

The possibility of using exchange-traded funds to meet your investment goals always exists. In this case, you can seek out an ETF that invests in dividend stocks. You will still receive dividend payments, and the fund will have built-in diversification. When looking at ETFs to use for dividend investing, be sure to focus on yield, and pick funds that have the highest yields. Many investors can do a mixture of both; you could invest in ETFs while also investing in specific companies like IBM.

Alternative Investments

The world of dividend investing isn't restricted to traditional stock investing. You can also invest in the following:

- REITS

- MLPs

- BDCs

A REIT is a real estate trust. This is a company that owns hard property assets and rents them out. The types of property are quite varied. For example, you can invest in REITs that own rental homes, apartments, or commercial real estate. There are also REITs that own hotels and resorts. In fact, any type of property that you can think of is represented by at least one REIT. But interestingly, there are REITs that have great prospects for the future because they are technology-related. For example, some REITs own cell phone towers, and there are others that own cloud computing.

REITs pay high dividends, and they trade like stocks on the stock market. Investing in REITs is a good way to get some exposure to real estate and other types of property ownership.

An MLP is a master limited partnership. These companies are midstream energy companies that transport oil and gas, own pipelines, or own refinement facilities. These are great investments to consider, and they also pay high dividends. You also invest in them by purchasing shares on the stock market. These types of investments are particularly noteworthy because the companies are partnerships and not corporations. When you invest, you become a limited partner. This means that you can deduct company expenses on your tax returns. Essentially, a large share of the income from an MLP is tax-free.

The final alternative investment that we are looking at is called a BDC, or Business Development Corporation. They also trade on stock exchanges and pay dividends. These are financial companies that invest in small to mid-sized companies that need cash. They can provide loans to companies or take an ownership stake.

When to Cash Out

Cashing out is a personal decision. By cashing out, in this case, we don't mean selling off your shares. What we mean is when should you stop reinvesting and start taking dividends as cash income. The answer is you start doing this when the level of dividend payments you receive starts matching your desired income.

Don't be afraid to shake up your portfolio. If you find an investment that suits your needs better than stocks you are currently invested in, then you should be ready to sell some of your shares and invest in the other stock. There is no reason for you to be locked into a particular stock, you can buy shares in other companies and then start getting dividend payments from them in the next upcoming cycle.

Fundamentals Always Matter

No matter which path you choose, when dividend investing, you want to pay close attention to the fundamentals. In the end, fundamentals are what matters. A company with good fundamentals is going to be a good investment. So, you'll want some trade-off between solid fundamentals, yield, and dividend payment that suits your goals. Remember to always think long-term.

Bond Investing

Finally, if you are looking for an income investing portfolio, consider buying exchange-traded funds that invest in bonds.

As we discussed earlier, there is a wide array of choices, allowing you to find the right amount of risk and the right interest payments. You'll want to look at the yields of the bond funds. Some have high rates of growth and high yields. That is, you can achieve growth as well as income by investing in bond funds too. The advantage of using ETFs is that you can avoid the hassle of trying to invest in bond markets.

Chapter 7. The Main Mistakes of a Beginner

Mistakes happen in every field, sector, and industry. Some are always anticipated, while others happened unexpectedly. When it comes to stock trading, there are several mistakes that you can make. Understanding these mistakes can help you avoid them, thus ending up successful in your stock investments. Here are some of the common mistakes made by most investors, beginners, and professional traders alike:

Failure to Understand the Trade

It is always wrong to invest in a trade or business you know nothing about. It is a great mistake to engage in stock trading when you do not understand the business and financial models involved. You can avoid this mistake by taking the time to research the stock market and stock trading before investing your money. Know the different markets, the driving forces, as well as trading procedures.

Most investors tend to buy stocks from the latest companies and industries they know very little about. Although such companies may look promising, it is difficult to determine whether they will continue to exist. Understanding a specific company gives you a better hand over other investors. You will be able to make accurate predictions about the company or industry, which may bring you more profit. You will quickly tell when the business is booming, stagnating, or closing way before other investors get this information.

Individuals who do not take time to study companies miss out on future trends of these companies. Failing to establish such trends leads to several missed opportunities. For instance, a person who invests in a company that is higher than his capital may quickly lose all his investment. That is why it is always advisable that you invest in the industry you understand better. For instance, if you are a surgeon, you can invest in stocks that deal with medicine or related stocks. Lawyers can invest in companies that generate income through litigation, and so on.

Impatience

The stock market is for patient investors. It is a slow but steady form of investment. Although it bears various opportunities that can bring you money, you cannot make enough profit in one day. Most stock investors are always faced with the challenge of being patient. Some end up losing trade positions before they mature in the quest to make quick money. Exiting the market too early will always cost you some returns. As a new investor, you must never expect your investment portfolio to perform more than its capability, as this will always lead to a disaster. Remain realistic in terms of the time, duration, and resources needed to earn from the market.

Failure to Diversify

Another mistake that easily causes disaster is the failure to diversify. Professional investors do not have a problem with this since they can easily profit from a single type of stock. However, young investors must be able to diversify to secure their investment. Some of them do not stick to this principle. Most of these lose a great fortune as soon as they get onto the stock market. As you seek to invest, remember the rule of thumb governing stock diversity. This states that you should not invest more than 10% of your capital in one type of stock.

Getting Too Connected with a Certain Company

The essence of trading in stock is to make a profit. Sometimes, investors get too deep into a certain company that they forget that it is all about the shares and not the company itself. Being too attached to a company may cloud your judgment when it comes to stock trading since you may end up buying stocks from this company instead of getting the best deal on the market. As you learn more about companies, always remember that you are into the business to make money, besides creating relationships.

Investment Turnover

Investment turnover refers to the act of entering and exiting positions at will. This is one other mistake that destroys great investments. It is only beneficial to institutions that seek to benefit from low commission rates. Most stock trading positions charge transaction fees. The more frequently you buy and sell, the more you pay in terms of transaction fees. You, therefore, need to be careful when entering positions. Do not get in or exit too early. Have a rough idea of when you want to close positions so that you do not miss some of the long-term benefits of these positions.

Timing the Market

Market timing results in high investment turnover. It is not easy to successfully time the market. On average, only 94% of stock trading returns are acquired without the use of market timing. Most traders time the market as a way of attempting to recover their losses. They want to get even by making some profit to counter a loss. This is always known as a cognitive error in behavioral finance. Trying to get even on the stock market will always result in double losses.

Trading with Emotions

Allowing your emotions to rule is one of the things that kill your stock investment returns. Most people get into the market for fear of losses or thirst to make returns too fast. As a young trader, you must ensure that greed and fear do not overwhelm your decision-making. Stock prices may fluctuate a lot in the short-term; however, this may not be the case in the long term, especially for large-cap stocks. This means that you may get lower profits in the short term, but these may increase in the long term. Understanding this will help you avoid closing trades when it is not the right time yet.

Setting Unrealistic Expectations

This always occurs when dealing with small-cap stocks such as penny stocks. Most investors buy such stocks with the expectation that the prices will change drastically. Sometimes this works, but it is not a guarantee. To make great fortunes, people invest a lot of capital in these stocks, and then the prices do not change much. If these investors are not prepared for such an eventuality, they may feel frustrated and may quit the business completely. However, this is something that you must be able to manage if you want to grow your investment. Do not expect more than what a certain type of stock can deliver.

Using Borrowed Money

This is probably one of the greatest mistakes that investors make. Some investors get carried away with the returns they are making. As a way of getting more profits, they borrow money and use it to enter more stock positions. This is a very dangerous move and can result in a lot of stress. Stock trading is like gambling. You are not always sure how much you take home at the end of each trade. It is therefore not advisable for you to invest borrowed money in it.

As you try to avoid these mistakes, you must also avoid getting information from the wrong sources. Some traders have lost a fortune because they relied on the wrong sources for stock information. It is important to isolate a small number of people and places where you will seek guidance from. Do not be a person that follows the crowd. Take time before investing in new stock opportunities. Carry out proper due diligence, especially with small-cap stocks since these involve a lot of risks. Remember, you must trade carefully and implement expert advice if you want to succeed in stock trading.

CRASH COURSE

Chapter 8. Insider Tricks Used by Professional Traders

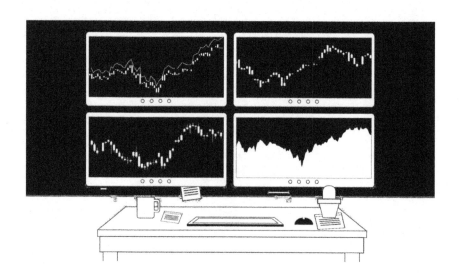

An investor should always be on the lookout for signals that might be clues about their investments. One signal you should be keeping an eye on is the actions taken by the insiders with a company. Are they sticking by the company and investing in it? Or do they seem to be running away from it despite amazing stock prices? These can be important clues as to the health and intermediate future of the company. One thing you need to keep tabs on is whether or not the insiders are buying or selling shares of the company. You'll also want to note major departures from the company. Of course, the company is going to make up some pleasant story about why some major figure is leaving. You know, they want to spend more time with their grandmother. But is that really what's going on? If other news or more signals are indicating otherwise, including insider moves, you might view such news with a negative eye. People often leave a sinking ship.

Insider Trading

Here we aren't talking about criminal activity, but rather a company members themselves who own shares of the company that they are associated with. A good indication that people are confident in the future of their company is finding out that they own and are buying more shares of stock in their own company. On the other hand, if they are selling off their shares, that can be a sign that the people actually running the company or involved with it don't have that much confidence in its future.

It's actually possible to find out what company insiders are doing when it comes to shares of stock in their own company. The Securities and Exchange Commission requires them to file publicly available reports. You can find publicly filed reports on a government website known as "Edgar." It can be found here:

https://www.sec.gov/edgar.shtml

"Insiders" will file various forms, including an initial form that they have to submit to the government indicating their insider status with the company. This is called form 3.

If you are researching this data, you're going to want to pay special attention to form 4 and form 144. On form 4, any transactions involving a large number of shares are recorded. So, if the insider bought a large number of shares, it would be recorded on form 4. Also, if they sold a large number of shares, it's going to be reported on form 4.

If a single insider is selling shares, that doesn't necessarily mean anything. However, if you notice that multiple insiders are off-loading their shares, pay attention. That might be an indication that a large number of people who are in the know about the company's prospects aren't confident about the company's future.

Form 144 is related to a special class of stock called restricted stock. This is stock that the insider was provided as compensation for employment. If they decide to unload it after a required holding period, this will be noted with form 144.

In summary, if insiders are confident that the company is doing well and has solid long-term prospects, they are probably going to be buying shares in the company, not trying to get rid of them. You will want to take this kind of information and incorporate it into the larger picture of course. It's important to consider all the indicators for the company and not get lost in the details of focusing on one sign. So, if you notice that there is a large sell-off, you'll want to check other information like the company's latest earnings reports.

Quantity also Matters

Don't get alarmed if people sell a small number of shares. When they are trying to divest their own portfolio of any interest in the company, it is when you should take notice.

Congressional Insiders

A few years ago, the news program 60 Minutes did an interesting investigation. They found that members of Congress were playing the role of insiders at many companies and getting advantageous stock buys as a result. Unfortunately, there isn't much we can do about that, but it's good to have awareness about it.

Stock Buybacks

Stock buybacks can be a good sign or a bad sign. If a company is doing well, a stock buyback can be used as a way for a company to pass on profits to investors. However, stock buybacks can also be an indicator that a company is heading for trouble. The first thing to consider is that the company has lower than expected earnings. In that case, a company might use a stock buyback in order to artificially boost their indicators on the stock market. Buying back shares of stock, if done on a large enough scale, can alter important metrics like the price per earnings ratio and earnings per share. If you have fewer shares but the same earnings, earnings per share are going to look more favorable. They can do this in the hopes of artificially boosting the value of the stock and hence it's the market price. Consider an example. Suppose that a company has $500 in earnings and 100 shares. The earnings per share are $5. If they buy back 50 shares, then you still have $500 in earnings, but with 50 shares, so now the earnings per share are $10. That looks better to investors taking a cursory look at the stock, but in reality, the company's prospects haven't changed.

Another negative possibility is that the company has stagnated. If companies are out of ideas and not pursuing new ones, they aren't investing a large amount of money into research and development. That means they have cash sitting around and using a stock buyback could be a simple way to unload the cash.

You'll also want to check the price-to-earnings ratio and look up to see if the stock is overvalued. It can be a bad sign when a company is buying back overvalued shares.

Another question to ask is, where is the company getting the cash used for the buyback? Hopefully, they have enough money on hand to do it. But if they are borrowing money for the share buyback, that is definitely a sign that the company is unhealthy.

If you have invested in a company and they engage in a share buyback, you'll want to investigate further to find out what's behind it. In many cases, it's not something to worry about. However, sometimes it's an indicator that the future with this company is not so bright.

Stock Splits

Another corporate action you will need to be aware of is a stock split. Companies can do stock splits or reverse stock splits. In a stock split, a share is converted from 1 share to 2 or 3 or more shares. That immediately changes the price per share and impacts metrics like earnings per share. Imagine that a company has a share trading at $100, and it has 100 shares outstanding, and earnings per share of $5, meaning they have a price to earnings ratio of $20. If they do a 2-1 split, now there are 200 shares. The amount of money invested in the company hasn't changed, so the share price immediately drops to $50 a share. Now you have twice the number of shares in your portfolio, so the value of your investment hasn't changed. Earnings per share would be cut in half and would be reported as $2.50. The price-to-earnings ratio would remain at $20.

One reason a company might do a stock split is to reduce the price of a share, in order to attract more investors.

A stock trading at $1,000 a share might be unaffordable for a lot of small investors. If a company was interested in attracting more small investors, they might to a 4-1 stock split and drop the share price to $250 per share. A stock split for a high-priced stock can also increase liquidity. That is, it will increase the ease with which you can sell your shares. Very high-priced stocks will have large bid-ask spreads, which can make them harder to sell. Doing a split and bringing the price back down to a lower level can reduce the bid-ask spread and make it easier for investors to sell their shares.

A reverse stock split is going to reduce the number of shares that you own. So, if you own 100 shares and they did a 1-2 reverse split, you would only own 50 shares after that.

If the share price had been $100, it would rise to $200 after the split. Remember that the amount of money invested remains the same before and after the split, so the share price also has to change if the number of shares changes.

Chapter 9. Tips and Tricks for Successful Stocks Trading

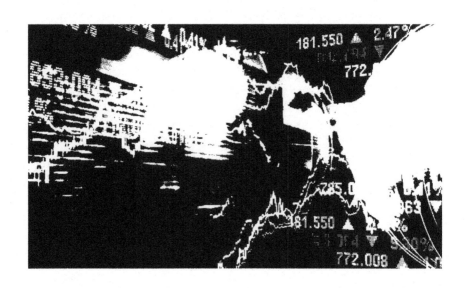

There are some tips and tricks that you can keep up your sleeve to help you invest in stocks. Let us look at some of them.

Always Be Informed

You need to be informed about what happens in the market. This is the only way you can trust your decisions. You should go through different resources and publications if you want to obtain more information about the various stocks in the market.

Buy Low, Sell High

This is a strategy that most investors will use. It is always good to buy low and sell high, and you must follow this to the tee. It is when you do this that you can expect to make large profits in the market. When you buy low and sell high, you will purchase a stock at its lowest value and sell it at its highest value. It will be easy for you to determine when the stock price will reach the highest rate based on some methods and data you collect. You need to ensure that you always act according to the data that you have collected. Experts recommend that it is a good idea to buy stocks the minute the market opens. Most stocks reach their highest price in the afternoon, and that is when you should sell them.

Scalping

This is a very popular technique in the stock market. When you use this technique, you can always buy and sell stocks within a matter of a few seconds. Your purchases and sales depend on how fast you are. This is a very strange method, but it is very effective, especially in volatile markets. Let us assume that you purchased a stock at 10:00 A.M. and sold it at 10:02 A.M. The price of that stock is $3, and the selling price is $5. So, in a matter of two minutes, you made a $2 profit per share, and this is a great profit for a scalper. This does not seem like a profit, but if you do this at least twenty or thirty times a day, you can make a huge profit. You should only use this form of trading once you have enough experience in the market. If you want to take up this technique, you should have at least a year's worth of experience to help you make the right decisions.

Short Selling

Many traders use the concept of short selling when they invest in the market. Short selling refers to when you need to borrow stock from the holder and sell it to another buyer. Then, you will wait for the stock price to fall before you give the stocks back to the lender. This is one of the easiest ways in which you can capitalize on the volatility of the prices. You must make the right decisions about the investments you make and not invest or borrow useless stocks. You must always ensure that you maintain a wide margin that will make a few mistakes. You should ensure that you have enough capital to support any other investments if things never work out. It is always good to buy shares back at the earliest if you believe that the price of the stocks will continue to increase.

Identify the Pattern

It is important to remember that stocks and every other stock in the market will follow a pattern. Once you notice this pattern and understand it, you can invest in stocks successfully. This pattern has all the information you need about the high and low points of the stocks and gathers some information on how you can trade between those points. It is important to have the history of the stock with you since it will help you determine the previous trend and predict the future trend of the stock.

Look at the Results

Every company is result-oriented, which means that the report published by the company will tell you how well the company is doing. The report that the company shares will shed some light on how well it is doing in the market. You should go through this report to ensure that you are making the right choice. The data collection results should show you that you could make enough profits when you invest in it. A small company will always aim to sell a large volume of stocks, and if you are impressed with the company and its numbers, you can invest in the stocks of that company. Remember that a company only publishes the results quarterly. Therefore, you need to look at all the results before you invest in the company.

Look at the Company Name

When choosing to invest in the stock market, you should understand that its name does matter. You must see if the company is well known and is doing well in the market. You can invest in a company that does not have any significant changes. Some people steer clear of such companies. If you are not a fundamentalist and are willing to take on a few risks, you can use technical analysis to help you make the decision. It is always good to learn more about the company if you choose to invest in shares in that company.

Understand the Company Better

You need to look at how the stock performs in the market, but it is important to spend some time understanding the company you are investing in. You need to know if the company is working on the right products and services. Understand the industry of the company. See if they are developing new products, technology, or services. Remember that whatever the company does affects the price of the stock. The best way for you to do this is to learn more about the company through fundamental analysis. You should always read the news about the company too. It is only this way that you can assess how well the company is doing. If you have any knowledge about the company or the products, you should spend some time to see where the company is heading.

When you start looking at a company, you need to ensure that you obtain the information from the right sources. Read this information carefully to understand whether the company is doing well or not. Ensure that the sources you use to obtain this information are reliable. If you get a fax, tip, or email from a person stating that one company is better than the rest, you need to make sure that you do not rush into investing. Take some time out and read about the company. Never invest in any company simply because of some information you may have received. Always conduct thorough research before you invest in the company. This is the only way you will learn if the company is doing well or not. Never waste your time or money. So, always stick to reliable sources and use that information to invest in the correct stocks.

Don't Trust Mails

You mustn't trust any emails that come from companies that claim to have enough knowledge about the stocks of other companies. These emails will also suggest the stocks that you should invest in, but the information in those emails is untrue. Companies cannot go through their investors' portfolios and suggest which stocks they should invest in. Even if a company does choose to do this, they may give you a suggestion that will not work for you. So, it is good to avoid these stocks and only invest in those stocks that you have all the information about.

Understand the Corrections

Remember that the price of stocks will be corrected in the market, and it is important that you remain patient. The price of the stock will drop when the market is correcting the price of the stocks in the market. If you are impatient, you will make a mistake and lose a lot of money. Always look at the company and make the right decisions about your investments. If a stock is either overpriced or underpriced, it means that the corrections will be made soon. Never sell your stocks in a panic and wait for the corrections to be made. You need to follow the news regularly, so you understand how or why the correction is being made.

Hire a Broker Only If Necessary

You should never hire a broker to do the job for you unless you need one. The only reason is that a broker will charge you a fee for helping you with your investments. They will also ask you to pay a commission, which will eat into your profits. You also need to remember that you need to pay your broker a fee regardless of whether you make a profit. So, they do not have to work hard to ensure that you make a profit. There are theories that companies hire brokers to increase the price of the stock in the market. They request the brokers to motivate investors to trade in a specific stock even if they do not want to invest in that stock. You will purchase these stocks if you can be swayed easily, which will lead to huge losses. You should always look for discounts online and see if you can trade independently. Avoid depending on your broker to buy and sell your stock.

Diversify Your Risks

This has been mentioned repeatedly across the book, so you can imagine how important it is for you to do this. You must always diversify your risks depending on the type of investment you make. This holds for any instrument. When you choose to invest in stocks, try to invest in stocks from different industries and sectors. If you invest in stocks only in one sector, you will lose a lot of money if the industry were to crash. It is because of this that you need to ensure that you diversify your capital. You must invest in different instruments in the market. Yes, one industry may be doing well compared to other industries, but this does not mean that you put all your money on stocks in that industry.

Money Movement

If you notice a sudden change in the price movement and the flow of money in the company, you know that the stock value will increase. If there is a sudden increase in the capital through external sources or it pumped its profits into its business, then it means that the company wants to expand. This will mean that the stock prices will rise, and it will benefit you as an investor. You must always keep track of the news and make the right decisions.

Look at the Stock Volume

If you notice that the volume of the stock has suddenly changed in the market, it is always a good idea to invest in that stock. The sudden changes in the price and volume of the stock will happen when there is some information in the news about the stock that makes people buy or sell stocks. Ensure that you capitalize on these situations so that you can make a huge profit. According to Timothy Sykes, you should always purchase a stock if you experience a high price after one year. The price of the stock will change only when the company talks about its earnings and bonuses.

Chapter 10. Advice to Minimizing Losses and Maximizing Gains

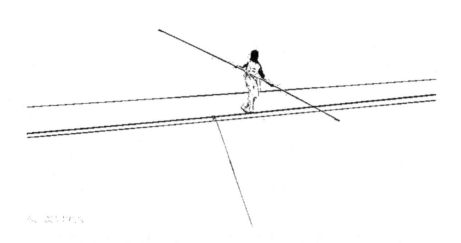

Some firms have different shares on the market. Some are good, and others are not so lucrative. How are you going to pick the right companies' stocks to make a full profit?

Well, the question is a million dollars one, but the answer is pretty easy. Before and unless you know the stock market, the answer to the million-dollar question cannot be sought. Yeah, business awareness is a must for anyone who wants to invest in stocks.

The good news is that trading on the Internet is very easy and hassle-free. All can invest in the stock at any time. Unlike other investment options on the market, there is no lock-in duration and restrictions.

However, you have to do some simple work in this sort of investment. At first, you will certainly reap the rewards of your investment if you prepare correctly and acquire ample knowledge of the workings of the stock market.

When the initial groundwork has been done, the answer to the million-dollar question can be sought. If a corporation issued public stock on the market — you bought those stocks, for instance, 100 shares at $10 each. Now, what factors will affect the price of the share? First and foremost, we must know why a specific company issues the public shares — the main purpose of shares issuance is to raise money for business expansion or pay the debt if any, and with the business increasing, the share prices often increase accordingly.

On the other hand, if you buy a share of a company and the share price falls in a few days, the company's growth curve is decreasing. Expert professionals, therefore, often recommend that investors keep an eye on major shares in the company.

Even if you have no idea what a company is, you can access information about a company, its growth curve, and its credibility in the previous industry. Many professionals recommend that they even purchase small-scale shares for full benefit.

Whenever you plan to buy a company share — gather all of the company's profile details and other important information. Following the study, purchase certain shares if you agree that a certain company share price will increase.

What Other Factors Affect the Trading Process?

Well, the website of the stock trading organization, the stockbroker, and the decision-making capacity impact the entire trading mechanism directly. It is always often easier to make a thorough market analysis on the Internet and then select the best alternative. If your fundamentals are simple, your investment will certainly give you maximum benefit. It is easier to do some simple work and then trade instead of jumping straight on the market. Now it is clear that professionals who make money on the same market have done all the required work required before the trade. So if you are a new investor and want to earn profits in a short time, first do your primary job, advise financial experts and then start trading online. Save money and build a good financial reserve to help your family better and effectively.

Options Trading — Losing Before Winning

Many options traders were frustrated when they set options to make a profit faster. Currently, nearly 90 % of the time, your options role will lose a lot until it would ultimately gain if it's raining at all. Sounds like something you've experienced?

Yeah, this is a reality of options trading and practice that seasoned traders like me learned to embrace. Many of my positions, especially single directional ones such as a long call, actually fall into a 60% loss until they eventually return to an astounding 100% profit. Yeah, most beginners took the loss early and missed the benefit.

What is the explanation for this phenomenon?

There are three key reasons why MOST options strategies lose a lot before making a profit.

The bid/work distribution of all the options involved in one position is first and foremost. The difference between the demand price and bid price of the options contract is the bid differential. Traders purchase retail options at the requested price and sell at the sale price.

An Options Contract with a $0.90 demand price and a $0.60 offer price has a $0.30 bid transaction range. This means that if you sell the option right as you purchased it, you instantly lose $0.30. The range of requests for options is considerably large for most inventories with spreads of $0.30 and spreads of up to $0.50 in some cases.

Only in extremely liquid inventories such as the QQQQ are there spreads of $0.10. Buying out money options costing about $0.70 with a bid of $0.20 could make you lose up to 30% right when you're in a spot! This is where most beginner options traders freak out, particularly if they commit the greatest sin of options trading—put all of their money into one trading.

Secondly, none of us, either George Soros or Warren Buffett, are stock market wizards. None of us will be able to trade reliably and move the stock exactly as planned at the moment it was launched (day trading excluded because periods are very limited in day trading).

As Jim Kramer said, we should always gradually develop a role over days because we are not geniuses. Yeah, unfortunately, most of the time, the stock seems to be heading in the opposite direction the very moment you sell.

The explanation seems that most traders enter trade emotionally when the shopping is heavy, which is also the point at which the stock retreats somewhat because of the over-compensation or over-sale when purchasing put options or shortcuts.

Leveraging in options trading now works in both ways. If it makes money faster, it will lose money faster, even though the stock just marginally shifts towards your favor.

Thirdly, Feedback!

Yeah, for a certain number of contracts, most options brokers will charge a minimum of $10 per trade. For beginner traders who take very small jobs, $20 ($10 for purchases and $10 for sales) may make considerable losses, particularly when money options are purchased. Committees often greatly sacrifice nuanced techniques for alternatives with multiple legs, such as the Condor Spread.

Combine the offer for spread loss with a pullback into the market, because we're not geniuses, and you'll end up losing 60% or more the very day that you placed a stock option. Sad but true, such a drastic and rapid loss would ruin most policy losses.

That is why many traders take losses too early to see stock recovery, ultimately in the right direction. Yeah, most losses are taken before the expiry of certain options! From a recent report, 60% of all available options were shut down before expiry!

When we use options trading strategies with limited risk, we can restrict this risk to a sum that we fully expect a loss, and we can tolerate loss if the trade goes wrong. When we transact directional options, we place some small "bets" over some time, and each time, ensure that the total is small enough to lead to negligible losses if the trade goes badly.

When you traded in this way, strength and control will overpower your emotions in the face of almost an immediate 60% loss in directional options trading.

Holding control also enables non-geniuses like us to wait for the reserves where they would ideal are, as most inventories won't move the way we want them to instantly (neutral tactics for options are very different, as you would expect the inventory not to move.

If you embrace the fact that your next trade option will possibly lose money considerably before they can benefit, it means you can use only the money that you intend to lose from the beginning to have a holding power that increases your chance of winning considerably

Chapter 11. Tax Implication and How to Reduce Their Impact on Your Earnings

Ah, we come to our favorite subject, taxes! The objective in the stock market is to make money, and every time that you make money, you are going to find yourself in a position of having to pay taxes on it. Unfortunately, it's a reality we can't escape. You might delay it, but at some point, you're going to have to pay.

There are many different issues you need to be aware of when it comes to taxes. This isn't a tax advisory book, and you should consult an accountant to make sure you're doing everything right. However, we'll take a brief look at some of the main issues.

Capital Gains

Suppose that you hold an asset, and the price appreciates. If you sell it, you'll realize a capital gain — in other words, you made money. When you make money by selling appreciated assets, you owe capital gains tax. The important thing to consider is how long you held the asset.

If you held the asset for one year or less, this is a short-term capital gain. The bad news about this is short-term capital gains are considered ordinary income. That means you'll pay the regular income tax rate on your gain.

If you hold the asset for longer than a year, even if it's just a day, then it becomes a long-term capital gain.

For some reason, Congress has decided that they know that holding assets for an arbitrary period that they made up is better, and so long-term capital gains have very favorable tax rates. These are much lower than income tax rates.

The bottom line here is that you'll want to take into account how long you have held an asset (aka stocks) when selling. If you are a long-term investor and planning to hold your investments until retirement, this means that you will be paying long-term capital gains taxes on your investments when you sell them off to get the money. Of course, if your retirement is in the distant future (more than ten years away), it's hard to say what the laws are going to be.

Dividend Income

The important thing to note about dividend income when considering taxes is that it's considered to be ordinary income. There isn't anything special to consider dividend income. The one exception is dividends paid by an MLP. That's because they aren't technically dividends and you're considered a "partner" in the business. In that case, you are able to deduct depreciation from your taxes. The company passes it on to the "partners." This has huge implications. Many investors in MLPs are able to enjoy their income from the investments virtually tax-free. It's a little complicated, so if you start putting money into MLPs, you'll want to consult an accountant. The company will be sending you the appropriate forms.

Individual Retirement Accounts

One of the advantages of individual retirement accounts or IRAs is that they allow investments to grow inside of them tax-free. You can utilize this to your advantage. One way to do so is to buy dividend stocks inside the IRA and then reinvest the dividends. That way, you can continually grow your account and grow it beyond the usual limitations.

Expenses

Deducting expenses related to your investment might be problematic. The IRS isn't too friendly when it comes to deducting expenses related to investing. There is one exception, and that is if you are a day trader. Then a day trader can deduct expenses like publications they read and all the computer equipment and software services that they sign up for. But if you are doing ordinary investing, that might be a hard sell.

One way to get around it is to set up a business to run your investing. Then have the business buy all the equipment and so forth. Of course, this will inject other complications into the situation, so you'll have to weigh the pros and cons in order to determine whether or not it's really worth the extra hassle. Quite frankly, in most cases, it's not going to be.

Understanding Your Brokerage Account and Statement

You'd be surprised to know that most extremely wealthy people have taxable brokerage accounts. It provides an avenue for them to benefit from the stock market and diversify their income stream. As we've discussed earlier in this book, if you want to invest huge amounts of money and be a successful investor, you have to open a taxable brokerage account.

What is a Brokerage Account?

A brokerage account is a taxable investment account that you can use to buy and sell stocks and other securities. As the name suggests, it's opened through a brokerage firm. It's much like a bank account. You have to deposit money into your account before you can start buying and selling stocks.

You can deposit money into your account through checks or electronic funds transfers. You can also wire money to your account.

Type of Investments a Brokerage Account Can Hold

Brokerage accounts are not just for stocks. There are a number of securities that a brokerage account can hold, including:

- **Common Stock** — This represents partial ownership of a company. It usually comes with voting rights.
- **Preferred stock** — This stock usually comes with high dividend payments, but it's more expensive

than common stock. Preferred stock shareholders typically don't have any voting rights.

- **Bonds** — A bond is a debt security. When you purchase a bond, the issuer (usually a government entity) owes you money. You earn money from bonds through interest rates.

- **Mutual Fund** — A mutual fund is funded by different shareholders. It's basically a pool of money that's invested in different securities. It's relatively easy to invest in a mutual fund. Plus, it's usually managed by a financial professional. You can buy different mutual funds, too, so you don't have to put all your money into one mutual fund.

- **ETF** — An ETF, or Exchange Traded Fund, is a basket of different securities that are traded like a stock. An ETF is a good investment because it has trading flexibility. It helps you diversify your investment portfolio and manage risk. It's also cheaper than a traditional mutual fund.

- **REIT** — A real estate investment trust, or REIT, is a company that either finances or operates income-producing real estate properties, such as commercial buildings. REITs usually own various income-generating real estate companies, such as hospitals, warehouses, hotels, and malls. You can invest in publicly traded REITs using your brokerage account.

- **Money Market and Certificate of Deposit** — A money market account generally represents pools of liquid mutual funds. It has higher interest rates and has a limited check-writing capacity. A certificate of deposit is basically a time deposit. For example, you agree to deposit $10,000 into your account. You can't withdraw that amount for five years, but you'll earn an interest rate throughout this period. So, if you earn $1,000 in interest per year, you're going to earn an extra $5,000 for your deposit after five years.

Cash Brokerage Accounts and Margin Brokerage Accounts

There are two main brokerage account types — cash accounts and margin accounts. A cash brokerage account requires you to deposit cash into your account. You'll have to pay for your transactions in cash and in full when you have a cash brokerage account.

A margin account, on the other hand, allows you to borrow from the broker using some of your assets as collateral to buy securities.

If you're a beginner, it's best to go for a cash brokerage account. Why? Well, margin brokerage accounts are complex and will get you buried in debt if you're not careful.

Limits of Money You Can Deposit in a Brokerage Account

As previously mentioned, other investment plans such as the IRA and 401(k) have limits, but taxable brokerage accounts do not, so you can deposit and invest as much as you want. That said, keep in mind that you do have to pay taxes for this type of investment.

How Many Brokerage Accounts Can One Have?

You can have as many brokerage accounts as you want, but keep in mind that most brokerage firms require a minimum deposit amount of $500 to $2000, so opening multiple accounts can be costly.

However, if you have unlimited resources, you can open multiple accounts with different brokerage firms.

Difference between a Discount Broker and a Full-Service Broker

There are two general types of broker:

- A full-service broker and

- A discount broker

A full-service brokerage account is great because it comes with a dedicated broker. You can call, text, or email him should you want to make an order. This broker usually knows you personally, and sometimes he knows your family. He also knows your finances intimately. He's like a financial advisor. You usually have to meet him regularly to discuss your portfolio.

Full-service brokers usually charge high commission fees. A discount broker, on the other hand, doesn't charge much. But, this type of broker usually operates online. A discount brokerage account is like a Do It Yourself (DIY) investment plan.

So, what should you choose? Well, it depends on what your priority is. If you are on a budget and you really want to save money, it's best to open a discount brokerage account. But, if you really want to have a financial adviser, it's a great idea to open a full-service brokerage account.

Understanding Your Broker's Statement

A broker's statement is a monthly report that contains the activities in your brokerage account. You can choose to receive a paper statement, but you can usually just check it online as well.

It pays to examine your statement carefully so you can spot some kind of fraud. When you first receive your income statement, you have to check to see if it looks professional. An unprofessional-looking statement is a red flag. Legitimate brokerage firms invest time and effort to make sure that their reports look polished and professional.

Here's what you'll find in your broker statement:

- **Statement Period Date** — A broker's statement reports how your investment is doing at a specific period of time, usually a month. If you don't see a statement period date, that's a red flag.

- **Account Number, Account Name, and Address** — This obviously contains your taxable brokerage account number, your name, and your present address. Be worried if this information is incorrect.

- **Contact Information** — This contains the contact information of your broker. If you don't see this anywhere in the statement, the brokerage firm you're dealing with may be dubious.

- **Name of the Clearing Firm** — This contains the name and the contact number of the clearing firm that holds your investments. FINRA rules require brokerage firms to place this information in their statements. So, be alarmed if you don't see this anywhere in your statement.

- **Account Summary** — This provides insight with regards to how your account is doing. This can help you review and assess your investment decisions.

- **Fees** — This covers the transaction and commission fees you've paid within the time period.

- **Account Activity** — This is where you can see the stocks you've bought or sold within that particular time period.

- **Margin** — If you have a margin account, you'll find this section. This contains the amount you've borrowed to purchase stocks and other securities.

- **Portfolio Detail** — This section breaks down your investment by types like stocks, bonds, or mutual funds.

Chapter 12. What to Do and What to Buy in a Down Market

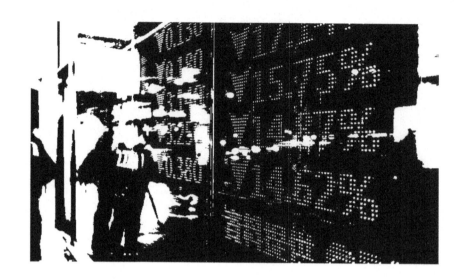

Now that you have an idea of why you need to invest and some fundamental principles in investment as well as asset classes, you can invest in it. For you to start winning in a big way, you would have to put in the time. You would have to put in the effort. You would have to have the proper experience and groundwork to make that happen. And in many cases, even with the best-laid plans and with the best strategies laid out, things still don't pan out.

The better approach is to do the best with the situation you are facing. In other words, use specific strategies that would enable you to position yourself to come out ahead. They might not necessarily result in you making tons of money or experiencing truly stupendous returns, but they can position you for solid gains. The following strategies enable you to do just that.

Buy Depressed Assets

Now, this might seem straightforward. After all, this is just a reiteration of the classic investment and commercial maxim of "buy low, sell high." However, the big challenge here is in determining what constitutes a "depressed asset."

You might be thinking that a stock that was trading at $50 and pops to $150 might not be all that depressed if it fell to $100. You might be thinking, where's the depression? This is not a fire sale. It hasn't fallen enough.

If you look at the stock's trajectory and how much growth potential and market attention, it might very well turn out that the stock is headed to $300. Do you see how this works?

If that's the case, then scooping up the stock at the price of $100 after it fell from $150 is a steal. After all, buying something worth $300 for a third of its price is one heck of a bargain.

Now, the big issue here is how do you know the stock's full future value? This is where serious analysis comes in. You can't just buy stocks on hype. It would be best if you looked at facts that would inform the growth trajectory of that stock.

For example, is it a market leader? Does it have certain drugs in the approval pipeline that have little to no competition? Is it on the cusp of a breakthrough drug patent? Is it in the process of buying out its competition?

There are many factors that you should consider, which can impact the overall future value of a stock. You should pay attention to its current developments, and you should pay attention to the news cycle surrounding the company.

You should also pay attention to its industry. Is its industry fast-expanding, or is it a "sunset industry" on its last legs? If it's in a sunset industry, there might still be opportunities there because, usually, such industries witness a tremendous amount of consolidation. Whatever the case may be, always be on the lookout for the future value of a stock based on what you know now, as well as its past performance.

Dollar-Cost Averaging

What happens if you buy a stock that subsequently crashes? This happens to the very best of us. If this happened to you, don't get depressed. Don't think that you suck at investing. Don't think that all is lost. If you get caught in a downturn, it might be an amazing opportunity.

Now, it's important to note that almost all stocks experience a pullback. I have yet to come across a stock that has appreciated positively with no dips in its trading history. I'm not aware of a stock that hasn't experienced a day-to-day dip in pricing. All stocks experience a pullback. Even stocks that are well on their way to becoming breakthrough or high-valued stocks will experience dips.

What happens if you bought a stock that drops in value tremendously? Well, you have two options at this point. You can wait for the stock to keep going up and then start buying some more. You're taking bets on its recovery.

The better approach would be to use this as an opportunity. For example, if you bought, for the sake of simplicity, one share of stock at $100 a share, and the price crashes 50% to $50 a share, you can buy one share at $50, and this would average out your holdings to $75 per share.

Ideally, you should wait for the stock to drop so much and then buy a whole lot. This enables you to set your break-even point at a much lower level. For example, using the same hypothetical facts mentioned above, instead of buying one share, you buy 9 shares at $50. So, what happens is, the average price per share gets reduced to $55.

Even if the depressed stock manages to limp along and possibly pop up here and there, it doesn't have to pop up all that much to get all your money back from your position because once it hits $55, you're at break-even territory. Compare this with breaking even at $75 or, worse yet, waiting for the stock to come back to $100 a share. It's anybody's guess whether it will back to that level.

This strategy is called dollar-cost averaging, and it is very useful. You must have free cash available, and you must use that free cash at the right time.

That's how you maximize its value. That's how you fully take advantage of opportunities that present themselves. Otherwise, you might be in a situation where the stock crashes so hard that you could have broken even very easily with little money spent, but unfortunately, you were locked out because you don't have the cash to do it.

Buy Self Liquidating Assets

Another investing strategy you can take is to buy assets that pay for themselves. For example, if you spent a million dollars buying a building, but the building generates rents totaling $100,000 per year, the building pays for itself in roughly 13 years or more, factoring in taxes and other costs.

Self-liquidating assets may seem too good to be true, but they are very real. Most of this applies to certain types of real estate, like commercial properties. However, this strategy also applies to stocks and bonds.

For example, if you buy stocks that have no dividend and you buy bonds, you can use the bond interest to start paying off your stock's portfolio. Of course, this can take quite a bit of time if you factor in interest rates as well as taxes.

Smart Money Valuation

Another winning strategy is to buy into private corporations as a sophisticated investor at a much lower valuation. Now keep in mind that many mobile app companies are popping up all over the United States. You don't necessarily have to live in Silicon Valley of California to have access to these types of companies.

The great thing about these companies is that in the beginning, they require very little capital. Many require

"Angel," "per-Angel," or even raw seed capital. The founder would have a rough idea of software, an app, or a website. This is the most basic stage of a company's evolution.

Now, when you come in as a source of seed capital, you can lock into a large chunk of the company's stock for a very low valuation. For example, somebody comes up with a startup idea, and the initial cost is a maximum of $1 million. If you were to invest $250,000, you have a 25% stake in the company.

You may be thinking that 25% of a company that's not worth that much, which is very, very risky, doesn't seem like a winning proposition. Well, keep in mind that after the seed stage, the company's valuation usually goes up. So, once your money has been used to push the company further along its developmental path, the company's valuation starts to go up, especially if they now have something more concrete to show other investors.

You may be asking yourself, okay, the smart money valuation thing sounds awesome. This is great in theory, but is it real? How can the Average Joe investor get in on such deals?

There are websites like Angel List and others, as well as LinkedIn groups that publicize startup projects that are actively recruiting investors. Of course, you need to do your homework and pay attention to the track record of the founders.

Chapter 13. How to Use Both Macroeconomic and Microeconomic Analysis

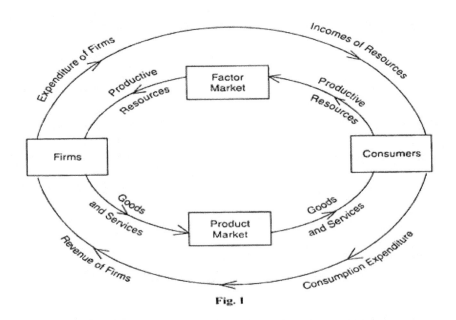

Fig. 1

You can't go to war without a weapon. You can't just buy a stock; you must do extensive research. You must learn to be your own stock analyst. This will help you make wise and sound investment decisions.

To do comprehensive stock research, you must apply two methods used in economics—microeconomics analysis and macroeconomic analysis.

Macro-Economic Analysis

As discussed earlier in this book, economic forces (such as the law of supply and demand) affect stock prices. So, before you invest in a stock, you have to use a top-down global research approach. You must look at the global trends. You must look at the big picture.

As of this writing, Airbnb is not a public company yet, but for the purpose of discussion, let's assume that it is. A lot of cities in Europe and in the United States have banned Airbnb, but it continues to grow in various cities in the world. In fact, you can find a lot of great Airbnb deals in Bali, Malaysia, Singapore, Zurich, Mykonos, and Faro. Plus, it still has a number of untapped markets. If you look at the big picture, you'll see that Airbnb is still a great investment because of its huge growth potential.

Aside from looking at the company's global overview, you must also consider other factors, such as:

Interest Rates

When the interest rate is high, it would be more costly for companies and individuals to pay their debts. This decreases their disposable income and their spending. This also affects business revenues and can drive down the stock prices.

But, when a country has a low-interest rate, people have more disposable income. They'll end up buying more stuff. This could lead to an increase in stock prices.

However, you have to take note that rising interest rates can benefit specific industries, such as the financial sector — banks, mortgage companies, lending companies, and insurance companies.

The Cyclical Nature of an Industry

Before you buy a company's stock, you have to determine if that company belongs to a cyclical industry.

Cyclical sectors such as the automobile industry and the construction industry are sensitive to the ups and downs of the economy. When the economy is good, their prices go up, but they go down when there's a recession.

Try to avoid investing in companies in cyclical sectors (unless you're very good at timing your investments). You'd want to invest in a stock that can withstand economic setbacks.

Stock Market Index

As previously discussed, an index tracks the performance of market leaders. So, in essence, it reflects the overall health of the stock market. If an index is trending up, it means that stock market players are a bit optimistic and a bull market may be happening.

Industry-Wide Research

Let's say that you want to invest in luxury brands such as Louis Vuitton (LVMH) or YSL. Before you do that, you must look into the overall health of that industry.

If you look closely, you might discover that luxury brands are not doing as well as they used to be because of online shops and China-made products.

Micro- Economic Analysis

When you do macro-economic analysis, you are looking at the economy and the industry, but understand that microeconomic analysis uses a "bottom-up" approach. This means that you have to do extensive company research.

You have to look into the different aspects of the company, such as:

- **The Company's Product** — Is the product good? Does it have loyal customers? Is the product going to be relevant ten years from now? Let's say that a music store is selling its stocks. Would you buy it? Well, let's face it: no one buys CDs anymore. We just download music from the internet or check YouTube.

160

Technology is changing by the minute. A widely used product may become irrelevant and unnecessary in the next few years. Just look at what happened to diskettes.

- **Sales and Revenue** — Are the company earning money? Are their products doing well in the market?

- **Debt to Equity Ratio** — Is the company's debt bigger than its equity? If so, then you should run as fast as you can.

- **P/E Ratio** — If the company has a high P/E ratio, it means that it has high growth potential. However, it also means that the stock is overvalued. A low P/E ratio means that the company has low growth potential, but it also means that it's overvalued. If you're into growth investing, choose a company with a high P/E ratio. But you have to choose a company with a low P/E ratio if you're into value investing.

- **Earnings per Share (EPS)** — A company with high EPS is really doing well. It's profitable. So, assuming other factors check out (e.g. it's not using a lot of unsustainable debt to generate the earnings), it's a good idea to invest in a company with a high EPS.

- **Company Management** — Do you trust the people managing the company? Do they engage in unethical business practices? If you don't trust the people running the company, then avoid it at all costs.

Also, make sure that the company's profit has been trending upward at least in the last five years.

Chapter 14. How to Create a Secure Financial Future

In today's scenario, where the economy hides and seeks some sort of position, financial security is a must for every individual. Although it is a broad category, financial security, however, means investment and income in the future. Look at the market, and you'll find different options for investment. Often it's hard to pick the right option.

Trading is yet another investment opportunity that offers no limits, unlike other investment strategies, but just good returns. However, as we all know, the stock market is a constantly changing environment, and we need technical analysis to learn from it; that will ensure your market success.

Unfortunately, many of us are not going to analyze it and continue to invest. The result is obvious, and that is why people often do not respond disproportionately to stock trading.

On the other hand, many of us profit from the same market, but attitudes and strategies differ. Why is one person a successful trader and another failing trader? If you know the difference in this small line, your investment strategy is guaranteed to succeed. Before you start trading, there are many things to consider:

- **Financial Strength** — Firstly, your financial strength — how much you want to invest — must be analyzed. You can start with small funds if you are a new trader. You can add more funds to your investment plan once you make money.

- **Experts in Finance** — investment is not a simple task. Proper planning is, therefore, a must. If you know market trends and trading experience, you can plan without assistance. However, if you are new and would like some assistance, please consult financial experts — they are available online and offer the best investment plan.

- **Comprehensive Market Knowledge** — A successful trader needs good market knowledge.

- **Online Stock Broke** — Because we are unable to trade directly, your broker makes all forms of trading and charges a small fee in return. It's like a connection between the trader and the stock market. You should therefore have a good broker who can also give you advice and let you know about the most profitable company shares.

- **Technical Analysis** — A complete competitive market analysis is a must. You have to analyze stock price trends in the last 3 to 5 days, and you can predict market mood further. This research, however, does not always succeed; it still gives us an idea of the market.

- **Positive Attitude** — it is not your attitude; it is your business attitude. Those who often see the market as a risky forum affect many of us and create a negative business attitude. In that very case, you can make the wrong decision, even if you are on the right track. Therefore, you must be optimistic and try to believe in yourself.

One of the main factors for successful trading is the ability to understand the market and to adapt to changing circumstances. Once you get to know the market moods, you can better reap the advantages. Invest now and build a strong future financial reserve.

How to Choose the Right Stocks to Invest In

Mia worked in a software development company for fifteen years. She's good at her job, but she was always stressed and tired. So, she decided to give stock market investment a try in order to build a passive income portfolio that would help her retire early. She met with an old friend named Kate, a financial analyst. Kate helped her invest in high-quality and fast-growing stocks.

After two years, Mia had earned $650,000 capital appreciation profit. She quit her job and traveled around the world. She soon used part of her earnings to establish her own graphic design company. Her $650,000 grew to over $2 million.

Mia is living her dream life. She owns her time. She has a successful business, and she even bought a beach house in Miami.

Chloe was Mia's former colleague. Like Mia, she's been working in the software development industry for about fifteen years. She was also tired. After she heard about Mia's success, she decided to invest in stocks, too.

Chloe didn't know anything about the stock market and didn't know how to choose the right stocks. She invested in companies that were buried in debt and engaged in unethical business practices. So, she ended up losing $10,000.

A lot of people get rich through stock market investment, but many people lose huge amounts of money too. This is the reason why you should be careful in choosing the right stocks to invest in. You have to be clear about your investment goals and use the right strategies that work for you and match your risk tolerance level. You must also do extensive research before you place your bet on a stock.

Setting an Investment Objective

Before you start investing, you should be clear about what your investment objectives are. You should also decide what type of investor you want to be. Do you want to be a long-term investor? Or, do you want to be a day trader, trading stocks by the minute?

You must be clear about what you want to achieve through stock market investing. How much are you willing to invest?

How much do you want to earn each year? What are you willing to risk?

You need to set financial goals like how much you want to earn in one year or in five years. You should also set non-financial goals. Why? Well, your investment earnings are just mere tools that you can use to support your non-financial goals. So, what do you want to achieve? Do you want to have a grand wedding? Do you want to travel to a foreign country at least twice a year?

Factors to Consider in Choosing a Stock

The key to building a profitable investment portfolio is choosing the right stocks. When you're starting, buying individual stocks is costlier than investing in low-cost mutual funds. Below are the factors that you should consider in choosing stocks to invest in.

- **Growth in Earnings**

  Before you invest in a company, you should check its earnings and make sure that it's consistently growing over time. The growth doesn't have to be huge. You just have to look for an upward trend in earnings.

For example, let's say that you have an extra $3,000 and you want to invest it in stock. You're looking to invest in two companies. Company A is one of the biggest steel manufacturers in the country, while Company B produces the nation's best-selling batteries.

Take time to examine the data below:

o **Company A: Leading Steel Manufacturer**

Year	Earnings
2005	$2,158,111,202
2006	$2,160,369,000

2007	$2,080,250,000
2008	$1,988,910,000
2009	$1,888,630,121
2010	$1,780,980,011
2011	$1,761,918,870
2012	$1,709,919,450
2013	$1,670,980,689
2014	$1,659,658,905

Year	Earnings
2015	$1,640,050,814
2016	$1,590,010,110
2017	$1,550,000,289
2018	$1,499,110,980

- o **Company B: Leading Battery Manufacturer**

Year	Earnings
2005	$750,000,905
2006	$805,963,960

2007	$815,750,690
2008	$909,530,066
2009	$915,784,210
2010	$918,974,560
2011	$990,741,632
2012	$1,101,890,390
2013	$1,156,120,450
2014	$1,190,110,000

2015	$1,220,000,980
2016	$1,240,780,360
2017	$1,310,000.550
2018	$1,399,222,080

If you look closely, you'll see that Company A has a lot more earnings than Company B. However, its revenue has been declining since 2008. This means that the company is facing problems. It could be mismanagement or a decreasing market share due to an aggressive competitor entering the space.

Company B, on the other hand, has had steady growing earnings since 2006. This company is doing something right and is more worthy of your hard-earned money.

- **Stability**

Sir Tim Berners-Lee published a paper about a proposed information management program called the "internet" in 1989. He then implemented the first successful communication between a Hypertext Transfer Protocol (HTTP) and a server a few months later.

In 1990, Berners-Lee began writing the World Wide Web (www) — the first-ever web browser. The next year, he launched the first-ever web page. This forever changed the world. This is what stock market players call a black swan.

According to risk analyst Nassim Nicholas Taleb, a black swan is an event that's hard to predict that can forever change the world. And if you're wise enough to predict or at least spot a black swan at its early stage, you're going to win big in the stock market and in business. This explains why early internet entrepreneurs like Jack Ma and Jeff Bezos are extremely wealthy.

And soon, promising internet companies decided to go public and the investors went crazy placing their eggs in the "internet business basket."

But after the tech industry got a little too crowded and the world experienced a stock market crash in 2008, the revenues of internet companies became volatile. So, a lot of investors ended up losing huge amounts of money.

Even so, this is just an example. It doesn't mean that you shouldn't invest in the tech industry. All companies are bound to lose their stock value at some point, especially during periods of recession and economic crisis.

To achieve long-term success in the stock market, you have to invest in companies that are strong and stable enough to endure unfavorable economic conditions. Erratic stock price fluctuation is not a good sign.

To illustrate this point, look at the graph below:

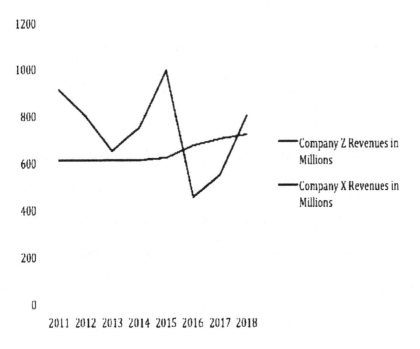

Notice that Company Z's revenue doesn't fluctuate as much as Company X's. This means that it's more stable and a good choice for long-term investment.

Chapter 15. Stock Market Strategies for Profitable Investing

Learning how to use successful bond market strategies will vary between the loss and possible profits of all your hard-earned money. These tips help you find the right investment strategies to use and avoid those that harm you more.

The Business Know

It is necessary to know the market before you can begin investment so that you can better understand how to use effective stock market strategies. Study the market as best as you can, including those stocks that are of interest to you — there are plenty of websites and other reference material that can help you get an understanding of the market.

Besides, partnering with a reputable financial advisor or creditable financial information provider is a perfect stock market strategy to understand better the market and what it can do for you.

Evite Fraud

Beginners are particularly vulnerable to fraud and schemes designed to draw prospective investors to divide their hard-playing cash. Many who fall for these sly stock market schemes won't do anything; in fact, only the scammers themselves profit from these scams!

The bottom line — most definitely if it sounds too good to be true. Equipped with the right investment strategies and expertise, you won't fall into these enticing schemes.

A Stock Broker Notice

An investment plan is a perfect way to use a stockbroker as a reliable broker will help you to decide on your portfolio and help you pick the right stock for your situation. A trustworthy broker can use his expertise to help you gain greater market knowledge, including trends, stock growth, and whether to buy or sell.

Furthermore, a stockbroker can show you even better investment strategies than you can buy. A reliable broker will happily assist you with your investments and will do everything possible to lead you in the right direction.

Learning how to play the stock market can be terrifying for beginning investors in particular. By learning about the market, avoiding schemes that are too good for you to be true, and finding a reputable stockbroker, you will learn successful stock market strategies to make your investment profitable.

It is crucial for beginners to have a solid understanding of the market and how to be as effective as possible before even beginning to invest in the stock market. The following bonds will lead you in the right direction.

Train Yourself

The first step towards being a good investor is to educate you. Take a few lessons in accounting, read as many books on investment as possible, and look online for different facets of the business and how it works for you.

Another suggestion that helps you become a better investor is to talk to a licensed stockbroker or financial advisor. A renowned advisor can provide you with direct personal information which you are not able to find in books or posts, and can also sit one-on-one with you and answer all your questions.

Take Stock Exchange Tools

Another smart tip is to use apps for some tasks. It is advisable to invest in personal finance software that can help you handle your money and track income and losses. A program that helps you monitor your stock market portfolio and trace when to buy or sell will be another software to consider; evaluate potential profits vs. risks of a specific stock, and track stock prices.

Continue to Train

One of the best investment tips, particularly for beginners, is to continue to practice until you have a good understanding of the market and its concepts. If you do not follow some other bond suggestion, it should certainly be a priority, regardless of what.

Many stock simulation programs, without taking risks and investing, will make you experience the real thing. Some of these systems are more practical than others, but all of them help you understand the idea of stock purchasing and trading.

Chapter 16.   COVID-19 Effects on Working with Stocks

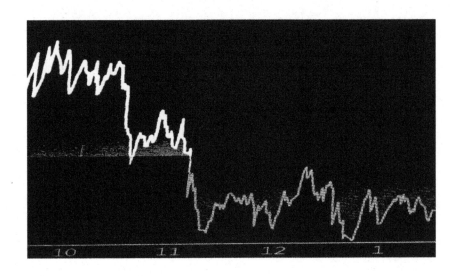

The stock market's reaction to the COVID-19 pandemic and the subsequent economic fallout has raised both fears and questions. This column delves into unexpected developments. There is evidence that shareholders favored the less distressed companies, and that credit facilities and government guarantees, lower policy interest rates, and stock price lockdowns helped to minimize the stock price decline. Fundamentals, on the other hand, only account for a limited portion of stock market fluctuations at the country level. Overall, it's difficult to argue that the correlations between stock prices and fundamentals have been shaky at best.

The World Health Organization (WHO) declared on June 8, 2020, that the COVID-19 pandemic was worsening around the world and cautioned against complacency: "the majority of people worldwide are still vulnerable to infection. "...With more than six months left in the pandemic, now is not the time for any nation to ease up on the gas." The US stock market started its fourth consecutive week of gains on the same day. The S&amp P 500 index has returned to where it was at the start of 2020, erasing the historical decline (one-third of its value) that occurred between February 20 and March 23, 2020, as if nothing had happened. As seen in the graph, this is absolutely unparalleled.

Is there something unusual about the stock market behavior during COVID-19? The reaction of financial markets poses serious concerns as the world suffers from the worst economic crisis since the Great Depression (Baldwin and Weder di Mauro 2020a, 2020b, Bénassy-Quéré and Weder di Mauro 2020, Coibon et al. 2020). Stock prices have been wildly fluctuating since the start of the crisis. They dismissed the pandemic at first, then panicked as it spread to Europe. They are now acting as if the millions of people who have been poisoned, the 400,000 deaths, and the containment of half the world's population has had no economic effects.

Paul Krugman (2020) said out loud what many people were thinking in one of his famous New York Times columns: "Whenever you consider the economic ramifications of stock prices, you want to remember three rules." To begin with, the stock market is not the same as the economy. Second, the stock market isn't the same thing as the economy. Third, the stock market is not a replacement for the economy (...). The correlation between stock performance and real economic growth, which is largely driven by the oscillation between greed and fear, has always been shaky at best. "Malkiel and Shiller (2020)," two other well-known economists, have also discussed the stock market's strange conduct in the face of the pandemic. The suspected stock market irrationality, according to Malkiel, is just "apparent," and the COVID-19 crisis does not "imply that markets are dysfunctional" since there are no arbitrage possibilities and stock markets remain difficult to beat. "Speculative prices can statistically mimic a random walk, but they are not as bound to genuine knowledge (...), says Shiller. The infectious stories about the coronavirus had their own internal complexities that were only tangentially linked to the truth."

What lessons can be learned about stock market actions from the COVID-19 crisis? This debate is particularly important for financial economists, but it is also important because the general public has a negative perception of stock markets, which should worry us (Rajan 2015) — especially after the COVID-19 crisis placed science and 'experts' to the test (Aksoy et al. 2020), without sparing economists.

A rapidly growing body of research looking at stock market reactions to the COVID-19 pandemic is already providing some insights. Although the stock market's actions during the pandemic could seem spontaneous, irrational, or even insane at first glance, closer observation shows that they did not respond randomly. Several studies have shown that stock markets are effective at discounting the most vulnerable companies: those that are financially fragile, vulnerable to international value chain disruption, vulnerable to corporate social responsibility, or less resilient to social distancing (Alburque et al. 2020, Ding et al. 2020, Fahlenbrach et al. 2020, Pagano et al. 2020, Ramelli and Wagner 2020). Furthermore, it appears that, at least in the medium term, stock market declines are linked to analyst forecast revisions (Landier and Thesmar 2020). We approach these papers from a macroeconomic standpoint. While the studies described above provide useful details, some questions remain unanswered.

What has been the response of the stock market to the COVID-19 pandemic? How do we understand the disparities in responses around countries? Are there any macroeconomic or institutional factors that influence stock market response across countries, and if so, which ones? Are these disparities the product of how governments treated the pandemic? How have financial markets responded to nationwide lockdowns and economic policies aimed at 'flattening' the curves of infection and recession? (2020 Gourinchas)

We discuss how stock markets have incorporated public knowledge about the COVID-19 pandemic and subsequent lockdowns in our recent paper (Capelle-Blancard and Desroziers 2020). Despite the fact that the COVID-19 shock was global, not all countries were affected in the same way, and they did not react in the same way. This high heterogeneity is something we take advantage of. We want to understand the differences in stock market responses by looking at the situation in each country prior to the crisis, as well as the subsequent containment measures (social distancing and stay-at-home orders) and economic policies (fiscal and monetary) that were introduced during the crisis. From January to April 2020, we consider a panel of 74 nations, which can be divided into four phases: incubation, outbreak, fear, and rebound. We gathered regular data on stock index prices, COVID-19 total cases and deaths, global market sentiment and volatility, government responses to the outbreak, and various indicators of mobility for each region (or lack thereof).

Three main results emerge about stock market reactions during the COVID-19 pandemic. First, after initially ignoring the pandemic (until February 21, 2020), financial markets responded strongly to the rise in the number of infected people in each country (February 23 to March 20, 2020), with volatility increasing as fears about the pandemic increased. Following central bank intervention (23 March to 20 April 2020), however, news of the health crisis no longer seemed to bother shareholders, and shares rebounded all over the world. Second, it appears that country-specific characteristics had little, if any, impact on stock market responses. Stock markets in countries more vulnerable to the pandemic did not respond as strongly, either because of systemic economic fragility (for example, indebted countries) or because of exposure to transmission vectors (for example, countries with 'at-risk' populations). Third, the number of COVID-19 cases in neighboring (but mostly wealthy) countries piqued investors' interest. Fourth, the fall in stock prices was mitigated by credit facilities and government guarantees, lower policy interest rates, and lockout measures.

Finally, do capital markets take into account all available information? In fact, we can see the glass as either half-full or half-empty. On the one hand, the stock market's behavior during the COVID-19 pandemic is not entirely coincidental. Our research indicates that the reaction of stock markets was affected by health policies introduced during the crisis to restrict virus transmission and macroeconomic policies aimed at supporting businesses, rather than the situation of countries prior to the crisis. Fundamentals, on the other hand, only account for a (very) small portion of stock market volatility. It's difficult to deny that the connection between stock prices and fundamentals has been anything but loose, as Krugman and Shiller have claimed.

Conclusion

There are also many different types of investments, orders, and such that the individual may make. It is crucial that the investor knows the differences between these and can decide on which methods the investor wishes to invest in. However, the investor must know the pros and cons of each to reach that conclusion. The investor must educate himself or herself before making any further decisions on their investments and strategies for trading. There are many elements of the stock market that one must familiarize themselves with; the more that you know, the better the chance of you receiving a high return on your investment is.

Stock market investing can be very powerful for any person looking to create wealth or build a side income. Among all the asset classes, stock investments have generated the best returns historically. Consequently, it is beneficial for you over the long term that you develop a sound understanding of this highly profitable investment avenue.

The next step is to follow this through and begin your quest as a stock investor. It is important to begin by setting goals for yourself as an investor. You must consider all of the variables involved in investing. Setting goals will help provide you with a sense of direction. By using this as a reference, you may decide on which path of investing you will choose. What will be the time period of your investment? Will you purchase individual stocks or ETFs? How much risk are you willing to take in your investments? These questions, among others, must be answered to provide you with clear goals in your investing. After this, you may create an account, fund your account, and start trading. There must be research done, and you must select your stocks. After this, you are on the path to success in trading.

After you have accomplished this, you must continue to conduct research on the market, monitor your stocks, and manage your portfolio. Being an investor is an ongoing process. This can really help you to get started in learning about stock, and it may serve as a reference guide throughout your stock investing career. There will constantly be changes in the economy, the stock market will fluctuate every day, and the stocks themselves will continuously move. However, the basic concepts of stock will always be helpful to know, and this provides its readers with those basics that are necessary for one to be successful in stock investing.

The goal is to help investors, especially those who are just getting started with investing in the stock market, to learn the basic concepts of the stock market that will help them to initiate the trading process and become both successful and profitable in their investments.

Stock investing requires discipline, patience, and thoughtful analysis. Diversification is an essential strategy for successful stock investing. Keeping your emotions in check is also a crucial part of becoming a successful investor. A long-term approach to stock investments provides many times good returns.

By reading it to the end, you are proving that you are disciplined and ready to work hard! Many rookie investors spend their money investing blindly. Unlike the majority, you have taken your time to acquire knowledge to make wise decisions. Good job!

OPTIONS TRADING

A Crash Course Guide to Making Money

for Beginners and Experts:

How to Invest in the Market through

Profit Strategies to Buy and Sell Options

Anthony Sinclair

Introduction

An option is a financial contract called a derivative contract. It allows the owner of the contract to have the right to buy or sell the securities based on a specified period's agreed-upon price.

As the name suggests, there is no obligation in this type of transaction. The trader pays for the right or the option to buy or sell a transaction such as security, stock, index, or ETF (exchange-traded fund). An option is a contract.

The option derives its value based on the value of the underlying asset hence the term derivative contract. This contract states that the buyer agrees to purchase a specified asset within a certain amount of time at a previously agreed-upon price. Derivative contracts are often used for commodities like gold, oil, and currencies, often in US dollars. Another type of derivative is based on the value of stocks and bonds. They can also be based on interest rates such as the yield on a specified amount of time Treasury note as a 10-year Treasury note.

In a derivative contract, the seller does not have to own the specified asset. All he must do is have enough money to cover the price of the asset to fulfill the contract. The seller also has the option of giving the buyer another derivative contract to offset the asset's value. These choices are often practiced because they are easier than providing the asset itself.

Securities come in several types. The great thing about securities is that they allow a person to own a specified asset without taking its tenure. This makes them readily tradable because they are good indicators of the underlying value of the asset.

The trader can exercise the option at the strike price up until the expiry date reaches. In Europe, a trader can only exercise the right to the option at the strike price exactly on the expiry date. We will more largely focus on the American way of trading options, which allows for exercising right on or before the expiration date.

Trading options and trading stocks are different because stocks and options have different characteristics. Stocks share ownership in individual companies or options, and this allows the stock trader to bet in any direction that he or she feels the stock price is headed.

Stocks are a great investment if you are thinking of long-term yields, such as for retirement and have the capital. They are very simplistic in the approach in that the trader buys the stock and wagers on the price that he or she thinks will rise at a certain time in the future. The hope is that the price will increase in value, thus gaining the trader a substantial yield.

The risk of investing in stocks is that stocks can plummet to zero at any moment. This means that the investor can lose his or her entire investment at the drop of a hat because stocks are very volatile from day to day. They react to world events such as wars, politics, scandals, epidemics, and natural disasters.

On the other hand, options are a great option for traders who would like flexibility with timing and risks. The trader is under no obligation and can see how the trade plays out over the time specified by the option contract. In that period, the price is locked, which is also a great appeal.

Trading options also require a lower investment compared to stocks typically.

Another great appeal for options reading is that the specified period is typically shorter than investing in stocks. This allows for regular buying and selling as options have different expiration dates.

The drawback that makes some people hesitate in trading options is that it is more complex than trading stocks. The trader needs to learn new jargon and vocabulary such as strike prices, calls and puts to determine how he or she can set up effective options. Not only does the trader have to learn new terms, but he also must develop new skillsets and the right mindset for options trading.

There are several advantages to trading options, and they include:

The initial investment is lower than with trading stocks. This means that the options trader can benefit from playing in the same financial market as a stock trader without paying as much upfront. This is called hedging.

The options trader is not required to own the asset to benefit from its value. This means that the trader does not incur the cost associated with the asset. Costs can include transportation and storage fees if applicable.

There is no obligation to follow the transaction. Whether the trader exercising a call or put option, at the end of the day, the loss is limited because the trader is only obligated to pay for the contract and nothing more. Only if the trader feels it worth it does he or she take action to move forward with exercising the contract.

The options trader has many choices. Trading options give the trader great flexibility.

The strike price freezes the price. This allows the options trader the ability to buy or sell the asset on or before the expiration date without the worry of fluctuating prices.

Options can protect an asset from depreciating market prices. This is a long-term strategy that can protect assets from drops in market prices. Exercising a call allows the trader to buy the asset at a lower price.

The trader can earn passive income from assets that he or she already owns. You can sell call options on your assets to earn income through traders paying you premiums.

Successful options traders weigh the pros and cons carefully and implement strategies to minimize the costs and potential losses while leveraging ways to make maximum profit.

BEGINNERS

Chapter 1. What Are Options

Trading and the Best Market

An option is an agreement that lets in (but doesn't require) a monetary expert to purchase or sell a hidden instrument like a security, ETF, or even list at a foreordained cost over a specific timeframe. Buying and selling options are achieved on the alternatives advertise, which exchanges agreements dependent on protections. Purchasing a choice that allows you to shop for shares sometime in the future is called a "name alternatives." However, shopping for an option that permits you to promote shares sometime within the no longer too distant future is referred to as a "put alternatives."

Nonetheless, alternatives are not a similar thing as shares considering they don't communicate to proprietorship in an organization. What's more, even though fates use contracts truly as options do, options are viewed as a lower risk because of the way that you may pull back (or leave) An option contract anytime. The price of the alternatives (its top rate) is, therefore, a degree of the hidden useful resource or security.

There are various types of alternatives — call and put options — which offer the speculator the right (however not commitment) to promote or purchase protections.

Call Options

A call option is a settlement that offers the monetary expert the privilege to purchase a particular measure of offers (regularly 100 for each transaction) of specific protection or object at a predefined fee over a selected take look at of time. For instance, name options might enable a supplier to purchase a selected movement of quantities of either stock, bonds, or even unique gadgets like ETFs or lists at a later time (via the termination of the agreement).

In case you're purchasing a name option, it implies you need the stock (or other security) to head up in price with the aim that you can make an advantage off of your settlement through training your entitlement to purchase those shares (and commonly quickly offer them to capitalize on the benefit).

The rate you are paying to buy the name alternatives is referred to as the top-notch (it's the expense of purchasing the agreement which will permit you to, in the long run, buy the stock or security). In this sense, the top rate of the name alternative is just like an in advance installment like you'll put on a house or vehicle. When buying a name, alternatively, you concur with the dealer on a strike fee. You are given the option to purchase the security at a foreordained price (which doesn't change till the agreement terminates).

Be that because it may, for what motive would a monetary expert use option? Purchasing alternatives are essentially wagering on stocks to go up, down, or to help an exchanging position in the marketplace.

The cost at which you consent to buy the fundamental protection utilizing the opportunity is called the "strike cost," and the cost you pay for purchasing that alternatives settlement is referred to as the "superior." When identifying the strike fee, you're wagering that the gain (in general, a stock) will go up or down in fee. The quantity you're deciding to buy that wagered is top-notch, which is a stage of the estimation of that benefit.

There are various types of options — name and put alternatives — which offer the financial expert the right (yet now not commitment) to sell or purchase protections.

Thus, call alternatives are additionally a lot of identical protection — you are paying for a settlement that terminates at a set time but allows you to buy protection (like a stock) at a foreordained cost (which won't move up regardless of whether or not the fee of the stock available does). In any case, you have to reestablish your options (typically week after week, month to month, or quarterly premise). Thus, alternatives are constantly encountering what's referred to as time rot — which means their well worth decompositions after a few times.

For name alternatives, the decrease in the strike fee, the extra inherent well worth the name alternative has.

Put Options

On the opposite hand, a put opportunity is an agreement that gives the speculator the privilege to sell a particular measure of offers (once greater, often one hundred for every transaction) of specific safety or ware at a predefined value over a specific time fashionable. Much the same as name options, a put option permits the broking the right (however no longer commitment) to sell security via the agreement's termination date.

Much the same as name alternatives, the fee at which you consent to sell the stock is known as the strike fee, and the top class is the fee you are purchasing the put opportunity.

Put options paintings likewise to calls, besides you need the safety to drop in fee in case you are purchasing taken care of alternative to make again (or sell the put alternatives and while you parent the fee will pass up).

On the despite name options, with put alternatives, the better the strike price, the greater the intrinsic well worth the put alternatives have.

Long As Opposed to Short Options

Not in any respect like distinctive protections like fates contracts, are alternatives changing usually a "long" — which means you're buying the alternatives with the expectancies of the cost going up (in which case you will buy call alternatives)? In any case, irrespective of whether you purchase put options (appropriate to sell the safety), you are as but shopping extended options.

Shorting an option is promoting that alternative. However, the blessings of the deal are restricted to the premium of the opportunities — and the hazard is boundless.

Chapter 2. How Much Capital Do You Need to Trade

There are too many risks in this type of trading. Capital is a basic requirement to start any business. Does options trading require too much capital? No. When starting on options trading, it is better to start with small capital to avoid massive trading risks.

Many are the individuals who utilize much of their cash for trading during their first days, which is so dangerous. Such individuals end up having too many risks to handle, and finally, they make up their minds to close their businesses. I do not want you to fall into such a mess. Do your thing with the right speed.

Start options trading with a reasonable small amount. Do not brag off that you got everything under control. You will lose even the only cash you had. Starting with less money has a high likelihood of fewer risks in trading. I bet you can now handle a few risks and be able to continue with your trading.

How to Start Options Trading

Now with the basic knowledge of options trading, I will provide you with a few details on how to start an options trading journey.

- You should look for an options trading broker. The key to successful options trading is your broker. There exist legit and non-legit brokers in options trading. Some of the tips for selecting a good broker include the following:

- Do some research on the broker first. You need to be keen and alert before opening a brokerage options trading platform. Different brokers will approach you with different platforms. Do not rush or assume everything is good; do some research on the best brokers. Make sure you spend your cash well by paying for a good options trading platform. It will help you a lot because your trading performance depends on your platform. Choose a broker with good ratings.

- Charges lower commissions. Some brokers tend to exploit traders by charging high commissions to beginners. You should weigh different commission offers of different brokers before settling on one. Some even charge no commission to traders. You should prefer brokers with fewer commissions. Payment of high commissions periodically can mess you up with losses, and you may find it even hard to secure your trading capital. Do not accept to pay high commissions. You also need to make some savings other than wasting money while paying commissions.

- A simple user interface platform. There is a wide variety of software with different functionalities and features. Some software has a simple user interface, while others are too complex for you to use. You should choose a platform with a simple and clear user interface that enables you to make your trades with less struggle. Some platforms can waste your precious time when you struggle too much searching on the Internet on how you operate them. Make your work easier by handling software that is according to your level.

- Trading tools for research. You should also consider factors like tools that are present on the platform. Do not purchase a platform with no tools. It will be hard for you. Platform tools ease your trading and make your performance excellent. The tools here may include charting tools, research tools, and even tools that alert you on any market changes that may arise.

- Do some testing on the brokerage platform. Do not be that kind of a careless trader who does things for the sake of doing with no precautions. You need to be cautious enough since this is an income-generating activity. You should test on a brokerage software before making up your mind about purchasing it. Check on the reliability and stability of the software and be 100% sure that this is the platform you will use for your trading. Ensure the software is not that type of platform that crashes down unexpectedly. You might miss crucial trade while fixing your software.

- Be approved to trade options. You need to be approved by the broker in charge before purchasing and offering options for sale. They normally have their ways of approving you, like checking your experience and the money that you have. It aids in avoiding risks for the customers. You cannot escape this step.

- Get a clear understanding of the technical analysis. Options trading is a technical field. You need to have the technical analysis techniques of trading options. The technical aspects include reading charts, know about the volume of stock, and also moving averages. Trading charts mostly analyze price behavior in the market. You will handle the aspects many times while trading. Perfect your technical knowledge and be cautious with them.

- Take advantage of mock trading accounts. Using real accounts when starting options trading is a risky game. You can lose a lot of cash within a short time duration. Mock accounts exist for a reason. You should test your trading skills in the mock accounts, learn a few tricks, and perfect your skills. The advantage of using a mock account is that there is no loss of money since they mostly provide virtual money. It prepares you for real trading. You should take advantage of them and learn a lot. Utilize them for a while and do some evaluations on your returns. When everything works out well, face real trading and shine.

- Utilize limit orders. It is risky to rely on market prices since price behavior change with time. You should utilize limit orders when trading. A limit order is a type of order that enables you to purchase market securities at an agreed price. Using this type of order shuns you from incurring losses in options trading.

- Revise your strategies with time. After entering into the options trading, with time, you need to revise your strategies. Utilize the working strategies more often and get rid of unsuccessful trading strategies. You should not have many strategies that do not bring good performance. Few working strategies are better than having multiple ones that do not help you.

- Register and join in options trading platforms. Joining forums comprised of other options traders is another way of how to get started in options trading. Forums are platforms for different people with different experiences and opinions. You can learn mistakes made by others in trading. It is part of growing in options trading. So why shouldn't you give it a try?

- Study and learn about trading metrics. Having your returns maximized is also another way of getting started in options trading. Traders normally use different trading metrics such as delta, gamma, theta, and Vega. You should learn and practice them for massive returns.

Chapter 3.   Basic Options Strategies

Traders often jump into options trading with little understanding of options strategies. With a bit of effort, traders can learn to take advantage of flexibility and power. Strategies are usually laid in the trading plan and should strictly implement in every options trading move that is likely to be involved.

Collars

The collar strategy was established by holding several shares of the underlying stock available in the market where protective puts were bought and the call options sold. In this kind of strategy, the options trader is likely to protect the capital used in the trading activities rather than the idea of acquiring more money during trading. This kind is considered conservative and somewhat much more critical in options trading.

Credit Spreads

It is presumed that the biggest fear of most traders is a financial breakdown. In this side of strategy, the trader gets to sell one put and then buy another one.

Covered Calls

Covered calls are the right kind of strategy where a particular trader sells the right for another trader to purchase his or her stock at some strike price and get to gain a proper amount of cash. However, there is a specific time that this strategy should utilize and, in a case where the buyer fails to purchase some of the stock and the expiration date dawns, the contract becomes invalid right away.

Cash Naked Put

Cash naked put is a kind of strategy where the options trader gets to write at the money or out of the money during a particular trading activity and aligning some specific amount of money aside to purchase stock.

Long Call

It is the most basic strategy in options trading and one that is quite easy to comprehend. In the long-call strategy for options trading, aggressive option traders who happen to be bullish are pretty much involved. It implies that bullish options traders end up buying stock during the trading activities with the hope of it rising shortly. The reward is unlimited in the long-call strategy.

Short Call Option

The quick-call strategy is the reverse of the long call one. Bearish kind of traders is so aggressive in the falling out of stock prices during trading in this kind of strategy. They decide to sell the call options available. This move considers being so risky by the experienced that options traders believe that prices may drastically decide to rise once again. It significantly implies that large chunks of losses are likely to be incurred, leading to a real downfall of your trading structure and everything involved in it.

Long Put Option

First things first, you should be contented that buying a put is the opposite of buying a call. So in this kind of plan, when you become bearish, that is the moment you may purchase a put option. Put option puts the trader in a situation where he can sell his stock at a particular time before the expiration date reached. This strategy exposes the trader to a mere kind of risk in the options trading market.

Iron Condor

The iron condor involves the bull call spread strategy, and the bear put strategy all at the same time during a particular trading period. The expiration dates of the stock are still similar and are of the same underlying stock. Most traders get to use this strategy when the market is expected to experience low volatility rates and with the expectation of gaining a little amount of premium. Iron condor worked in both up and down markets and was believed to be economical during the up and down markets.

Married Put

On this end, the options trader purchases options at a particular amount of money and at the same time to buy the same number of shares of the underlying stock. This kind of strategy is also known as the protective put. It is also a bearish kind of options trading strategy.

Cash Covered Put

Here, one or more contracts sold with 100 shares multiplied with the strike price amount for every particular contract involved in the options trading. Most traders use this strategy to acquire an extra amount of premium on a specific stock they would wish to purchase.

Long Butterfly

This strategy involves three parts where one put option is purchased at particular and then selling the other two options at a price lower than the buying price and purchasing one put at an even lower price during a specific trading period.

Short Butterfly

In this strategy, three parts are still involved were a put option sold at a much higher price and two puts then purchased at a lower price than the purchase price and a put option is future on sold at a much lower strike price. In both cases, all put bear the same expiration date, and the strike prices usually are equidistant as revealed in various options trading charts. A short butterfly strategy is the opposite way of a long butterfly strategy.

Long Straddle

The long straddle is also known as the buy strangle, where a slight pull and a slight call are purchased during a particular period before the expiration date reaches. The importance of this strategy is that the trader bears a high chance of acquiring reasonable amounts of profits during his or her trading time before the expiration date is achieved.

Short Straddle

In this kind of strategy, the trader sells both the call and put options at a similar price and bearing the same expiration date. Traders practice this strategy with the hope of acquiring reasonable amounts of profits and experience various limited kinds of risks.

Reverse Iron Condor

This kind of strategy focuses on benefiting some profits when the underlying stock in the current market dares to make some sharp market trade moves in either direction.

Iron Butterfly Spread

Buying and holding four different options in the market at three different market prices is involved in the trading market for a particular trading period.

Short Bull Ratio

The short bull ratio strategy is used to benefit from the amounts of profits gained from increasing security involved in the trading market in a similar way in which we usually get to buy calls during a particular period.

Strap Straddle

Strap straddle strategy uses one put and two calls bearing a similar strike price and with an equal date of expiration and also containing the same underlying stock that is usually stagnant during a particular trading period. The trader utilizes this type of strategy for the hope of getting higher amounts of profits as compared to the regular straddle strategy over a specific period of the trading period.

Strap Strangle

This strategy is strong, where more call options are purchased as compared to the put options and a bullish inclination is then depicted in various trading charts information.

Limit Your Risk

A good reason to go with buying options is that you will be able to limit your risk down to just the amount of money that you pay for the premium. With other investment options, you could end up losing a lot of money, even money that you did not invest, to begin with, but this does not happen when you are working with options.

Let's say that you saw that the prices of cows were about to go up. You could pay some money upfront and enter into a contract with someone else to sell your five cows for $ 2000. At this point, since you are working with an options contract, you did not buy the cows upfront.

On the other hand, if you had gone up to the other person and purchased those cows straight up for a cost of $ 10,000, you could end up in trouble. For this example, the price of the cows may end up falling by $ 500, rather than going up by $ 500, and you would end up losing $ 2500 in the process. Since you went into the options contract though, you would stand to lose no more than $ 250 if the prices were to fall afterward. You still stand to lose some money, but it is a lot less than you would have lost otherwise.

You will find that when you are working with options, it can provide you with some good leveraging power. A trader will be able to buy an option position that will imitate their stock position quite a bit, but it will end up saving them a lot of money in the process.

Let's say that you saw that there was an opportunity to make a profitable trade, you were only able to spare about $ 1000 to purchase the stock, but you didn't know that options were available. If we were still talking about the cows from before, you would not be able to purchase even one cow for the money (remember that they are about $

2000 each without the options contract). So you would completely miss out on the possibility of making a profit.

But, if you decided to purchase with an options contract, rather than buying the underlying asset outright, the dynamics have completely changed. If you look into options contracts, you will be able to make more purchases and potentially more money compared to some of the other stock choices you can make.

Going back to the idea of the cows, the market price at the beginning of this trade is $ 2000. For a regular cattle trader, one who doesn't know anything about options had the $ 2000 in hand and believed that the price of the cattle is going to go up; he would only have the opportunity to purchase on a cow. If the cost of the cows goes up to $ 2500, this trader will only be able to make a profit of $ 500. It isn't bad, but since there is a significant risk with this option, it is not always the best.

On the other hand, a trader who knows a bit about options will be able to do things a bit differently. If you had $ 2000, you could choose to purchase eight options contracts, with a premium of $ 50.t

Chapter 4.   Risks Management in Options

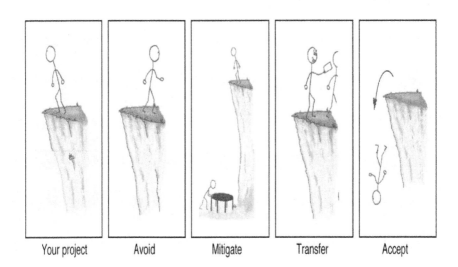

| Your project | Avoid | Mitigate | Transfer | Accept |

Many experienced options traders find it relatively easy to make money but holding it can prove harder. As anyone can do, there must be another dimension to the trading option that has been ignored so far; otherwise, any trader would be through. This is the risk management dimension. Most of what professional traders can do is manage Risk; play defense and try to keep profits. If a market maker manages to keep a third of the bid-ask range, it will be very successful in the long run. Danger management tension is a key differentiator between amateurs and experts. There are two things to remember when putting risk management in perspective.

At times, it's fun to "take a shot" when you make a trade. This could have been for some reason. You might want to start trading with a new strategy. You might have a hunch that you simply can't get the hard evidence to validate. And you might need to do a swap to help the trader. It is never necessary, however, to "take a shot" when handling the Risk. Risk management is far too important to take the chance. You just don't need to have any patience for errors.

Professional option trading is not about making significant, unforgettable trades. It is about making low, predictable gains and keeping risks under control.

We should take care of the risks in the order of their Risk. We will split the risks into three groups.

- **Primary Risks**
  - Inventory
  - Delta
- **Secondary Risks**

  • Gamma

  • Jump risk

  • Vega (including skew and calendar risk)

- **Tertiary Risks**

  • Correlation risk

  • Rho

  • Dividend risk

  • Buy-in risk

  • Early exercise

- Strike risk

- Pin risk

Stock Risk – Dividends and Buy-in Risk

Let's have a look at the case when a corporation declares a special dividend. Assume the stock is at $100, so we're long 1,000 out of a one-year 80 strike order. Assume the interest rate is negative, and the conditional uncertainty is 30%. The sum of this option is 23.53. When the corporation pays a dollar dividend, the interest of the call will decrease to 22.73. We're suddenly wasting $80,000. Remember that this is not going to support being hedged in the underlying. The dividend is a gain to those who hold the shares, not to those who own the options.

It doesn't happen very often. So, when it does, it can be a huge concern. In 2004, Microsoft paid a special dividend of $3.08 as the shares traded $29.97. Beware of businesses sitting on a lot of funds. It is, of course, entirely probable to be harmed if we have a long stock, and the planned dividend is that.

Nonetheless, the business option tends to be better at forecasting this. Generally, the rumors of payout cuts are beginning to surface well in advance of the real reduction, and the option sales are continuing to be sold at a lower cost. Finally, regular dividend yields appear to be much smaller than special dividends, so the cut in the normal dividend will not be as expensive as the declaration of a special dividend.

Pin Risk

Pin risk arises as the underlying interest reduces the effective interest of the option at expiration. Anyone short of these options is exposed to pin risk. The main Risk is that it is difficult to determine whether the decision will be exercised.

Note that since the Risk of a pin is triggered by the probability of a given investor having an unplanned role in the underlying stock that he eventually must liquidate, it is not a matter of cash-setting options. There we earn cash for any expiring shares. Cash does not need to be unwound or liquidated until the economy is reopened. Nevertheless, cash-setting options have their expiration wrinkle.

Forward Risk

For most options, as the in-the-money option expires, we will obtain the corresponding position at the bottom (a long position for long calls, a short position for medium calls, a short position for short calls, and a medium position for short calls). As we keep the offset position as a buffer at the start, we're not going to have a net advantage until expiry.

That is not the case for cash-setting options. Here we usually have a future or another traded commodity, but at the end of the day, we obtain cash. As a result, our expiry status does not balance our shield. If we don't want to be directional, we need to flatten our options for deltas in the month to come.

Irrelevance of the Greeks

As the expiration approaches, the utility of most Greeks as Risk controls declines. Vega and rho are now obsolete, as the trend towards zero, as the time to expiration tends towards zero. More specifically, gamma and theta become confusing.

At the time of expiration, gamma is infinite if our preference is at the money and zero otherwise. That's because we're precisely at a point where the option switches from being equal to the underlying situation to being useless. The delta will transform from one to zero when the underlying price passes the hit. To avoid incurring huge hedging costs, the investor will postpone worrying about persistent delta hedging and then wait until he is confident that the delta option has exceeded its expiring value and then hedged. This isn't as troubling as it seems, because it is expected to entail a change of less than a buck.

Theta is also becoming unreliable. Less significance of theta starts earlier than gamma, sometimes yielding very odd numbers many days before the expiry date. The main issue here is that theta has been configured to display the deterioration of option interest over one day. Normally, this is a good thing as it transforms theta into a number that is directly relevant, however close to its expiry, it becomes irrational when theta shifts too rapidly for one day.

Expiring at a Short Strike

As the expiration approaches, the utility of most Greeks as Risk controls declines. Vega and rho are now obsolete as they move towards zero, as the time to expiration tends towards zero. More specifically, the gamma and theta become confusing.

At the time of expiration, gamma is infinite if our preference is at the money and zero otherwise. That's because we're precisely at a point where the option switches from being equal to the underlying situation to being useless. The delta will transform from one to zero when the underlying price passes the hit. To avoid incurring huge hedging costs, the investor will postpone worrying about persistent delta hedging and then wait until he is confident that the delta option has exceeded its expiring value and then hedges. This isn't as troubling as it seems because it is expected to entail a change of less than a buck.

Theta is also becoming unreliable. Less significance of theta starts earlier than gamma, sometimes yielding very odd numbers many days before the expiry date. The main issue here is that theta has been configured to display the deterioration of option interest for one day. Normally, this is a good thing as it transforms theta into a number that is directly relevant, however close to its expiry, it becomes irrational when theta shifts too rapidly for one day.

Chapter 5. Volatility in the Market

We can define volatility as a statistical measure of the levels of fluctuations of stock, shares, or the entire market. The value is calculated as the ASD or annualized standard deviation of the price swings of security in terms of daily percentage. The value is expressed as a percentage.

Historical Volatility

Historical volatility is simply a measure of a security's volatility in the past. When computing this figure, you will have to define a specific period for consideration. One of the most common figures used for historical volatility is 20 days. This specific measure approximates total trading day numbers within a month.

Implied Volatility

Another useful term is implied volatility. This measures the volatility that is implied by the prevailing market price of the stock's options. Implied volatility is computed using one of the main option pricing models, like the Black Scholes Model. Using this or similar models, you can work out volatility where a mathematical relationship has been established relating to the price of an option and the volatility of the underlying stock.

Implied volatility provides insights into the market's view of the options contracts' underlying security. It can be determined by making use of the following:

- Option's current market price

- The value of the underlying security

- Expiration dates

- The strike prices

- Any applicable interest rates

- Any applicable dividend yields

In an ideal situation, we would expect the implied volatility figure to be the same for all options that have the same expiry date. This is regardless of the strike price that was used in our computations. In practice, however, this is hardly accurate because the figures we get vary mostly due to strike prices. This variation in volatility is known as the volatility skew.

The Impact of Volatility on Options Trades

We have already established what the term volatility means in options trading. It is simply a measure of the size and rate of the price change of the underlying security. High volatility implies a high option premium. The reverse is also true.

If you can accurately assess the value of statistical volatility for the underlying security, you will be able to use this value in a pricing model for purposes of computing a fair market price for the option. It is crucial that, as an options trader, you keep in mind the fact that changes in volatility can greatly impact your trades either negatively or positively.

Historical volatility generally measures the speed at which a futures commodity or stock price has moved in the past. This enables you to predict with some degree of accuracy, its expected movement in the future.

For instance, if we have a vehicle that is traveling at 50 miles per hour, we can determine how many miles it will travel for the entire year.

Distance = speed * time

In our case, distance = 50 mph * 24 hours/day * 365 days/year = 438,000 km

If everything remains constant, then we can accurately predict the distance that the car will cover. However, in real life, this is hardly the case because the car could make stops, break down sometimes, and so on. The same is true for stocks and options. Although our calculations depend on known factors, if the variables keep changing, the outcome could be different.

How to Compute Historical Volatility

Historical volatility is quantifiable and is based largely on previous changes to a futures or stock options contract. To calculate this figure, you need to consider the past prices and all price changes, then average them out into a percentage.

For instance, you can consider the historical volatility for 10 days. If you have the price change for 10 days in percentage terms, you should subtract the daily percentage price variations to find deviations from the average daily change for the period.

One of the most common methods that can be used to compute historical volatility is the close-to-close changes in percentage for daily values. There is another method known as the high minus low prices. Another approach would be to take an average of low, high, and median prices. The purpose of all these models is to obtain some intraday information that is usually not included in a close-to-close system.

It is also advisable to spend a few moments calculating historical volatility as well as the trending vs. trading range markets. A stable trend will likely emerge, and it can go either up or down but will not affect the size of percentage price changes.

While the changes in average daily price may increase, historical volatility as calculated may become smaller. Also, it is possible to demonstrate that historical volatility figures can increase if the average daily price reduces in size regardless of the market trends. One of the most popular methods uses 10 days of daily percentage price changes. This information is then used also to compute a standard deviation. Commonly used are 20 and 30 days and specific time frames for your computations.

How to Compute Implied Volatility

It is a lot easier to look at implied volatility with common pricing models such as the Black-Scholes model. You will need to have at least five inputs or variables. These variables are:

Chapter 17.   Historical volatility (or statistical volatility)

Chapter 18.   Strike price

Chapter 19.   Stock price

Chapter 20.   Risk-free interest rate

Chapter 21.   Number of days to expiration

With these inputs, you will receive a more accurate and reliable theoretical option price. However, most of the time, the markets do not set the fair value price for the same option. Options prices will normally deviate from these theoretical values. The fair price is a result of the input of five independent variables.

In general, if the market price exceeds the theoretical price of an option, then market participants such as traders and investors have added a premium to the price. A lot of these concepts are best viewed with real-life examples.

Commodity options usually portray excellent volatility. When the markets portray high volatility, then traders should be careful of buying options straight up. It would be a lot better to sell than to buy at this point. When the volatility is low, then options buyers should start buying.

Chapter 6.   Typical Beginners

Mistakes in Options

"Well, now we know what not to do."

Inexperienced traders are often warned away from purchasing options that are out of the money as being a greater risk than the ultimate reward is likely to be. While it is true that a short expiration time coupled with an out of the money option will frequently look appealing, especially to those with a smaller amount of trading capital to work with, the issue is that all of these types of options are likely to look equally appealing which leaves them with no way to tell the good from the bad.

As a more experienced trader, however, you have many more tools at your disposal than the average novice which means that, while risky, cheap options have the potential to generate substantial returns, as long as you keep the following in mind while trading them.

Ignoring the Statistics Behind Options Trading

One of the biggest mistakes that most newbie options traders make is that they forget the probability is a real thing. When you check a potential stock before purchasing an option, it's important to understand that the history of an option is important when deciding whether or not you should be investing in it, but so are the odds and probability surrounding whether or not a particular event is going to occur.

For example, a common strategy that investors use is to leverage their money by investing in cheap options so that this will help to prevent big losses on a stock that they actually own shares of. Of course, this is a good strategy, but nothing works one-hundred percent of the time. Make sure that if the rules of probability and simple ratios are telling you to stay away from a deal, you listen to the facts staring you in the face. Wishful thinking will come to bite you later on.

Being overzealous: Frequently, when new options traders finally get their initial plan just right, they become overzealous and start committing to larger trades than they can realistically afford to recover from if things go poorly. It is important to take it slow when it comes to building your rate of return and never bet more than you can afford to lose.

Regardless of how promising a specific trade might seem, there is no risk/reward level at which it is worth considering a loss that will take you out of the game completely for an extended period of time. Trade reasonably and trade regularly and you will see greater results in the long-term guaranteed.

Not Being Adaptable

The successful options trades know when to follow their plans but they also know that no plan will be the right choice, even if early indicators say otherwise. There is a difference between making a point of sticking to a plan and following it blindly and knowing which is one of the more important indicators of the separation between options trading success and abject failure. This means it is important to be aware of when and where experimentation and new ideas are appropriate and when it is best to toe the line and gather more data in order to make a well-reasoned decision.

This also means having several different plans in your options trading toolbox and not just resolutely sticking to the first one that brings you a modicum of success. This is crucial as there are certain plans that will only work in specific situations and knowing which to use when, in real-time, will lead to significantly greater returns on a more reliable basis every single time.

Likewise, an adaptive options trader knows that market conditions can change unexpectedly and is prepared to respond accordingly. This means understanding when the time is right to go in a new direction, regardless of the potential risks that doing so might entail.

Sometimes a good trader has to make a leap of faith, and a trader who is successful in the long term knows what signs to look for that indicate this type of scenario is occurring in real-time. Unfortunately, this type of foresight cannot be taught and instead must be found with experience.

As long as you keep the appropriate mindset regarding individual trades, any new strategy that is attempted will result in valuable data, if nothing else. It is important to understand that learning not to use a specific course of action a second time is always valuable, no matter the costs. Working to build this into your core trading mindset will lead you to greater success in a wider variety of situations in the long term.

Ignoring the Probability

Always remember that the historical data will not apply to the current trends in the market at all times which means you will always want to consider the probability as well as the odds that the market is going to behave the way it typically does. The odds are how likely the market is to behave as expected and the probability is the ratio of the likelihood of a given outcome. Understanding the probability of certain outcomes can make it easy to purchase the proper options to minimize losses related to holdings of specific underlying stocks.

When purchasing cheap options, it is important to remember that they are always going to be cheap for a reason as the price is determined by the strike price of the underlying stock as well as the amount of time remaining for the option to regain its value, choose wisely otherwise you are doing little more than gambling and there are certainly better ways to gamble than via options trading.

Not Considering Exotic Options

An exotic option is one that has a basic structure that differs from either European or American options when it comes to the how and when of how the payout will be provided or how the option relates to the underlying asset in question.

Additionally, the number of potential underlying assets is going to be much more varied and can include things like what the weather is like or how much rainfall a given area has experienced. Due to the customization options and the complexity of exotic options, they are only traded over the counter.

While they are undoubtedly more complex to get involved with, exotic options also offer up several additional advantages when compared to common options, including:

• They are a better choice for those with very specific needs when it comes to risk management.

• They offer up a variety of unique risk dimensions when it comes to both management and trading.

- They offer a far larger range of potential investments that can more easily meet a diverse number of portfolio needs.

- They are often cheaper than traditional options.

They also have additional drawbacks, the biggest of which is that they cannot often be priced correctly using standard pricing formulas. This may work as a profit instead of a drawback, however, depending on if the mispricing falls in favor of the trader or the writer.

It is also important to keep in mind that the amount of risk that is taken on with exotic options is always going to be greater than with other options due to the limited liquidity each type of exotic option is going to have available.

While some types are going to have markets that are fairly active, others are only going to have limited interest. Some are even what are known as dual-party transactions which means they have no underlying liquidity and are only traded when two amiable traders can be found.

Not Keeping Earnings and Dividend Dates in Mind

It is important to keep an eye on any underlying assets that you are currently working with as those who are currently holding calls have the potential to be assigned early dividends, with greater dividends having an increased chance of this occurrence.

As owning an option doesn't mean owning the underlying asset, if this happens to you, then you won't be able to collect on your hard-earned money. The early assignment is largely a random occurrence which means if you don't keep your ear to the ground, it can be easy to get caught unaware and be unable to exercise the option before you miss the boat.

Along similar lines, you are going to also always want to be aware of when the earnings season is going to take place for any of your underlying assets as it is likely going to increase the price of all of the contracts related to the underlying asset in question.

Chapter 7.   Important Trading Principles to Follow

You need to take it a step further by applying principles that will reinforce that plan. Think of that trading plan as the foundation of your house of success. The policies below are the bricks to develop your home into what you want it to be.

Ensure Good Money Management

Money is the tool that keeps the engine of the financial industry performing in good working order. You must learn to manage your money in a way that works for you instead of against you as an options day trader. It is an intricate part of maintaining your risk and increasing your profit.

Money management is the process whereby monies are allocated for spending, budgeting, saving, investing, and other procedures. Money management is a term that any person with a career in the financial industry, and particularly in the options trading industry, is intimately familiar with because this allocation of funds is the difference between a winning options trader and a struggling options trader.

Below you will find tips for managing your money so that you have maximum control of your options day trading career.

Money Management Tips for Options Traders

- Define money goals for the short term and the long term so that you can envision what you would like to save, invest, etc. Ensure that these are recorded and easily accessed. Your trading plan will help you define your money goals.

- Develop an accounting system. There is a wide range of software that can help with this, but it does not matter which one you use if you can establish records and efficiently track the flow of your money.

- Use position sizing to manage your money. Position sizing is the process of determining how much money will allocate to entering an options position. To do this effectively, allocate a smart percentage of your investment fund toward individual options. For example, it would be unwise to use 50% of your investment fund on one option. That is 50% of your capital that can potentially go down the drain if you make a loss in that position. A good percentage is using no more than 10% of your investment fund toward individual option positions. This percentage allocation will help you get through tough periods, which eventually happen without having all your funds lost.

- Never, ever invest money that you cannot afford to lose. Do not let emotion override this principle and cloud your judgment.

- Spread your risks by diversifying your portfolio. You expand your portfolio by spreading your wealth by investing in different areas, add to your investments regularly, being aware of commissions always, and knowing when to close a position.

- Develop the day trading styles and strategies that earn you a steady rate of return. Even if you use scalping where the returns are comparatively small, that constant flow of profit can add up big over time.

Ensure That Risks and Rewards Are Balanced

To ensure that losses are kept to a minimum and that returns are as high as they can be, options day traders should use the risk/reward ratio to determine each and to make adjustments as necessary. The risk/reward ratio is an assessment used to show profit potential concerning potential losses. It requires knowing the potential risks and profits associated with an options trade. Potential risks manage by using a stop-loss order. A stop-loss order is a command that allows you to exit a position in an options trade once a certain price threshold has reached.

Profit targeted using an established plan. Potential profit calculates by finding the difference between the entry price and the target profit. It is calculated by dividing the expected return on the options investment by the standard deviation.

Another way to manage risks and rewards is by diversifying your portfolio. Always spread your money across different assets, financial sectors, and geographies. Ensure that these different facets of your portfolio are not closely related to each other so that if one goes down, they don't all fall. Be smart about protecting and building your wealth.

Develop a Consistent Monthly Options Trading System

The aim of doing options trading is to have an overall winning options trading month. That will not happen if you trade options here and there. You cannot expect to see a huge profit at the end of the month if you only performed 2 or 3 transactions.

You need to have a high options trading frequency to up the chances of coming out winning every month. The only way to do that is to develop a system where you perform options trades at least five days a week.

Consider a Brokerage Firm That is Right for Your Level of Options Expertise

There are four essential factors that you need to consider when choosing a broker, and they are:

- The requirements for opening a cash and margin account.
- The unique services and features that the broker offers.

- The commission fees and other fees charged by the broker.
- The reputation and level of options expertise of the broker.

Look at these individual components to see how you can use them to power up your options day trading experience.

Broker Cash and Margin Accounts

Every options trader needs to open a cash account and margin account to be able to perform transactions. They are simply tools of the trade. A cash account is one that allows an options day trader to perform operations via being loaded with cash. Margin account facilitates transactions by allowing that to borrow money against the value of security in his or their account. Both types of accounts require that a minimum amount deposited. It can be as few as a few thousand dollars to tens of thousands of dollars depending on the broker of choice. You need to be aware of the requirements when deliberating which brokerage firm is right for you.

Broker Services and Features

There are different types of services and features available from various brokerage firms. For example, if an options trader would like to have an individual broker assigned to him or her to handle his or her account personally, then he or she will have to look for a full-service broker. In this instance, there minimum account requirements that need to meet. Also, commission fees and other fees are generally higher with these types of brokerage firms. While the prices are higher, this might be better for a beginner trader to have that full service dedicated to their needs and the learning curve.

On the other hand, if an options trader does not have the capital needed to meet the minimum requirements of a full-service broker or would prefer to be more in charge of his or her option trades, then there is the choice of going with a discount brokerage firm. The advantage to discount brokerage firms is that they tend to have lower commissions and fees. Most internet brokerage firms are discount brokers.

Other features that you need to consider when choosing a brokerage firm include:

- Whether or not the broker streams real-time quotes.
- The speed of execution for claims.
- The availability of bank wire services.
- The availability of monthly statements.
- How confirmations achieve, whether written or electronic.

Commissions and Other Fees

Commission fees paid when an options trader enters and exits positions. Every brokerage firm has its commission fees set up. These typically developed around the level of account activity and account size of the options trader.

These are not the only fees that an option trader needs to consider when considering brokerage firms. Many brokerage firms charge penalty fees for withdrawing funds and not maintaining minimum account balances — the existence of costs such as these cuts on options trader's profit margin. Payment of fees needs to be kept to a minimum to gain maximum income, and as such, an options trader needs to be aware of all charges that exist and how they are applied when operating with a brokerage firm. It needs to be done before signing up.

Broker Reputation and Options Expertise

You do not want to be scammed out of your money because you chose the wrong brokerage firm. Therefore, you must choose a broker that has an established and long-standing reputation for trading options. You also want to deal with a brokerage firm that has excellent customer service, that can aid in laying the groundwork for negotiating reduced commissions and allows for flexibility.

Ensure That Exits are automated

Even though I have stated that emotions should set aside when trading options, we are all human, and emotions are bound to come into the equation at some point. Knowing this is imperative that systems develop to minimize the impact of emotions. Having your exits automated is one such step that you can take to ensure that emotions are left out when dealing with options day trading. Using bracket orders facilitates this.

A bracket order is an instruction given when an options trader enters a new position that specifies a target or exit and a stop-loss order that aligns with that. This order ensures that a system is set up to record two points — the goal for-profit and the maximum loss point that will tolerate before the stop-loss comes into effect. The execution of either order cancels the other.

CRASH COURSE

Chapter 8. Buy an Equity at a Lower Price

$$\frac{30 \text{ Owned Shares}}{100 \text{ Total Shares}} = 30\% \text{ Equity Stake}$$

$$\frac{30 \text{ Owned Shares}}{150 \text{ Total Shares}} = 20\% \text{ Equity Stake}$$

Low margins can be very useful when trading. To use them successfully, they must be integrated into the overall pattern. The basic idea is to enter the market as soon as it breaks out of the state of equilibrium that exists. If the price rises sharply from this point on and then falls back down there, an increase in demand is expected. This is a classic double bottom. In combination with the Accumulation / Distribution, this becomes the basis for an interesting trading approach. Choose only the trades in the direction of the thrust. Place stops at the opposite end of the short bar.

Trading Beams with Large Margins

A wide-span bar can be either bullish or bearish, depending on where it appears in the formation. If it appears at the end of a buy peak, then it is to be classified as bearish, at the break from a formation, however positive. Most beams with a large span are followed directly by a correction beam. The buy zone is in the lower half of the bar, and the profit-taking area is located at around 50% to 100% of the span above the high of the bar. Of course, this only applies to short-term traders. The course tends to be varied, with a short track following a long bar. Of course, this is not always the case, and the definition of a wide-span bar is subjective. This is where the art of chart reading comes into play. This ability can only be learned by analyzing many charts over the years.

Purchase Zones

The buy zone describes the lower half of a push. While the relapses are causing the price to rise, the buying zone also moves upwards. In these areas, you should look for opportunities to get started. Before you open your position, you should know where to set the stop and set a price target. Mark the buy zone, the stop loss, and the area of the price target in the chart. Do not chase after a quick course! Among the countless stocks, there is always a good candidate for a better start. Opt for a boarding area. The following steps could help:

- Buy only in the purchase zones.

- Place your stop loss immediately after opening your position.

- Be sure to close the position when you reach the winning zone. Is this done by means of a stop, or are you simply selling? Any possibility is a compromise: if you sell, the price could rise even higher. Waiting for the stop to be triggered will often result in significant portions of the potential win.

The following options are available:

- Make the stop tighter.

- Close only half the position. So, your decision is only half wrong or half correct.

- Close your position at the first sign that the supply outweighs the demand.

- Use a shorter time frame to set the stop. For example, if you trade on a daily chart, choose a 30-minute chart to place your stop more accurately.

The Stop

If you do not know what you are risking, you risk everything. There is no stop-loss option that is equally satisfactory for everyone. Everyone has to find out for himself which ratio of risk to the potential profit he feels comfortable with. Here are some suggestions for placing stop orders:

- Three ticks below the low of the last or penultimate fulcrum

- An average range below the closing price or the low of the day on which the purchase was made

- 50% of the breakout or break-in after opening the day after entering the position. This stop works especially well when combined with the other possible stops. For example, a value sometimes opens below a stop at a level, which then turns out to be the low of the day. We like to see it move about eight ticks or half the span of the previous bar after opening.

- Three ticks below the lower low or lower end of the last two bars

- Close the position after three bars, if it is not yet in the profit zone.

- Release the trade and try to exit without loss if the trade runs too far against you after the opening and your stop is not triggered. Do not think about a possible profit anymore. Their only interest is the stopping and preservation of your capital.

It is of utmost importance to always have a good plan ready for your investment. When opening a position, ask yourself if this is a long-term investment for five or ten years or not. Then you should not panic in the face of short-term price fluctuations. Are you a trader? Unfortunately, many people set their exit point or stop loss according to the following criteria:

- The stop-loss is at a point where the losses are already huge.

- The stop is based on the general market situation. If the whole market collapses, my positions will be closed.

- As soon as everyone is frantically trying to close their positions in my stock quickly, then I sell too.

Profit Taking

If you have a long position and the price goes into profit, then you can protect your profit by:

- Best selling

- Sell when a closing price is below an opening.

- Sell when the price falls after the opening by half the average range.

- Set the stop below the previous day's low.

- Sell when the price closes below the two previous closing prices and below the opening.

- Sell at the third strong positive bar of the next smaller time frame. For example, if the price breaks into the profit zone on the weekly chart, then you sell after the third consecutive day in a row.

Anticipation

The following factors are important in anticipating the completion of a pattern or reversal. You can build parts of a position at an early stage before all criteria are met. Remember: The stated goal is to make profitable trading and not to be in the market at 90% of all price moves. Learn to settle for small pieces of the market. Either you secure your profits by means of a best-order, or you sell at the first sign that the supply exceeds the demand.

- The seven possible times to anticipate a pattern are:

- The closing price of the bar, if a short spread indicates a low supply or low demand.

- An opening course in the direction of completing the pattern.

- An outbreak after opening in the direction of completing the pattern.

- An outbreak after 30 minutes towards the completion of the pattern.

- The course is midway through the opening and in the direction of completing the pattern.

- At the closing price if the pattern is fully developed.

- For a correction movement after completing the pattern.

For many patterns, it can be seen that the price will fall back into the buy zone, but the pattern will be completed above the buy zone. Then it has to be decided on a case-by-case basis which measure is the right one.

The Time-Break-Out Rule

A common approach is to trade the breakout from the first 30-minute bar, with the stop loss at the other end of this bar. This approach has been tested using S & P's market data over 14 years. Trading according to this rule leads to huge losses. It should be noted that this method has been profitable in recent years. But one must always keep in mind the fact that how dangerous it can be, if too short a test period is chosen to check a method. When entering a position, the 30-minute rule may be useful, but as with most tools, isolated use will not work.

Price Gaps

Normally, a positive price gap is considered a sign of strength and a buy signal. In verifying this assumption, it turned out that the exact opposite is true. The review was based on two methods:

- Sale with a positive price gap.

- Sale on a positive price gap, but only if the price falls back to the previous day high.

For purchases, the opposite applies. Both approaches were tested by computer without stops and as day trades. The second approach turned out to be almost twice as successful as the first. It is used approximately 60 times a year per future. The course must go in your direction before doing anything. This signal provides a clear market advantage, but in most cases does not make up for the fees and slippage.

But when combined with other filters and more meaningful stop management, this is a valuable addition to your trading arsenal. Coincidentally, the review found that this could be a profitable trading system for bonds.

This pattern is very similar to a pattern developed by Larry Williams called Oops. The starting point is the same, but we do not know which entry and exit criteria were used by him. The information can be reused as follows:

- The signal is likely to be more reliable if the price has already gone one way and the expected end of that price movement is within range. Then this could be a good way to realize profits and perhaps build up counter positions.

- Other ideas are:

- Watch out for introductory signals on reverse movements of the last closing price, several previous closing prices, and several previous highs and lows.

- Consider setting a half-span stop after boarding.

- Watch price gaps above or below a cluster of close closing prices.

- Look for a reversal after half the gap in the price gap before opening a position.

These simple computer tests will tell you quickly whether such an opening with a price gap will give you a technical advantage in view of past price developments or not. Larry Williams and Toby Crabel have made a name for themselves in this field. Whole volumes could be filled solely with the study of price movements in relation to the opening and the movement away from the opening price.

Chapter 9. Options Pricing

Stock:	AMZN	Price	38.70			Expires:	1 month
	Call Option				Put Option		
Intrinsic Value	Time Value	Option Price	Strike Price	Intrinsic Value	Time Value	Option Price	
3.70	0.30	4.00	35.00	0.00	0.17	0.17	
0.00	0.65	0.65	40.00	1.30	0.55	1.85	
0.00	0.05	0.05	45.00	6.30	-0.20	6.10	
		= In the Money					

Stock:	AMZN	Price	38.70			Expires:	9 months
	Call Option				Put Option		
Intrinsic Value	Time Value	Option Price	Strike Price	Intrinsic Value	Time Value	Option Price	
3.70	6.41	10.11	35.00	0.00	4.00	4	
0.00	7.50	7.50	40.00	1.30	4.80	6.10	
0.00	4.97	4.97	45.00	6.30	3.00	9.30	
		= In the Money					

Options traders need to comprehend extra factors that influence an option's price and the complexity of picking the right technique. When a stockbroker becomes acceptable at foreseeing the future price movement, the person may believe it is a simple change from options, but this isn't accurate. Options traders must deal with 3 shifting parameters that influence the price: the underlying time, volatility, and security. Changes in any of these factors affect the option's value.

Option pricing hypothesis utilizes factors (exercise price, stock price, interest rate, time to expiration, volatility) to value an option hypothetically. It estimates an option's reasonable value, which traders join into their techniques to maximize profits. Some ordinarily utilized models to value options are Black-Scholes, Monte-Carlo, and Binomial Option Pricing. These speculations have wide margins for error because of deriving their values from different assets, typically the cost of an organization's basic stock. There are scientific formulas intended to compute the fair, reasonable value of an option. The broker inputs known factors and finds a solution that depicts what the option should be worth.

The essential objective of any option pricing model is to compute the probability that an option will be worked out or be in-the-money (ITM) at lapse. Basic asset value (stock value), interest rate, exercise price, time to expiration, and volatility, which is the number of days between the computation date and the option's exercise date, are usually utilized variables that are input into logical models to derive an option's hypothetical fair value.

Here are the general impacts that factors have on an option's cost:

Strike Price and Underlying Price

The value of puts and cuts are influenced by changes in the fundamental stock cost in a generally clear manner. When the stock cost goes up, calls should gain value since you can purchase the underlying asset at a lower cost than where the market is, and puts should diminish. In like manner, put options should increase in value, and calls should drop as the stock value falls, as the put holder gives the right to sell stock at costs over the falling market cost.

That pre-determined price to purchase or sell is known as the option's exercise price or strike price. Suppose the strike price permits you to purchase or sell the basic at a level that allows for a quick profits purchase, discarding that exchange in the open market. In that case, the option is in-the-money (for instance, a call to purchase shares at $10 when the market cost is currently $15, you can make a prompt $5 profit).

Like most other monetary resources, options costs are affected by prevailing interest rates and are affected by interest rate changes. Put option and call option premiums are affected contrarily as interest rates change lose value while calls benefit from rising rates. The inverse is genuine when interest rates fall.

The impact of volatility on an option's price is the most difficult concept for beginners to comprehend. It depends on a measure called statistical (also known as historical) volatility, SV for short, looking at past value developments of the stock over a given timeframe.

Option pricing models necessitate the trader to go in future volatility throughout the life of the option. Normally, options traders don't generally know what it will be and need to guess by working the pricing model "in reverse." The merchant knows the cost at which the option is trading and can inspect different factors, including dividends, interest rates, and time left with a bit of research. Subsequently, the main missing number will be future volatility, which can be evaluated from different information sources.

Factors That Affect an Option's Price

You cannot price an option until you realize what makes up its worth. An options trade can turn into a mind-boggling machine of legs, numerous orders, Greeks, and adjustments. However, if you don't have the foggiest idea about the essentials, what are you attempting to achieve?

When you take a look at an option chain, have you considered how they generated every one of those prices for the options? However, these options are not created randomly but rather calculated out utilizing a model, for example, the Black-Scholes Model. We will dive further into the Black-Scholes Model's seven components and how and why they are utilized to determine an option's cost/price.

Like all models, the Black-Scholes Model has a shortcoming and is a long way from perfect.

History of the Black-Scholes Model

The Black-Scholes Model was distributed in 1973 as The Pricing of Options and Corporate Liabilities in the Journal of Political Economy. It was created by Myron Scholes and Fisher Black as an approach to evaluate the price of an option after some time. Robert Merton later distributed a subsequent paper, further extending the comprehension of the model. As with any model, a few assumptions must be comprehended.

- The rate of profit for the riskless asset is constant.

- The more the option will be worth, the underlying follows, which expresses that move in an unpredictable and random path.

- There is no riskless profit, arbitrage, opportunity.

- It is possible to lend and borrow any amount of money at a riskless rate.

- It is possible to purchase or short any amount of stock.

- There are no charges or costs.

The model has seven factors: strike price, stock price, interest rates, types of option, dividends, time of expiration, and future volatility.

Stock Price

If a call option permits you to purchase a stock at a pre-determined cost later on, then the higher that cost goes, the more the option will be worth.

Which option would have a higher worth:

- A call option permits you to purchase TOP (The Option Prophet) for $100 while it is trading at $80 or

- A call option will enable you to buy TOP for $100 while it is trading at $120

Nobody will pay $100 for something they can purchase on the open market for $80, so our option in Choice 1 will have a low worth.

All the more alluring is Choice 2, an option to purchase TOP for $100 when its worth is $120. In this circumstance, our option worth will be higher.

Strike Price

The strike price follows the same lines as the stock price. At the point when we group strikes, we do it as in-the-money, at-the-money, or out-of-the-money. When a call option is in-the-money, it implies the stock price/cost is higher than the strike cost. The stock price is not exactly the strike price when a call is out-of-the-money.

A TOP call has a strike of fifty while TOP is presently trading at $60. This option is in-the-money.

The stock price is not exactly the strike price when a put option is in the money. A put option is out-of-the-money when the stock price is greater than the strike price.

A TOP put has a strike of twenty while TOP is presently trading at $40. This option is out-of-the-money.

In-the-money options have a greater value contrasted with out-of-the-money options.

Type of Option

This is likely the easiest factor to comprehend. An option is either a call or a put, and the option's estimation will change appropriately.

- A call option gives the holder the option or right to purchase the basic at a predefined cost within a particular timeframe.

- A put option gives the holder the option or right to sell the hidden at a predefined price within a particular timeframe.

If you are long a call or short a put, your option value increments as the market moves higher. Suppose you are short a call or long a put your option value increments as the market goes lower.

Time to expiration

Options have a constrained life expectancy; thus, their worth is influenced by the progression of time. As the time to expiration upturns, the value of the option increments. As the time to termination draws nearer, the value of the option starts to diminish. The value starts to quickly diminish within the last 30 days of an option's life. The additional time an option has till termination/expiration, the option needs to move around.

Interest Rates

The interest rate has a nominal effect on an option's value. When interest rates rise, a call option's value will rise, and a put option's value will decrease.

To drive this idea home, how about we take a look at the dynamic procedure of investing in TOP while trading at $50.

- We can purchase 100 shares of the stock altogether, which would cost us $5,000.

- Instead of purchasing the stock altogether, we can get long an at-the-money call for $5.00. Our all-out expense here would be $500. Our underlying cost of money would be littler, and this would leave us $4,500 leftover. Also, we will have a similar prize potential for half the risk. Presently we can take that additional money and invest it somewhere else, for example, Treasury Bills. This would create a guaranteed return on our investment in TOP.

The higher the interest rate, the more appealing the subsequent option becomes. In this manner, when interest rates go up, calls are a superior investment, so their cost likewise increments.

On the other side of that coin, if we look at a long put versus a long call, we can see an impediment. We have two options when we want to play an underlying drawback.

- You can short a hundred shares of the stock that would produce money into the business and earn interest in that money.

- You long a put which will cost you less money by and large but not put additional money into your business that produces interest income.

The higher the interest rate, the more appealing the primary option becomes. Accordingly, when interest rates rise, the value of put options decreases.

Dividends

Options don't get dividends, so their value varies when profits are discharged. When an organization discharges dividends, they have an ex-dividend date. If you own the stock on that date, you will be granted the dividend. Additionally, on this date, the estimation of the stock will diminish by the number of dividends. As dividends increment, a put option's value likewise increments, and a calls' value declines.

Volatility

Volatility is the main evaluated factor in this model. The volatility that is utilized is forward. Forward volatility is the proportion of implied volatility over a period later on.

Implied volatility shows the "simplified" development in a stock's future volatility. It discloses to you how traders think the stock will move. Implied volatility is constantly communicated as a percentage, non-directional, and on a yearly premise.

Chapter 10. Tips and Tricks in Stocks

This is a much better and more successful strategy. Here are some helpful tips and tricks that should guide you as you trade online in options.

The Price of Any Stock Can Move in 3 Basic Directions

These directions are up, down, and no movement at all. Depending on the kind of call that you have, you can leverage this movement to make a profit or at least avoid incurring losses.

Plenty of first-time traders and investors assume that prices of securities will go either up or down. However, this is the wrong school of thought because sometimes there is no movement at all in the price of stocks and shares. This is a very important fact in the world of options trading.

There are plenty of real-life, practical examples that show a particular stock or share which did not move significantly for quite a lengthy period. For instance, the KOL share traded within a $4 range for a total of 23 days. If you had invested money in either a call option or a put option through this stock, you would have lost money.

A purchase of a call option is usually with the hope that prices will go up. In the event that prices do rise, then you will make a profit. At other times, the prices will remain the same or even fall. In such events, if you have an out-of-the-money call, the option will most likely expire, and you will lose your investment. In the event that the price remains stagnant and you have an in-the-money option, then you will at least recoup some of the money you invested.

There will be sometimes when frustrations engulf you. This is when you just sit and watch prices start to skyrocket just a couple of weeks after the options you purchased had expired. This is often an indicator that your strategy was not on point and you did not give it sufficient time. Even seasoned traders sometimes buy call options that eventually expire in a given month and then the stock prices rise sharply in the following month.

It is therefore advisable to purchase a longer-term call option rather than one that expires after a single month. Now, since stocks move in 3 general directions, it is assumed that close to 70% of options, traders with long call and put options suffer losses. On the other hand, this implies that 70% of options sellers make money. This is one of the main reasons why conservative options traders prefer to write or sell options.

Before Buying a Call or Put Option, Look at the Underlying Stock's Chart

Basically, you want to find out as much information as possible about the performance and worth of an underlying stock before investing in it.

You should, therefore, ensure that you take a serious look at the chart of the stock. This chart should indicate the performance of the stock in the last couple of days. The best is to look at a stock's performance in the last 30 and 90 days. You should also take a look at its last year's performance.

When you look at the charts, look at the movement of the shares and try and note any trends. Also, try and observe any general movement of the shares. To identify the trend of a particular stock, try and draw a straight line along in the middle of the share prices. Then draw a line both above and below so as to indicate a channel of the general flow of the share.

Chart Readings and Buying Call Options

Let us assume that you wish to invest in a call option. Then you should ask yourself if the stock price is likely to rise and why. If you think that the stock will rise and trade at a higher level, then you may be mistaken, unless something drastic happens or new information becomes evident. New information can be a shareholders' meeting, impending earnings announcement, a new CEO, product launch, and so on.

If there is a chart showing the presence of support at lower prices and stock prices fall to that level, then it may be advisable to buy call options. The call option will be a great bet when prices are down because prices will very likely head back up. However, never allow greed to occupy your mind. When you see a profit, take and do not wait too long.

Chart Readings and Buying Put Options

Now, supposing the stock chart indicates a solid resistance at a higher price. If the stock is beginning to approach this higher level, then it is possible that the price might begin to move in that direction as well. So as the price moves, expect to gain small but significant profits. Avoid greed, so anytime the stock price falls, simply move in and make some money.

Chart Readings for Purchase of Call and Put Options

Now, if your chart readings indicate that the shares are within the lower levels of their range, then it is likely that daily changes in price will send it towards the middle of the range. If this is so, then you should move in and make a profit as soon as the price tends upwards. Even minor profits such as buying at $1 and selling at $1.15 mean a 15% profit margin.

Find Out the Breakeven Point Before Buying Your Options

Now, you need to identify a call option that you wish to invest in, especially after studying its performance on the market. Before buying, however, you should work out the breakeven point. In order to find this breakeven point, you will have to consider things such as the commissions charged and the bid spread.

It is very important that you are positive that the underlying stock of your options will move sufficiently so as to surpass the breakeven point and earn a tidy profit. You should, therefore, learn how to work out the breakeven point in an options trade.

Calculating the Breakeven Point

As an options trader, you need to know how to calculate and find the breakeven point. In options trading, there are basically 2 break-even points. With short-term options, you need to make use of the commission rates and bid spread to work out the breakeven point. This is if you intend to hold on to the options until their expiration date.

Now, if you are seeking short-term trade without holding on to the options, then find out the difference between the asking price and bid price. This difference is also known as the spread.

If You Are Dealing with Call and Put Options, Embrace the Underlying Stock's Trend

As an investor and trader in options, you need to consider the trend of the underlying stock as your friend. This means that you should not fight it. Basically, if the stock price is headed upwards, you should find a strategy that is in tandem with this movement. If you oppose it, you are unlikely to win.

Similarly, if the stock is on a downward trend, then do not oppose this movement but try and find a strategy that will accommodate this trend. You need to understand, however, that this saying is intended to guide you but is not necessarily a rule. This means that you apply it even while you consider all other factors. For instance, the major news may have an immediate effect on the price trend of a stock or shares.

As a trader, you should learn to jump successfully on a trend and follow the crowds rather than go to extremes and oppose it.

When Trading Options, Watch Out for Earnings Release Dates

Call and put options are generally expensive with the price increases significantly if there is an earnings release announcement looming. The reason is that the anticipation of very good or very bad earnings reports will likely affect the stock price. When this is an underlying stock in an options trade, then you should adjust your trades appropriately.

As an example, stocks such as Google may rise insanely during the earnings announcement week only to dip significantly shortly thereafter. Consider Apple shares that were trading at $450 at the markets. Call options with Apple as the underlying stock were trading at $460. However, the market had targeted a price of $480 within 3 days, which did not happen. This cost investors' money. Such underlying assets are considered volatile due to the high increase in price, rapid drop shortly thereafter and related risk of losing money.

Chapter 11. How to Double or Triple Your Returns

You are the one responsible for turning your venture into foreign exchange into a successful endeavor. That is one of the great things about the stock. You do not have a boss screaming down your neck, telling you to do something you do not agree with. You can come up with your trading plan based on your own research and your knowledge. That being said, success can come more quickly for some than for others, and a lot of the time, this has to do with approaching this endeavor with the right strategy. We will provide you with three strategies designed to help you make this stock as profitable as possible (with as little loss as possible).

Buy Low and Sell High

If you began stock trading today with $25,000 in your pocket and access to a trading platform, all ready and raring to go, how would you know what is low and what is high? It's your first day. Naturally, for you to understand what would represent a good low investment and conversely what is high, you need to know the exchange rate history of that currency. Maybe the exchange rate for the Japanese yen seems low, but actually, compared to last year or a few months ago, it's a little high. Now it would not be a good time to buy.

Maybe the pound seems low right now, but yesterday the British government announced that the first round of the Brexit negotiations with the EU failed, and therefore, the pound may have room to go lower than it is when you logged onto your trading platform. You can wait and see what the pound is today or tomorrow and buy then.

The point here is that buying low and selling high requires understanding the patterns associated with that stock and what might cause it to go up or down. And that's merely the buying side of things. Once you have bought low, you need to figure out when you are going to sell. This is where a good trading plan will come into play. A good plan will prevent you from selling too soon, or even not selling soon enough.

Focus on Not Losing Money Rather Than on Making Money

This may not be an easy strategy to understand initially, in part because not losing money and making money seem like two sides of the same coin. They are, but they are not identical. One of the personality types that is associated with difficulty in finding success in trading is the impulsive type. This type of person wants to make money and they want to make it quick. They have a vague strategy about how they plan on doing that, but the most important thing to them is that they have a high account balance to make as many trades as they need to turn a profit. This is the wrong approach. Currencies are not the same as stocks. A stock's value may change very little even over a week, so the strategy that involves a lot of trades to make money is usually not the best strategy. You need a clear idea of when you are going to but, yes, because you want to make money, but mostly because you don't want to lose.

Every market that involves exchanges, like the stock market, has some implicit risk, and stock trading is risky, too, because you may be tempted to give up the advantage you have to try and make money quickly.

Develop a Sense of Sentiment Analysis

All right, the third strategy was going to be about Fibonacci retracement, which is a type of technical analysis of the market, but as this is the basics of stock trading, we are going to go into a different strategy that is not any easier than a Fibonacci retracement, just different. Sentiment analysis is a term that is used in many different specialties, not just finance, and it is not easy to describe.

It is essentially a type of analysis that is not based on a chart showing exchange rates over time (technical analysis) or understanding a factor that might today be affecting the value of the stock(fundamental analysis). Sentiment analysis attempts to gauge the tone of the market, the direction the market is heading in, by parsing all of the available information.

A key to understanding sentiment analysis is likening it to public opinion. The economy may be booming, people have more money in their pocket, so this hypothetical country's stock should increase in value, but maybe it doesn't. Maybe there is something that is causing the market to be bearish, which might cause the stock to drop.

As you perhaps can tell, as this analysis is not based on any concrete information, it can be thought of as intuitive and no one has intuition on day 1. Let's be honest about that.

Intuition comes from experience. But the purpose of this strategy is to introduce to you the idea that not the foreign exchange market, like any market, is not going to behave like a machine because it's not a machine.

Markets are places where human beings come together and humans are unpredictable, often in a frustrating way. Perhaps one day, stock trading may be handled by machines (that wouldn't be fun), but that day is far off and so you will have to develop your own sense of where the market seems to be going and use this as a strategy to achieve success in this endeavor.

Regardless of the investment that you make, be sure always to do your research. Doing research is a must. It is what will increase your chances of making the right investment decision.

The more that you understand something, the more likely it that you will be able to predict how it will move in the market. This is why doing research is essential. It will allow you to know if something is worth investing in or not. Remember that you are dealing with a continuously moving market, so it is only right that you keep yourself updated with the latest developments and changes. The way to do this is by doing research.

Whether you will start forex trading or trade in general, it is always good to have a plan. Make sure to set a clear direction for yourself. This is also an excellent way to avoid being controlled by your emotions or becoming greedy. You should have a short-term plan and a long-term plan. You should also be ready for any form of contingency.

Make your plans practical and reasonable. Remember that you ought to stick to whatever project you come up with, so be sure to keep your ideas real. Before you come up with an idea, you must first have quality information. Again, this is why doing research is very important.

What if you fail to execute your plan? This is not uncommon. If this happens to you, relax and think about what made you fail to stick to your plan? Was it favorable to you or not? Take some time to analyze the situation and learn as much as you can from it. Indeed, having a plan is different from executing it. It is more challenging to implement a plan as it demands that you take positive actions.

Learn from Your Competitors

Pay attention to your competitors and learn from them. Studying your competitors is also an excellent way to identify your strengths and weaknesses. You can learn a great deal from your competitors, especially ideas on how you can better improve your business.

Your competitors can also help you promote your trading goals and draw more techniques. This way, you get a better idea of how to trade. You do not have to fight against your competitors; you can work together.

It is prevalent for people online to support one another. , it is a good practice that you connect with other traders, especially those who are in the same niche. Do not think of them as your direct competitors, and you might be surprised just how friendly they can be.

Now, a common mistake is to consider yourself always better than others. This is wrong as you are only deluding yourself, making you fail to see the bigger picture. Instead of still seeing yourself better than your competitors, learn from them, and see how you can use this knowledge to improve your trading endeavors.

Cash-Out

Some people who trade forex or invest in cryptocurrency commit the mistake of not making a withdrawal. The reason why they do not cash out is so that they can grow their funds. Since you can only earn a percentage of what you are trading/investing, having more funds in your account means making a higher profit return. Although this may seem reasonable, it is not a recommended approach. It is strongly advised that you should request a withdrawal. You should understand that the only way to enjoy your profits is by turning them into cash; otherwise, it is only as if you were using a demo account. Also, by making a withdrawal, you lower your risks since the funds you withdraw will no longer be exposed to risks.

You do not have to remove all your profits right away. If you want, you can withdraw 30% of your total profits, allowing the remaining 70% to add up to the funds in your account. The important thing is to make a withdrawal still now and then.

Take a Break and Have Fun

Making money online can be exciting and fun but it can also be a tiring journey. Therefore, give yourself a chance to take a break from time to time. When you take a break, do not spend that time thinking about your online business. Instead, you should spend it to relax your body and clear your mind. You will be more able to function more effectively if you do this. This is an excellent time to go on a vacation with your family or friends or at least enjoy a movie night at home. Do something fun that will put your mind off of business for a while. Do not worry; after this short break, and you are expected to work even more.

Making money online is a long journey, so enjoy it. Making money online can be lots of fun. Do not just connect with people to build a good following, but also try to make friends with your connections. You do not have to take things too seriously. Keep it fun and exciting.

Chapter 12.

How to Become a Millionaire with

Option Trading

Most investors and traders at the securities markets often aim to buy low then sell high and make a profit. However, options traders are the key layers in any market. This is because they can earn large amounts of money regardless of market conditions.

The options traders can make money in any market environment, even where there are no trades up or down. The reason is that options contracts are flexible in different ways. This versatility is what makes them such powerful market tools for continued profitability. Here are some profitable approaches that you can adopt to become a millionaire with option trading

Writing Options

One of the best ways of winning at options is to write options. You can write some pretty sophisticated strategies which are capable of earning your top dollars.

As a writer, you get to earn what is known as a premium. This is money that you earn even if the investor does not eventually use it. It is possible to write profitable commodities-based options regularly. Speculators can come up with profitable options that they believe will fare well in the options markets.

The Straddle Strategy

This is another approach that can help you get rich with options trading. Options mostly involve the buying of security that then turns profitable when the underlying commodity moves in a particular direction. It could be up or down but all that is necessary is a movement. A straddle is a great choice of options investment vehicle because it does not desire a specific outcome as is the case in other situations.

With a straddle, you can purchase both calls and put options with the same expiry dates and at similar strike times. The straddle strategy can be successful if and only if the underlying security of the option sees movement in either direction just so long as the movement is sufficiently large to cover the cost of premiums in both directions. Speculators can write straddle options if they believe that it is going to do well in the market.

The Collar Strategy

We also have a strategy known as the collar strategy. It is considered a pretty challenging options strategy to understand. However, a seasoned speculator can write one for you but only if he owns the underlying asset. By owning the asset, he can take the risk.

In this instance, the best option is an out-of-the-money put option. This is beneficial because should the commodity price go down, then the losses will only be minimal as it is a put option. However, should the commodity move upwards, then the trader will make a tidy profit.

The Strangle Strategy

The strangle strategy is in some ways similar to the straddle. This is because they both include the buying of a call and put option as well as the same expiration date. The only difference is that they have different strike prices. For speculators, it is possible to use the information available to enter a low-cost position.

When a trader or speculator opts for this strategy, they choose a low-cost entry because either or both of the options contracts may be bought out-of-the-money. As such, it may not be worthwhile exercising the right afforded by the shares. Both the straddle and strangle can be written by a speculator or even the trader.

So, what is the Most Profitable Options Strategy?

We have now looked at several options trading strategies, all of which are profitable and easy to execute. There are more than 40 different variations of options trading techniques. This makes it a pretty difficult job to determine the most profitable options trading strategy.

A lot of the time, traders try to find trades that will not lose their money. Also, there is a lot of varied opinions out there about the best and most profitable strategies. Fortunately, most options trading strategies offer very attractive returns with huge margins being quite common. However, it can be a risky venture, so it is advisable to proceed with caution even as you seek to become a wealthy millionaire.

Options Trading is Quite Profitable

Some express concern about profitability as well as risks posed by options trading. Fortunately, it has been proven, over the years, to be quite profitable.

Trade-in options provide you with leverage which offers you the inherent right to control a huge number of shares. This kind of leverage offers returns far greater than what selling stocks only can offer.

If you can make use of the leverage afforded by stock options, then you stand a great chance of making huge profits. These are profits made from just minuscule movements of the underlying stocks. By identifying the right strategies, then you will be able to make money regardless of the prevailing market conditions.

This means making profits even when there is no movement in the market. However, with some strategies, you may lose money if you make a wrong move. Therefore, sufficient care needs to be taken to mitigate any such losses as they can be significant.

The Most Profitable Options Trading Strategy

It is advisable, to begin with, the most basic options trading strategies first. This is the way most options traders start. By using these simple options trading strategies, you stand to make huge returns on your investments and trading skills. It is very possible to enjoy a 100% return on investment within a couple of days and sometimes even in just a couple of hours.

You can also find plenty of websites and advisory services that provide advisory services and trading assistance to traders. Some trades may fail. But it is also likely that most of your trades will be successful. Therefore, a good strategy, or approach to this challenge would be to ensure you place multiple trades on each occasion. Ensure that your strategy will win you money even though one or two trades may lose some money.

What you need to do to achieve this level of success is to work hard on your technical analysis skills. With excellent analysis skills, you will be able to analyze trades and be able to accurately determine which ones are winners and which ones you should possibly avoid. Therefore, learn to use your technical analysis tools and skills and then put them to practice often. It is only with deep knowledge of technical analysis and lots of practice that you will then be able to hone your skills and become and wealthy and successful options trader.

Consistently Profitable Strategies – Selling Puts & Credit Spreads

There are some studies conducted by credible institutions that the two most profitable options trading strategies are selling credit spreads and selling put options. The study found that the profits from such trades are consistent and regular over a long period.

However, the study found something else. The study reveals that buying call options and put options is more profitable in the long run even though it is not as consistent. You stand to make 7%-12% per month on the total portfolio which is about 84% to over 144% per annum. Considering that the techniques used are very simple, easy to apply, and require the most basic of technical analysis, then your chances of making stress-free money are very high. You can expect to win over 80% of your trades if you come up with the right trading plan.

Overall Best Options Trading Strategy

According to finds, it is widely accepted that you will make the most profits selling puts. If you invested a lot of your trading resources into selling put options, then you stand to make a lot of money consistently and with very little risk of loss.

The only challenge with the selling option is that it has certain limitations. This is because selling put options works best in a market that trends upwards or is on the rise. You can complement selling puts with selling ITM puts for long-term contracts. These are contracts that last 6 months or longer. They will make you tons of money simply because of the effect of time decay.

Also, when you sell, as a trader on the options market, credit spreads, you will be able to take advantage of the market in both directions. This means you will profit from an upward as well as downward market trend. This is great as even smaller traders can make some money regardless of experience. Therefore, always remember not to search for the size of the profits. When searching for the most profitable and successful options strategy, focus on factors like;

- Ability to come up with a reliable and safe plan

- Have a plan that generates regular income

- Associated risks are low

- Technical requirements are manageable

Sell Naked Puts is one of the most lucrative ways of making money trading options. The return on margin is almost as lucrative as selling credit spreads. However, it does not carry a similar level of risk. In short, anytime that you sell a put option, then you make it possible to purchase a stock at a price of your choosing.

A Closer Look at Naked Puts

It's the end of June and XYZ stock is at $50. However, the market is fluctuating and you prefer to buy this stock for $45. What you need to do at this stage is to sell a $45 put option for $2. You can put the expiration date on this option as the third week of July. Once you post the option, you will immediately receive $200 into your trading account. Now should the XYZ stock price fall below $45, you will be required to purchase 100 units. This will cost you $4,500.

However, you already have $200 in your account so the cost of buying the shares is reduced by this amount. If you sell a put option each month for the following six months, you will receive a total of $1,200. This will drastically lower the cost of buying XYZ shares. However, if the stock starts rising, you will not need to buy it but will keep selling the put option. While there is a slight risk due to liquidity issues, this strategy is quite a winner and can lead you to immense profits in just a short while.

ROI or Return on Investment

The Term ROI stands for Return on Investment. ROI is a measure of performance and is used by both investors and traders to measure the effectiveness and efficiency of an investment. This includes your trading capital. ROI deliberately endeavors to measure directly the total return derived from a particular investment.

For instance, if you invest a total of X amount on a particular trade and then received a return of Y from this investment, then ROI will endeavor to indicate the performance of your investment amount and what you received for your efforts. If you want to calculate the rate of return of an investment, you will need to know the total return which is then divided by the investment amount.

One of the most important aspects of your investment portfolio is its profitability. You need to regularly monitor your investments which are best achieved using the ROI or return on investment. It is advisable to work out what each dollar invested has generated.

R.O.I = (Profits — Costs) / Costs

Even then, investors need to understand that the ROI depends on numerous other factors such as the kind of investment security preferred and so on. Also, note that a high ROI implies a higher risk while a lower means reduced risk. For this reason, appropriate risk management must be undertaken.

Chapter 13. How COVID-19 Will Affect Option Trading

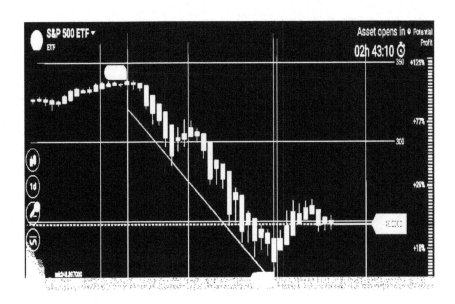

Coronavirus has had a variety of effects on global financial markets. It's difficult to say to what extent the epidemic affected people now that it's not over; between February 19 and March 23, the S & P 500 lost more than a third of its value. Over the same time frame, the Dow Jones Industrial Average has lost even more (up to 36 percent). Despite the return to growth, both indicators point to a massive disruption in the global economy that hasn't been seen in the last five years. Furthermore, the economic effects of the world's most recent pandemic may not be limited to that. It's likely that there are already undiscovered or delayed effects that will be found later.

Despite the recent recovery, the economic downturn in China, the United States, and Europe still have the potential to cause a full-fledged financial crisis. The current year's global GDP is very likely to experience a setback.

What should we expect?

The 'Fast Recovery' scenario, according to Roland Berger, an independent European consulting firm, is already out of the question. Their experts also predict that the outage will last between 4 and 12 weeks. China has moved further down the coronavirus curve, and its economy has regained its foothold (at least, according to the Chinese government itself). COVID-19's results, on the other hand, are still unknown in Europe and the United States. It might take a lot of time for them to recover.

Certain sectors will be affected harder than the overall economy. Airlines, leisure, and retail (with the exception of FMCG) will be hit hard. The automobile, logistics, and oil/gas industries are all in the same boat. Financial services, on the other hand, would be significantly less impacted. Nonetheless, the pandemic's impacts would be felt to some degree by all sectors. It will definitely take some time for the global economy to recover.

The COVID-19 stay-at-home requirement has spawned a major sub-industry of options trading, which is increasing in tandem with a rise in equities trading that shows no signs of slowing down.

In November, stock options trading reached new highs, continuing a pattern that started earlier in the year.

On all options markets, equity options trading is up 50% year to date compared to last year.

Optional Equity (Volume)

- NASDAQ has a 49 percent market cap.

- CBOE has a 51% market share.

- ICE has a 58 percent share of the market.

"As you can see from the volumes, the public is accepting alternatives in a completely unparalleled manner," Interactive Brokers' Steve Sosnick told me. "I think the lockdown led to some of the popularity... Many people were stranded at home, with $1,200 checks or rent/loan moratoria, with no sports to watch or wager on. So they went to the stock market, where they discovered that options have payout mechanisms that are identical to sports bets."

The comparison to sports betting is intentional: "The psychology [of sports betting versus stock betting] is quite close." "With sports betting, I have a chance to win a portion of the money. It's the same with stocks and options, only there are thousands of bets you can make every day with stocks and options, and when you're in an upmarket like we have been, you can start to believe that the odds are really in your favor."

Most of the trading activity has happened in out-of-the-money options that are nearing expiration, with most of it day trading: purchasing in the morning and selling in the afternoon, according to Kyle Robinson, who monitors trading activity at Piper Sandler.

What makes you want to do that? "They're selling options because a lot of people don't have enough money to buy a lot of stocks," he said. "You can purchase options for a fraction of the price, and if your options move at the same percentage as the underlying stock, you can profit as if you owned it."

Many day traders are right to aim options trading, according to Sosnick, and are not behaving irrationally.

He pointed out that buying out of the money calls has low initial investment, so you can only lose what you put in. "You will only lose a dollar if you buy a call for a dollar." "They might be poorly capitalized," Sosnick hypothesized when asked why so many people are doing basic day trading, in the morning and out by the close. They might crave the opportunity to sleep at night. It's possible that it's their only option."

Zero commissions on many trades, as well as the presence of social media and chat rooms full of debates on high-profile names, are all contributing to the day trading phenomenon.

Another important aspect is the availability of instructional materials that instruct traders about how to trade options.

"We have seen no decline in interest in educational content on our website," says JJ Kinahan, TD Ameritrade's Chief Market Strategist. "Stock fundamentals and getting started with options are the two most popular videos on our site." He pointed out that viewing of that content is already three times higher than a year ago.

Equity Trading is Also on the Rise

The rise in options trading is being accompanied by a similar rise in stock trading. For example, trading volume at Fidelity increased by 97 percent year over year in the third quarter.

According to Rich Repetto of Piper Sandler, regular average revenue trades (DARTs) at Interactive Brokers increased by 174 percent in November compared to the same time last year. They have added 29,000 new accounts to their scheme.

In a recent note to clients, Repetto wrote, "We are raising our 4Q20 EPS forecast due to better than expected trading, continued account expansion, and good margin balance and customer equity growth."

Robinson noted that trading in futures contracts, which are more often used by practitioners as hedging vehicles, and index options have not seen the same drastic rise.

How long will this high level of trading last?

What could probably go wrong in the midst of all this bullish call buying? The greatest risk, according to Sosnick, is simple mean reversion: "You may get into a losing streak." "If you buy risky calls, it doesn't take much to lose money after a few days or weeks."

Sosnick also hypothesized that, regardless of market dynamics, all of this day trading might have a finite shelf life.

"I wonder how far does this has to do with the fact that many people haven't had to pay student loans in a long time and will have to do so next month," he said. "If you use the typical student loan payment of $400 to bring in the economy, and I have to start paying that back, that is money that will come out of the markets."

Robinson concurred. Robinson told me, "We don't expect these levels to last." "Those who have stayed at home will return to work once the pandemic is over. When the vaccine is released, volatility will likely decrease, making day trading more difficult."

Sosnick decided that if the large amount of call buying stopped, volatility would decrease. He pointed out that the massive amount of call buyers has inflated implied volatility, which is one of the reasons the CBOE Volatility Index (VIX) has remained trapped at the elevated 21 levels amid a major rally.

How many people will be around for the next round of corrections?

According to Sosnick, the next correction would be the ultimate test to see if these new traders hang around. "People are knowledgeable, and they are attempting to educate themselves. A full market cycle, on the other hand, is the best education for traders, and we haven't seen one yet. Many of these traders just entered the market after March, so they haven't seen the whole cycle."

Sosnick doesn't blame the younger generation for enjoying a good time with stocks and options when they can: "And betting on NASDAQ was much more likely to pay off than betting on the Jets," he joked.

Conclusion

Thank you for making it through to the end of this book. You've now had a careful stroll through the key standards and ventures in options trading we feel are fundamental to progress as an options trader. You've figured out how the options markets function, the best trading strategies and why it's basic to pick the best possible fundamental assets for the procedures you need to utilize. You've additionally observed that great exit strategies are nearly as imperative as discovering great trades to enter, that focusing on the points of interest is basic, and that achievement is virtually inconceivable without a decent money-management plan — and the discipline to follow it.

At last, you've got lots of pages loaded with vital inquiries to consider in your search for the best online options broker. At the end of the day, it's a great opportunity to control up, plugin — and profit. You have all the data you have to appreciate 24-hour access to the options markets, fast and programmed execution of your orders and the most reduced commissions in the history of options trading. In any case, to share these advantages, you should confront the bigger individual duties that accompany coordinated access to online trading.

You should have the discipline to do your very own research, screen your own positions and monitor every one of the points of interest you may leave to your full-benefit financial firm. You can never again depend on a broker to watch your positions and call with guidance or suggestions. You are currently an autonomous administrator — and, all things considered, must be absolutely in charge of your own behavior.

You should likewise be mindful and be prepared to react to both fast moves in everyday trading designs and consistently evolving longer-term economic situations.

In case you think tolerating such difficulties and practicing such discipline is simple, think of one as a little preventative portion of the real world. An investigation — "Online Investors: Do the Slow Die First?" by Brad M. Barber and Terrance Odean, published in Economic Intuition.

DAY TRADING SWING & FOREX FOR BEGINNERS

A CRASH COURSE TO INVEST IN THE STOCK MARKET:

MAKING A LIVING BY BUYING AND SELLING STOCKS, OPTIONS AND CURRENCIES,

AND USING PASSIVE INCOME STRATEGIES

Introduction

It is near impossible to predict market movements, and that is why day traders, swing traders, and forex traders place trades of any length in which they take a position with the hope that the price will move favorably for them. Day trading, swing trading, and forex trading can all be profitable in the long term if done correctly. Give one or more of these strategies a try!

Day Trading

Day trading involves making short-term trades on assets such as stocks or currencies with the goal of making a quick profit when you buy an asset and sell it at a higher price before its value decreases. To do this, day traders generally enter a position and then exit it if the price does not move in their favor. In the long term, day trading can be profitable for traders who know what to do to make correct trades at optimal times and avoid losing money due to falls in the stock market. Day trading can be very high risk, and taking excessive risks can lead to devastating losses over time.

Swing Trading

Swing trading involves taking a position in an asset over a longer period of time (ranging from days to years). When a swing trader first enters a trade, it is called a long position because they will be holding the asset for some time. If the price does not go up or down in their favor, they will be happy with their profit or loss. But if the price increases significantly by the end of the time frame, then they are considering taking an opposite position by selling the shares or contracts at that point. This strategy takes more effort and can take more than one year to make money, but it also has less risk than day trading.

Forex Trading

Forex trading involves buying and selling currencies. The market is open 24 hours a day, so it is possible to trade on the short-term fluctuations in the market. Just as with stocks, currencies can be more volatile than others at times. A successful forex trader should be able to identify trends, determine their risk tolerance and time frame for trades, manage risks accordingly, and be able to stick with a plan through thick and thin.

Day Trading VS. Forex Trading VS. Swing Trading

Before I go any further, let me define what these terms mean. The most basic concept is that they refer to the same groups of conditions. But to be clear, Forex involves currency trading; day trading involves the buying and selling of stocks or futures; swing trading involves both stocks and futures.

The average Forex trade takes about 40-60 days to make money on a short-term basis (2-4 weeks). It might take even longer if the market is moving too fast or if it's in a tight range for too long. A long-term trend will generally move at a faster pace than short-term trends.

If you are going to day trade, then I recommend day trading the trend. Always trade what the trend is doing. I can make more money on a trend than on a range, and while I was trading in one of my previous blogs, I had a 15-year streak of daily winning trades where my little brother could not beat me. I made money. It might be different in your account but it makes sense that the following something works better than trying to anticipate and trade against it (when you should never do that).

Swing trading is in between and generally involving very few trades. I've noticed that swing trading sometimes takes a longer time than day trading due to the fact that you are not looking for explosive moves up or down, but a slow gradual move. But it can be done much quicker than forex if the market is volatile, so keep that in mind.

Here's where trend following comes in. Momentum begets more momentum, while range-bound markets are very hard to trade in the short term because there's nowhere to go but up or down when the range is too small.

Day trading is a versatile strategy that can be used to earn a profit without taking any risk. For example, traders can buy a stock and hold it for several weeks to months in order to collect dividends or sell short.

Swing traders are generally more risk-averse than day traders because they are not trying to capture small gains; instead, they aim at higher profits over longer time periods. Investors who are willing to take the time to learn how to swing trade from the start will likely be rewarded in the long term.

What You Will Discover in This Book_

I am a straightforward guy, so you will find that I like to get right to the point. There will be no beating around the bush. I will not spout out terms at you like this is a textbook. All the words in this book are meant to be understood by a complete newbie.

Before we get to these explanations, one thing needs to be stated: day trading is a business. I will remind you that throughout this book, it's such an important thing to understand. Companies do not just spring up and become successful overnight, even though it sometimes appears that way to outsiders. Businesses take hours of devotion every day and months of behind-the-curtain work to become successful. In the case of day trading, it usually takes between 3 and 6 months of regular time and effort to get your feet firmly planted on the ground to see the results you want.

Trading is not a get-rich-quick scheme. If you do not have the time it takes to learn the business's ins and outs, this is not your career. In fact, you must commit the right amount of time, be able to handle a challenge or the excitement of an ever-changing career, and have the will to learn and grow.

It is possible to make money through all three of these strategies, but it takes practice and knowledge. If you like the idea of any of these three methods, it is important that you practice your trading strategy and learn more about technical analysis. Technical analysis involves examining past price behavior to predict future price movement.

With some determination and a lot of effort, you can be a successful trader in any of these fields.

This book will discuss these three strategies, and how they are related to one another.

Are you ready to be serious about gaining new tools and skills that will allow you to take control of your financial future? If so, then read on! I promise that this book will let you hit the ground running with day trading, even though you are starting with zero knowledge and experience.

Don't wait and miss out on the opportunity to take control of your finances and your life. Procrastination will keep you chained to financial slavery. Read this book in its entirety to see how YOU can be the master of your destiny!

We have a lot of ground to cover in a few pages. So, let's get started.

Chapter 1: Day Trading

What Is Day Trading?

The stock market is a vast place and there are millions of trades that take place all over the world, within a single day. There are both buyers and sellers in the market, and they will all have the same motive in mind; to increase their wealth potential.

Of all these trades, not everything will be of the same nature. Some will be long-term investments and some short. Long-term investments refer to those that are held for a long period of time. They are preferred by those who are not in a hurry to make money. Short-term investments, on the other hand, are those that are liquidated within a short period of time. They are not intended to be held for a long time, as owners will be interested in disposing of them early.

Short-term investments can be of many types based on the time that they are held. Some can be held for a month, some for a week, and some will be disposed of on the same day. This book will focus on the last option.

Better known as Intraday trading, day trading is one of the most preferred ways to trade in the stock market. Preferred mostly by those willing to part with their investment within a single day and realize a profit, or loss, from.

Intraday traders are interested in realizing a profit by capitalizing on the difference in the rates of these securities as opposed to long-term investors who will be in it for the Dividends.

Dos of Day Trading

Risk Capital

You have to understand that the stock market is a very volatile place, and anything can happen within a matter of a few seconds. You have to be prepared for anything that it throws at you. In order to prepare for it, you have to make use of risk capital. Risk capital refers to money that you are willing to risk. You have to convince yourself that even if you lose the money that you have invested, then it will not be a big deal for you. For that, you have to make use of your own money and not borrow from anyone, as you will start feeling guilty about investing it. Decide on a set number and invest it.

Research

Before you invest in the market, you need to research it thoroughly. Don't think you're going to learn as you go along. That is only possible if you at least know the basics. You have to remain interested in gathering information that is crucial for your investments, and it will only come about if you put in some hard work towards it. Nobody is asking you to stay up and go through thick texts books. All you have to do is go through books and websites and gather enough information to help you get started on the right foot.

Diversification

You have to stress diversification in your portfolio. You don't want all the money to go into the same place. Think of it as a way to increase your stock's potential. You have to choose different sectors and diverse stocks to invest in. you should also choose one of the different types of investments as they all contribute towards attaining a different result. Diversification is mostly seen as a tool to cut down on risk, and it is best that you not invest any more than 5% in any one of the securities.

Stop Loss

You have to understand the importance of a stop-loss mechanism. A stop-loss technique is used to safeguard an investment. Now say, for example, you invest $100 and buy shares priced at $5 each. You have to place a stop loss at around $4 in order to stop it from going down any further. Now you will wonder as to why you have to place the stop loss and undergo one. Well, by doing so, you will actually be saving your money to a large extent. You won't have to worry about the value slipping further down and can carry on with your trade.

Take a Loss

It's okay to have losses from time to time. Don't think of it as a big obstacle. You will have the opportunity to turn a loss into profit. You have to remain confident and invested. You can take a loss on a bad investment that was anyway not going your way. You can also take a loss on an investment that you think is a long hold and will not work for you in the short term. Taking a few losses is the only way in which you can learn to trade well in the market.

These form the different dos of the stock market that will help you with your intraday trades.

Don'ts of Day Trading

No Planning

Do not make the mistake of going about investing in the market without a plan in tow. You have to plan out the different things that you will do in the market and go about it the right way. This plan should include how much you will invest in the market, where you will invest, how you will go about it etc. No planning will translate to getting lost in the stock market, which is not a good sign for any investor.

Over Rely on Broker

You must never over rely on a broker. You have to make your own decisions and know what to do and when. The broker will not know whether an investment is good for you. He will only be bothered about his profits. If he is suggesting something, then you should do your own research before investing in the stock. The same extends to emails that you might receive through certain sources. These emails are spams and meant to dupe you. So, don't make the mistake of trusting everything that you read.

Message Boards

You have to not care about message boards. These will be available on the Internet and are mostly meant to help people gather information. But there will be pumpers and bashers present there. Pumpers will force people to buy a stock just to increase its value, and bashers will force people to sell all their stocks just because they want the value to go down. Both these types are risky, as they will abandon the investors just as soon as their motive is fulfilled. So, you have to be quite careful with it.

Calculate Wrong

Some people make the mistake of calculating wrong. They will not be adept at math and will end up with wrong figures. This is a potential danger to all those looking to increase their wealth potential. If you are not good at calculating, then download n app that will do it for you or carry a calculator around to do the correct calculations. The motive is to make the right calculations and increase your wealth potential.

Copy Strategies

Do not make the mistake of copying someone else's strategies. You have to come up with something that is your own and not borrowed from someone else. If you end up borrowing, then you will not be able to attain the desired results. You have to sit with your broker and come up with a custom strategy that you can employ and win big.

These form the different don'ts of the stock market that will help you keep troubles at bay.

Chapter 2:   Conservative Strategy of

Day Trading

Awareness Is Power

Monitoring chief exchanging measures isn't sufficient. Informal investors likewise need to screen and stay up with the most recent occasions and news on the securities exchange considering the monetary viewpoint, rate plans, and the Fed's revenue.

In this way, achieve your home assignment. Draw up a list of must-dos of the stocks you might want to exchange and be constantly kept insider savvy of the overall business sectors, and chose organizations. Monitor business news and search for solid monetary sources.

Put Aside Funds

Gauge how much cash you need to roll the dice for each exchange. Various everyday brokers lose under 1% to 2% in their exchange accounts. For example, on the off chance that you hold a $40,000 exchanging portfolio and decide to lose 0.5 percent of your cash for each arrangement, the potential trade misfortune is $200 (0.5 percent * $40,000).

The overflow measure of monetary assets ought to be saved to exchange. You ought to consistently be prepared to lose them. Remember, it could conceivably occur.

Put Aside Time, as well

Day exchanging takes as much time as is needed, so that is the reason its name is day exchanging. Indeed, you should spend the fundamental piece of your day on it. Try not to try and take a gander at it if you are limited on schedule.

The exchanging method needs a dealer for all time to monitor the current circumstance available and to gauge spot openings, which can seize any time inside exchanging hours. On-the-spot choices are the key.

Get Started with Small

As a beginner merchant, focus on a limit of 1-2 stocks over the span of a meeting. Observing and searching for promising circumstances are all the more effective with a couple of stocks. These days, it is amazingly unavoidable to realize how to exchange with fragmentary offers, so you can explain explicit, more modest dollar sums you need to contribute.

Avert Penny Stocks

Likely you are chasing at exchanges and low costs yet avoiding penny stocks. Often, these stocks are illiquid, and the opportunity to hit a bonanza is hopeless.

The greater part of the stocks, valued under $5 per share, are de-recorded from the significant financial exchanges and may just be traded absurdly (OTC). Stay far from these until you have a specific opportunity to take care of your job.

Time Those Trades

At the point when financial backers and brokers put in the requests, they begin to carry out when the business sectors open up in the first part of the day, which prompts the unpredictability of a cost. An accomplished player can settle on a satisfactory decision and perceive examples to make benefits. Notwithstanding, it tends to be better for novices to peruse the market without taking any actions for the initial 15 to 20 minutes.

Generally speaking, the center hours are less delicate. Accordingly, elements toward the end chime begin to go up once more. Albeit the times of heavy traffic guarantee openings, it's more secure for novices to deflect them interestingly.

Reduce Losses with Limited Orders

Tackle what sort of requests you will use to enter and leave exchanging. Is it accurate to say that you will utilize limit requests or market orders? At the point when you post a market request, it is executed at the most sensible cost available as of now—subsequently, the cost is ensured.

In the interim, a limited request guarantees the cost, however, not the execution. The restricted requests help you exchange all the more precisely, wherein you provide your cost estimate (not unreasonable but rather executable) for purchasing and selling too. More prepared informal investors may utilize alternatives techniques to ensure their positions as well.

Be Down-To-Earth Concerning Profit

To be worthwhile, a methodology doesn't have to win constantly. A ton of merchants just advantage 50-60% from their complete exchanges. Ensure that the danger for each exchange is restricted to a particular level of the record and that techniques for passage and exit are resolved and brought down unmistakably.

Keep Calm

There are events when the securities exchange evaluates your nerves. In the limit of an informal investor, you need to dominate the abilities to keep trepidation, eagerness, and expectation, under control. Your choices ought to be solemnly controlled by the presence of mind but not by feelings.

Adhere to the Plan

Prepared merchants need to act rapidly, yet not to think for quite a while. Why? Since they have a planned exchanging technique heretofore, close by the control to hold fast to that methodology. Following your recipe intently instead of attempting to seek after the benefits is additionally of an extraordinary significance. Try not to let your sentiments and feelings run over you, and put your arrangement away. Among informal investors, there's an expression: "Plan your exchange and exchange your arrangement."

We should consider a portion of the reasons why day exchanging can be so confounded before we jump into a portion of the intricate details of day exchanging.

Chapter 3:   Advanced Strategy of

Day Trading

When you are looking forward to capitalizing on the small frequent price movements, day trading strategies are the best for you. Any effective strategy that you will choose must be consistent and must rely on in-depth technical analysis that utilizes charts, market patterns, and price indicators predicting future price movements.

It is your responsibility to choose the most appropriate strategy that best fits your requirements. As a trader, it is good that you know the average daily trading volume.

Fallen Angel

A Fallen Angel is a strategy that involves a bond that has been reduced to junk bond status from an investment-grade rating as a result of the issuer's weakening financial conditions. In terms of stock, a fallen angel refers to a stock that has always been high and now has fallen considerably. Fallen angel bonds can be a sovereign, corporate, or municipal debt that a rating service has downgraded. The main reason for such downgrades could be attributed to revenue decline that generally jeopardizes the capabilities of issuers to servicing debt. The potential for downgrade often experiences a dramatic increase when expanding debts are combined with expanding debt levels. The securities of fallen angels are at times so attractive, particularly to contrarian investors who seek to capitalize on the potential. This enables the issuer to recover from the temporary setback.

Example:

Due to the ever-falling oil prices over several quarters, an oil company has reported sustained losses. The company, therefore, can decide to downgrade its investment-grade bonds to junk status as a result of the increasing risk of default. This will result in a decline in the prices of the company's bonds and, in addition, increase yields, which will make the contrarian investors to be attracted to the debt as they only see the low oil prices as a temporary condition. However, there are conditions where you are likely to go at a loss, especially when the fallen angel bond issuers do not recover. For example, if there is an introduction of superior products by a rival company, the issuers may fail to recover.

ABCD Pattern / Reverse ABCD Pattern

The ABCD pattern is a pattern that shows perfect harmony between price and time. ABCD pattern usually reflects the common and rhythmic style in the market movements. The geometric price/time pattern consists of three consecutive price trends with a leading indicator that can guide a trader to determine when and where to enter and exit a trade. As a trader, ABCD Pattern can be very important in identifying the available trading opportunities in any market (be it futures, forex, or stock) on any timeframe (be its position, intraday, or swing), and in any market condition (be it range-bound, bullish or bearish markets). Before placing a trade, ABCD Pattern can help you determine the reward and the risks of trade.

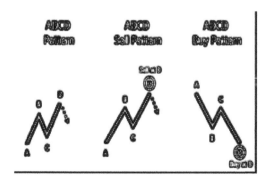

A representation of the ABCD Pattern (Above)

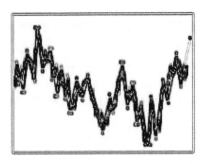

ABCD pattern on a trading chart

Bull Flag and Bear Flag

With technical analysis, a flag refers to a price pattern that can explode and move within a shorter timeframe to the prevailing price trend that has always been observed in longer time frames on a price chart. With the flag patterns, a trader can identify the possible prevailing trend that is continuing from a given point where the price has drifted against the same trend. Therefore, in the case that the trend resumes, by noticing the flag pattern, there will be a rapid price increase, and this makes the timing of a trade advantageous. Flags are areas of tight consolidation in price actions, and they show a counter-trend sharp directional movement in price. This pattern has 5 to 20 price bars.

Bullish Flag Formation

These are formation patterns observed in stocks that have a strong uptrend. Bull flags got their names from the fact that the pattern closely resembles a flag on a pole. A vertical rise in stock results in a pole, and a period of consolidation results in a flag. The flag is usually angled down away from the trend that is prevailing but also can be a horizontal rectangle. The bullish flag pattern starts with a strong price spike that is almost vertical. The prices then peaks and forms an orderly pullback where the lows and the highs become almost parallel to each other, making them almost form a tilted rectangle.

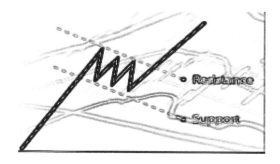

Bullish Flag Formation

The parallel diagonal nature is reflected by the plotted trend lines (both lower and upper trend lines). The breaking of the upper resistance trend line forms the first breakout.

Another uptrend move and a breakout are formed when there is an explosion of the prices, causing prices to surge back towards the high of the formation.

Bearish Flag

The bearish flag is an inverted version of the bull flag. In this case, an almost vertical panic price drop is formed by the flagpole because the sellers make the bulls get blindsided and, as a result, there is a bounce having parallel lower and upper trend lines, forming the flag. The panic sellers are triggered when the lower trend lines break.

This flag is similar to the bull flag in that the severity of the drop on the flagpole will determine how the strength of the bear flag can be.

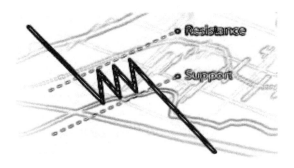

The Bearish flag

Develop Trading Skills

To become a trader, you are required to not only know about just finance or business but also hard science or mathematics. You must be an individual who can do deep research and analysis that can mirror the economic factors from a broader perspective, as well as the day-to-day chart patterns impacting different financial markets. As a trader, it is crucial that you need to sharpen your ability to concentrate and focus, especially in a fast-moving environment containing different people with different goals and ideas. You must also be able to practice self-control and regulate your emotions even when in situations upsetting you. Lastly, you should always be able to keep an accurate record of your trades to check on your account and to provide you with a learning opportunity that will help you become a better trader.

Chapter 4:   Typical Beginner's

Errors in Day Trading

Lack of a Plan

While trading, it is important that you have a plan. A plan acts as a compass direction while trading; it shows you the move that you should take to ensure that it is a wise trade decision. In a plan, we have different goals while trading. Some of these goals make our investment in day trading worth our while. They give us hope to achieve more out of life and, at the same time, inspire us to push beyond our abilities. A person's failure to create a plan results in failure. You find that you make investments without properly evaluating all the underlying factors. In case there are some risks involved, you find that you are not aware of them. In turn, these risks exposed you to the possibility of encountering a loss. When such incidences occur, you are not well-prepared with risk management strategies since you failed to have a plan. It goes without saying that a plan will help you achieve a lot in the trading industry. Most of the time, it provides a bearing for the direction that one is taking while trading.

The biggest challenge comes when you are a beginner, and you do not know much about trading. At that point, it is very easy to make a mistake. Any slight move that you take matters and has a big impact on your future. A single move can either sabotage what you have built for years or make you stronger than you were before. We have seen people succeed at trading, and then, at one point, they lose all that they have worked hard to build. Your success in this industry is dependent on the plans that you have regarding your trading future. Any slight mistake will cause you to go down faster than you could climb up. As you trade, you may come to a point where you encounter a series of wins. Such incidences make you feel confident in trading, and, at some point, you may be deceived to think that you can easily achieve success. At that point, you may decide to do away with having a plan. Such simple decisions can make a huge change in your trading, and you end up making a loss that you may not be able to recover from.

Trading to Cover Up for Previous Losses

Most traders are victims of this strategy. After conducting your daily trades, things may not move as planned. You find that you might have expected to get a profit out of the trades made, but instead, you end up with a loss. To cover up for the losses, you decide to engage in another trade, hoping that things will be different. Contrary to your expectations, you end up encountering more losses than you would have imagined. It gets worse if you spent more money on that investment as compared to the previous investments. You get to a situation where you are full of regrets due to the wrong decision that you made. It is important to note that rushed decisions barely lead to anything good. In most cases, they end up in sabotage, and you may not be able to recover from some of these incidences. We ought to learn that two wrongs do not make a right. Once you have made a mistake, the first step does not involve bouncing back to the same thing that caused you to make a mistake. You need to calm down and identify where you went wrong and start reorganizing from that point.

At times, we keep trading even after we make losses because we are in denial. You find that you are in a phase where you find it difficult to admit that you can make a mistake. These difficulties, at times, arise due to the fact that we have high expectations. Anything that does not lead us to achieve the dreams we created for ourselves automatically makes us regret the decisions that we made.

At that point, one becomes frustrated since things are not moving as planned. Instead of taking some time off to realize where you went wrong in the previous trade, you immediately engage in another without carefully thinking it through. This is perhaps one of the biggest mistakes that most traders make. While it is good to have big dreams and ambitions, it is important that you do not make wrong decisions while trying so hard to achieve some of these dreams. Well, since the whole point of investing is earning more from the investments that we make, it may not always be the case. Some days, we will encounter some losses, and they should not lead us in making rush decisions.

Overtrading

As a beginner, you may have started trading with huge expectations. You have this big dream of becoming an overnight success. You decide to invest heavily in your trades, especially after hearing what other traders are earning out of trading. Ideally, it is healthy to have self-belief and imagine that you, too, can get to the point that other investors have reached. While at it, it is essential that you have practical dreams that are achievable. Some people have managed to sell out the idea that trading is an easy task that can result in earning within minutes. However, many people start trading and end up with huge frustrations when they fail to achieve their dreams as fast as experts. You find that with the excitement of engaging in trading, you end up engaging in multiple trades as a way to earn quick money. In this instance, most trade executions are not carefully planned; they are randomly selected. This means that you do not take time to come up with the right strategies to succeed in the different trades, and eventually, you end up losing.

At the same time, we have individuals who spread their risks across different trades. You are uncertain if you will end up making a loss or a profit. In this instance, you decide to spread your risks so that regardless of how the trade goes, you will not experience a total loss. In the beginning, this looks like an attractive strategy, and it almost feels like it is impossible to make a complete loss. However, you should remember that you are taking a gamble. This means that you can either earn a loss or a profit in both situations. It might occur that you experience a loss in all the investments that you made. In this case, that strategy will not benefit you in any way, especially since you still encounter a loss at the end. While coming up with the decision to conduct multiple trades, you need to be open to the idea that anything can happen. At the same time, you need to be well aware of the different option strategies that you can utilize while carrying out different trades. This allows you to remain focused and that you note some red flags before you end up making certain mistakes.

The Belief That a Big Investment Leads to Profits

Some people tend to have a misplaced belief that they need to make a big investment for them to earn a profit. This belief has caused a lot of individuals to make numerous mistakes while trading. We have had people invest a huge amount of their earnings, only to end up making a huge loss. For instance, you have $100 in your account, and you end up investing $90. With such an investment decision, you cannot afford to make a loss. Any wrong move can result in sabotage and make you lose what you worked so hard to get. At this point, with such an amount, you may end up feeling depressed after you have made a loss. Remaining with $10 can be challenging, especially considering that you had more, yet you lost it from making a trading mistake.

At this point, it is important that we learn to avoid placing all our eggs in one basket. In case of an accident, we may end up losing all the eggs and have none that is spared.

If you are a beginner, you should learn the importance of starting small. We find that most beginners are suffering from such decisions. You find that with the excitement of starting a new investment, you tend to overspend. This causes you to spend much of your time and energy on the new investment, and you barely take time to think things through. You end up making rash decisions that prove to be wrong later on, especially when things do not work in your favor. After experiencing a loss, you get to the point of self-realization that the move you took was wrong. We tend to have a misplaced perception that if we make a small investment, we equally receive small returns. Well, we have some trades that demand little from us and can result in huge incomes later on. We need to come to the point of understanding that the strategies that we utilize while trading can create a huge impact on our trading career. With a small investment and the right strategies, one can make a huge impact as they would make with a huge investment. At times, it all narrows down to the mentality that we have and uphold regarding different instances in life.

Ignoring the Expiry Date

Trades have a certain period where they are regarded as valid; after this period, the underlying stock becomes useless. You might have purchased some stocks and failed to be keen on the expiry date. Before you know it, you end up making a big loss after your stocks have been regarded as invalid. This is a sad way to lose the money that you have invested in your stock. To avoid being caught up in such, you need to watch the stock market carefully and make a move when it becomes favorable to you. This way, you avoid reaching the expiry date with nothing. To accomplish this, one way is to keep a record of your trades. If this is something that you keep referring to on a daily basis, it becomes difficult to overlook some of these things.

Lack of an Exit Plan

We are too fast in identifying the signals that lead us to engage in a certain trade, but we barely take time to identify when to exit a trade. This is a mistake that we end up regretting deeply. Mainly, if you engage in a trade, it is expected that you identify all the factors that can sabotage what you have built. At times, you find that one is in a position to earn a lot from a particular trade strategy. However, if they keep holding on to their position, they may encounter a loss. To avoid finding yourself in such situations, learn to note the signals that point out that you need to leave a given trade. Staying will make things worse, so exiting is the best solution at this point. At times, you might be betting on the possibility of making a huge profit or making a huge loss. In such times, you would rather exit the trade and earn a small profit than take the risk of staying. When you stay, you might not be sure if you will earn a huge profit or experience a huge loss.

All of the above are some of the key mistakes that the majority of us make while trading. However, if you feel like you are already making some of these mistakes, there should be no cause for alarm. I will provide some guidelines on how you can avoid making these mistakes while engaging in day trading options. There are more mistakes that traders make that have not been highlighted. You can learn more about them from other platforms. After all, as a trader, learning is something that you have to embrace.

Chapter 5: Swing Trading

What is the Swing Trading?

Swing trading is indeed a form of trading that seeks to grab short to medium returns on a stock (or another financial instrument) over even a span of weeks or months. Swing traders mainly utilize fundamental analysis to search for trading possibilities. In order to assess cost patterns and trends, these traders could use significant analysis.

Money Required for Swing Trading

Let's look at how large an account you'd like to swing a trade for livelihood.

If someone advises you that someone wants $X to sell for a livelihood, they wouldn't realize what they really are speaking about.

Several factors determine how long it costs to swing a trade for livelihood, so it isn't easy to have a total amount that would appeal to us.

Here are all the key topics to understand:

- The basic life expenditures

- The standard of lifestyle people chooses to sustain.
- Who else do people support?
- How much would you like to save per month?
- What other costs will you have incurred by investing full-time (hospital services, etc.)?
- The effectiveness and benefit of your trading strategy.
- How are you going to deal with a trade recession?

The smartest thing you could do is get a stable income when you're learning to exchange. Build your assets from the trading revenue.

Once you are ready to generate 2–3 times the existing trading revenue, you should try swing trading on a full-time basis. When it becomes clear that you're wasting funds by heading to work, it's definitely time to leave your work and trade. Or perhaps not.

It would be best if you still held your career and even served part-time to provide a stable income stream. It depends on one's priorities, what they are comfortable doing, and the other responsibilities.

The easiest way to start is to monitor your expenditures. Remember to implement any protection to deal with emergencies. Perhaps you might not notice how much you're investing.

On the other hand, you do not know how minimal your monthly expenses are. If that's the situation for you, perhaps it would be simpler to substitute your earnings with trading. Often, swing trading means keeping a stake either longer or shorter for far more than a trading day, but normally not longer than a few weeks and months. It is a generalized timeline since certain trades can last much longer than a few months, but the trader could also deem them swinging trades. Swing trades could also occur on the day of a trading session, but this is an unusual scenario that is caused by highly unpredictable circumstances.

The aim of swing trading is to catch a fraction of a possible market shift. Although some traders are looking for dynamic stocks with a lot of change, others might choose more subdued stocks. In any way, swing trading seems to be the method of determining where the investment's price is expected to move ahead, entering a spot, and then gaining a portion of profit if the move suddenly appears.

Efficient swing traders are indeed trying to catch a fraction of the anticipated market change, and then carry on to the next chance.

Often swing trader's measure trading on even risk or reward basic principle. By studying the map of the commodity, they decide where they would reach, where they could put an end to the loss, and afterward predict where they should make a benefit. If they lose $1 per stock on the setup that might fairly generate a $3 profit that is a reasonable risk to reward ratio. On the other hand, actually, losing $1 to raise $1 or just earn $0.75 is not quite as beneficial as that.

Swing traders mainly use fundamental analysis owing to a short-term habit of the exchange. That being said, a critical approach could be used to improve the analysis. For instance, when a swing trader perceives a constructive setup in a portfolio, they might like to check that the dynamics of the commodity are either favorable or strengthening.

Swing traders would also search for openings on regular charts and therefore will follow one hour or fifteen minutes charts to identify accurate admission, prevent loss, and take-for-profit amounts.

Swing Trade Strategies

Swing trader continues to search for multi-day graph trends. Many of the much more popular patterns include shifting average crossovers, triangles, cup-and-handle trends, flags, head and shoulder patterns. In relation to other markers, main reversal candlesticks could be used to develop a strong trading strategy.

At the end of the day, every swing trader formulates a scheme and tactic that brings them an advantage on certain trades. This includes searching for trading arrangements that aim to lead to stable fluctuations in the price of the commodity. It's not quick, and there's no technique or configuration that works every single time. With a desirable risk or reward, success is not expected at all times. The more amenable the risk to reward of a trading approach, the less necessary it is to succeed in order to generate net benefit over multiple trades.

The Real-World Example of the Apple's Swing Trade

The chart given above illustrates the time when Apple (AAPL) had a significant price increase. This was accompanied by the tiny cup and handle design that always signifies the continuity of the price increase if the stock shifts past the top of that handle.

In any case:

The price rises just above the handle, causing a potential purchase of about $192.70.

One potential stop-loss location is under the handle, labeled with a rectangle, close to $187.50. It typically depends on entry and the stop-loss, the approximate trading cost is $5.20 for each share ($193.70-$186.50).

If you are searching for a possible payoff that is at minimum double the potential risk, every price over $204.10 ($193.70 + ($2 * $5.20)) would offer this.

Apart from the risk to reward ratio, the trader may also use other escape strategies, such as that waiting for a fresh low price. For this approach, the exit sign was not provided until $226.46, when that price fell far below the previous pullback level. This will have ended in the profit of $24.76 for each share. Think of another way—12 percent benefit in return for much less than three percent uncertainty. This swing of trade consumed about two months.

Such escape approaches might be when a price is below the shifting average (never shown) or when the indicator, just as a stochastic oscillator, exceeds the signal point.

Pros and Cons

Swing traders typically keep a short to a long portfolio for at most a trading day but not longer than just a few days.

This is a common time, but certain traders still prefer to keep positions indefinitely before their goal is met.

Swing trading is quite common with Forex retailers for two key factors. First, the Forex swing trade methods typically include entry and exit tactics that include a chart search just once or twice a day, and at most for some hours. This very flexible schedule is quite convenient for individuals with hectic lives and maximum work.

The core theory behind swing trading is to capture a bit of possible price fluctuation. Many swing traders favor higher-volatility assets (like foreign currency pairs), whereas others choose more stable market environments. In fact, swing involves purchasing lows and selling highs.

Anyhow, swing trading is mostly about forecasting the next market movement, getting into trading, and focusing on price movements. Productive traders aim to grab the only portion of the expected market shift and then search for another trading possibility. Another bonus of swing trading is that you do not have to waste the whole week in front of screens when the business lasts for hours or days.

This method of trading is very common among successful traders pursuing short and medium trading with the aid of various forms of research. Technical assessment is the most critical method of analysis that can be used in swing trading due to the comparatively short-term length of the transactions. In addition, the fundamental review should be carried out in order to allow an even clearer evaluation. Swing traders are normally looking for trading options on 4-hour and regular charts. Effective swing traders aim to make small trades over the span of one month.

Swing trading enables you to gain the benefit of the normal rise and fall of the Foreign exchange markets. Stock markets rarely move in one direction indefinitely, and by being eager to draw advantage of all that, you would maximize your gains when you theoretically make profits as the Forex price increases for the next several days and afterward make more as that market pulls down, which it would inevitably do eventually. You could find more openings by being in or out of markets. If you glance at every financial map, you could notice that there seems to be often a clear long-term pattern, but the stock will not necessarily be in the region of support or opposition. By getting in or out of the market in a couple of days, you will (usually) collect money and locate other established platforms for other transactions. This helps you propagate the uncertainty around and link up quite a bit less money instead of always trying to step up with the margin for the latest positions when you discover new trades. By ending your first spot, you won't need to deposit any funds into your savings to fund the second position.

Stop setbacks are usually less than long-term transactions. The limit loss on swing trading may be 110 pips depending on a four-hour chart, while the stop loss on the weekly chart, depending on an overall pattern, may tend to be 500 pips. This encourages you to put broader positions rather than relatively poor leveraged positions by long-term patterns.

You've got good limits. The swing trader is a much more complex trader and thus would usually have a particular region that they consider to be an indication that trading is going against them. That's why you understand precisely when the exchange doesn't work and can minimize the harm that poor trade could do. Longer-term traders typically have to lend themselves to the Forex market while they look for them all to "go for the fundamentals."

Some of the drawbacks of swing trading include that you will also get dragged down. That's because the market demonstrates support or opposition in a certain region, it does not guarantee that it will be rewarded today. Also, if you do a deal, you lose money. As a swing trader, you will have to take such risks quite often. You are likely to have setbacks periodically, regardless of how competitive you are. In the technical evaluation, you ought to be well-versed. It doesn't actually indicate "drawback," but it means hard effort. Usually, everyone can see the pattern on a chart that is moving from the bottom left to top right with time, so anybody attempting to swing the chart has to locate the entrances and exits. That is something that technical research could do, so you have to understand it first. This is time taking, it requires a unique mindset than long-term investing, with more ease. Although not generally scalping, swing traders face the risk of getting "startled out of stocks" when pullbacks in all of these narrower ranges tend to be much more aggressive than those staring at the weekly map. It is the psychological condition that several traders will inevitably have to struggle with throughout their careers.

Chapter 6: Conservative Strategy of

Swing Trading

Keep it Simple

You may have heard of the term "paralysis by analysis." This happens when you analyze something to the point where you cannot make a decision. Some swing traders overcomplicate their analysis of security by using multiple indicators that all have to line up for them to enter a trade. In real life, everything does not often line up perfectly and you have to go with what you feel is right.

I have thus far covered many different tools and indicators you can use to help you to make a decision. You do not need to use all of them to be a successful swing trader. Once you find 1 or 2 that work well for you, you should then stick with those. If you decide to use a few different tools that all need to align, it will likely mean that you are not going to be trading very often. That is not necessarily a bad thing though. It is better to sit on your hands and wait for a good trade versus jumping in and out of marginal trade setups and slowly lose your money. The only one who wins, in that case, is your broker, as they collect fees for all of your trades (the successful ones and the losing one's).

Find several indicators that work well for you and focus on using them. Don't trade often, but trade smart, by knowing why you are entering a trade and, most importantly, knowing your risk to reward ratio and exit price points. As you gain more experience in swing trading, you will be able to better recognize trades that are going to work out even if everything is not perfectly aligned.

Having said this, when you do happen to find a number of indicators that are all aligned with the trade you are considering taking, it can certainly provide some level of confidence that you have a potentially profitable trade.

Treat your Swing Trading Activity Like a Serious Business

Should you decide that swing trading is a right fit for your personality, and that it is able to fit into your life along with all of your other interests and responsibilities, then you need to treat this activity as a very serious business. It will require an investment of time and effort, which hopefully will lead to some very good rewards.

Have a designated area where you do your research and keep all of your records. You are essentially becoming a professional money manager for yourself, so you should keep your work organized at all times. Everything you do with your business should be oriented toward making sure you are a success. If you feel like a professional, then you are more apt to trade like one.

Develop a Work Plan

Have a work plan and stick with it. Your work plan should include checking the market at the open and before the close. During this time, you should monitor your positions, set alerts and possibly enter orders at target levels that you think might get filled during the trading day.

I also recommend that you review your portfolio and market performance every night from Sunday to Thursday to ensure your assumptions about your positions and portfolio are still valid. On the weekend, you should try to do a more thorough review.

It is important to establish a work plan and keep it consistent. By keeping your work plan relatively consistent, you can measure your performance without introducing additional variables. Measuring your performance allows you to find areas to improve and make changes as you see fit.

Actively Manage Your Risk to Reward Ratio; Focus on the Entry

As a swing trader, your first and most important tool is your capital or cash. As I have said before, without cash, you cannot be a trader. I have written at length already about the necessity of assessing the risk to reward ratio on every trade and also on how much capital you should put into each trade. Following your rules on these points will prevent you from quickly losing all of your capital. You will be wrong on your trades some of the time and you need to make sure you live to trade another day.

Just planning and knowing your stop-loss and profitable exits are not enough for swing trading. Your entry becomes the next important step in your trade. You have already determined your stop-loss point and your target price(s) for a profitable exit. However, you calculated the risk to reward ratio based on an assumed entry price point.

Let's assume you found a good setup during a scan in the evening after the market has closed. The security closed the day at $10.50, and you see an upside to $12.00 with support at $10.00 where you would stop out. Therefore, you have a potential $0.50 loss compared to a $1.50 gain to the upside. That is a 1 to 3 risk to reward ratio, which is very good, and you are ready to pull the trigger and place a buy order in the morning. The market opens the next morning and the security you are ready to buy opens up at $11.00. What do you do? The novice trader is already invested mentally in the trade, so they buy. Unfortunately for them, their risk to reward is now 1 to 1, with the downside to $10.00 and upside to $12.00. This is no longer a good trade at that entry point.

The rational trader reassesses the situation. They may put a buy order in at $10.50, hoping to catch the entry they wanted on the security during the normal daily price gyrations in the market. This will give them the risk to reward ratio that they need to make a good swing trade. If they do not get a fill, then they need to reassess again, and maybe move on to finding another trade with a more appropriate risk to reward ratio.

The bottom line, do not get emotional and chase a trade. The "fear of missing out" can motivate you to make a bad trade and you should be aware of this when picking your entry price on a trade.

Measure Your Results and Adjust Accordingly

As a trader, you must track your results to measure your performance. Nothing gets improved that does not get measured first. Every trader should use a tool to record the different aspects of each trade, from initial assessment through to the risk to reward expected, the entry point, and, finally, the exit. The tool can be a spreadsheet, it can be done on paper or it can be web-based. It does not matter how you do it as long as the process allows you to track the details of each trade as well as your performance.

Once you have your trades recorded in detail, you can go back at any time and review how the trade worked. You can compare your performance using the different indicators, i.e., is one working particularly well versus the others you use? Are you getting good entry points on your trades or do you need to exercise more patience? Are your exits working or are you consistently exiting a trade too early and not getting all of the money you could on a profitable trade? Are you respecting your stops?

Having all of this information to review will help you adjust your trading process and plan accordingly to maximize your performance without letting emotion enter into your decision-making.

Chapter 7: Advanced Strategy of

Swing Trading

To become a perfect trader using the swing style, the major thing you need to know is how to identify any potential trade. When you have identified such trade, you can now begin to apply the various concepts that we have covered so far in this book. The steps we have given here are simply to show you how to apply all concepts you have learned so far. You can easily use some of these approaches to quickly execute and identify trade as well as direct potential traders to the techniques.

Sizing Up the Market

Any swing trader should definitely know more or less about the market; to be a complete trader, you should know about the currency market, state of equity, fixed income, etc. You need this because hardly will you find any market that is not related. So, if there is an increase in the prices of a currency, you should expect that there will be a bear market in the case of bond prices. There will almost be an immediate flaw in equity if the bond price keeps falling rapidly. Commodity prices go up if the dollar weakens. We can continue to show how all these things are related.

The main thing is that you will be able to improve your trading ability when you look at all these major markets; this will allow you to be able to predict the possible directions of any other market.

Identifying the Top Industries

There are numerous ways you can use to identify the leading industries. You can use the top 10 % list to identify the stocks on the long side of the market. You can make use of the High Growth Stock Investor (HGS Investor) software which is a better tool than focusing only on the top 10 %.

Ensure that you look out for swing trades that are promising in the industry group within the top 10 % for long candidates and the short candidates' lower 10 %. Doing this will make you know the leading group and you can easily select from the candidates within the top two industries.

Selecting Promising Candidates

Many traders opt for technical analysis when they are selecting promising candidates but it will be better to use the fundamental analysis first; this will facilitate easy selection of your promising candidate. Then, you can now use technical analysis to time your entries and exits.

- Screen securities: When you screen security, you are sure to have filtered out penny stocks and thinly traded securities. We recommend you use the format below to screen

Market capitalization ≥ $ 250 million

Average daily volume ≥ 100,000 shares

Stock price ≥ $ 5

- Access chart patterns and rank the filtered securities: You can easily rank filtered securities using the price to cash flow ratio or earnings rank. After that, you can access the charts of promising stocks.

Determining Position Size

Now that you may have found your trade, you may be having problems with allocating it. You will know by now that we recommend that you set your position by risk level rather than by percent of capital, this will easily allow you to get your position size through knowing your stop loss, and limiting losses level should usually be between 0.25 % and 2.0 % of the value of your account in case the security comes to the level of the stop losses.

Executing Your Order

Ensure that your swing trading time commitment is in consistency with your order entry. If you are a part-time swing trader, you can enter near the closing price by using the limit orders at the exact day the signal was generated. Full-time traders can buy at a better price if they add the intraday trading overlay.

It is important that you enter a stop-loss order as soon as you execute your trade whether you are a full-time or part-time trader, except you are a full-time trader who tries to watch your position during market hours every day.

Recording Your Table

Recording of your table should follow the execution of your trade. The recording serves to keep your journal up-to-date and you can easily find some helpful details there. This book has dealt with the information that your journal should contain. Ensure that you keep such information simple and always strike a balance so that you do not enter too much irrelevant detail.

Monitoring the Motion of Shares and Exiting at the Right Time

When you might have recorded your positioning in your journal, you should be keen on monitoring them and ponder on your best exciting strategy. We recommend that you use the following scenario to know when exactly to exit.

- When you see the position meandering sideways.
- When you notice that the position is unprofitable.
- When the position is profitable.

Enhancing Your Swing Trading Skill

We may have given you some insights into trading but keep in mind that no trading system works efficiently 100 % at every time, likewise, you cannot be 100 % perfect as a swing trader. Expect to lose but know the numbers of losses you can accommodate. One of the ways by which you can become an efficient trader is that you should try as much as possible to evaluate your journal every month; this will make you able to easily detect your winning and losing pattern of position.

You can then alter your trading pattern based on the winning or losing position, but do not change this often because of one or two losses that you may eventually work upon. If you lose hugely, then it is possible that you will not need to adjust your entry and exit strategy but rather your risk management strategy.

Chapter 8: Typical Beginner's

Errors in Swing Trading

Mistakes are always part of the game in any trade. Traders in swing trading also make mistakes that cause them to fail. Others commit mistakes due to ignorance of the different rules and strategies used in swing trading. This is all about giving details of the various mistakes committed by the different traders in swing trading.

Below are the various mistakes swing traders commit while trading:

Lacking a Trading Plan

Most of the traders starting off on swing trading lack a well-defined plan. What do you normally think of when you do this? Swing trading is a risky arena. You need to be well-armed and prepared before entering into trading. Lacking a proper trading plan makes you misbehave in your trading, which is a very bad idea.

You normally lack a trading routine when you fail to have a plan. You find yourself lacking the objectives and goals for your trading. A trading plan enables you to stick to the plan and work hard for your objectives. Failing to have a plan makes you do things when you feel like it is so risky in the swing trading environment.

A plan is basically composed of objectives and strategies. Without it, it is like going to a war with no weapons with you. Prepare yourself with a good plan to be able to know the risks involved in the market since it enables you to formulate your own trading strategies.

Lacking a Time Horizon for Your Trading

Always known as a swing trader the duration you have for investment reasons. It enables you to be aware of the time duration you have before expiry. When you select your time horizon to be until retirement, it tells that you have to invest for a while before the time of retirement.

Failing to Utilize the Stop-Loss Orders

Stop-loss orders are very crucial for all kinds of traders. You need to implement it for safety reasons during trading. A trader who fails to utilize stop-loss orders strategies ends up with huge losses on their trading. You find yourself making big losses that could be controlled.

Losses all times turn down the success of any business. Failing to arm yourself so well in trading is just a total failure for your swing trading. You need to be alert with the crucial strategies in swing trading so as to survive and succeed.

Lacking Control over the Trading Losses

Losses will normally occur in most businesses, but does that mean you should have no control over them? You need to make fast and efficient actions when losses occur in your swing trading, even the smaller losses. Ignoring the smaller losses will make them accumulate so hard, and time will reach you will have no control over them.

You need to be serious about the losses that come up and be able to handle them before they shut down, you're trading. Losses promote no growth in swing trading. You need to have policies with you on how to handle losses. Most of the traders neglect this mistake which makes them fail in swing trading tremendously.

Putting Much Trust in Financial News

Watching and following up on news is not a bad thing, however, you need to be extra careful with what you hear or come across online. Some bloggers mislead novice traders a lot on how to handle their trading. You should be alert with all the information. Some people just want to see fail. Do not apply all the information you hear from other people. Have your own ways of how to handle things in swing trading. You do not need to copy what others are doing, people have different abilities. Rely only on the trusted sources and swing trading forums. Consult the experts in swing trading for any information that you have heard and you are not sure about it. Have trust in yourself that your ways will also succeed in swing trading.

Working on Too Many Markets at Once

A high number of swing traders fail in their trading due to being over-occupied with too many markets at once. You are not like a robot machine; you need to decide on a reasonable number of markets that you can handle. Do not be greedy for money, you need to calm down and at least focus on a few and perfect your skills rather than being involved with too many markets.

This will make you get out of control. Concentrating on many markets is even not healthy for your body and mind. You do need to select every market. You should choose the ones you are highly interested in, perfect your skills on them, and ace swing trading.

Being Overconfident

Being a confident swing trader is a good thing, but being extra than that is really a poor thing to do. Overconfidence has killed the dream of many swing traders. Traders are normally over certain with what they are doing and fail to list down even the risks that may be involved in their trading. You need to remember both the worst-case and the best-case scenarios in swing trading while planning. Consult others when you need help with your strategies, you may learn a few things that will help you in your trading. Do not be that kind of a bold trader who does things alone with no trainer or some sort of master in swing trading. Do not trust yourself that much, you might be doing things the wrong way.

Lack of Patience

Good things take time. This saying is also relevant in our case here. Most traders have no patience at all with the huge profits. They only want money to be accumulated in the first days after joining swing trading. That is not possible unless all you want to accumulate are huge losses. You need to give yourself more time before you begin to earn more money.

The kind of traders who rush in trading for their greed for money end up nowhere. You need to be realistic sometimes to succeed in swing trading. Do not rush the trade, the money will keep coming. Do the right thing at the right speed. Do not implement too many strategies in your trading and get confused. Work with at least one successful trading strategy and relax.

Indiscipline

It is not advisable to be undisciplined in swing trading. Success is directly related to discipline. When you are disciplined in your trading, you are able to handle your trade with caution and with the right mindset. Traders who mix their trading procedures and activities with other things end up mixing everything up. You need to be aware of all of your strategies and objectives at your fingertips to be able to know what you want to achieve. Not being disciplined makes you even forget your targets and your policies. This, of course, leads to total failure in your trading.

Too Much Focus on Profit

Profit-making is one of the main objectives of all businesses, but why focus too much on profit and forget about other crucial factors in swing trading? Factors like risk management and loss handling losses also need attention. Do not be the kind of traders who just think of making a profit and end up making big losses in their trading.

You need to have a balance on how you handle your trading activities. Do not allow to accumulate high profits which have the same amount as losses. There will no earn since the losses made will decline both your trading capital and your profits.

Failing to Trust Your Abilities

You need to have trust in your capabilities. As a beginner, you should not compare yourself with the expert successful traders. This will make your esteem to decline. You need to be yourself and remind yourself that you will succeed. All you need to do is to comply with the strategies and objectives that you wrote down. You also need to learn a lot and do much research in swing trading in order to succeed.

Using Much Money on the Investment

The amount of money you are dedicating for investment should be a good amount of your disposable income that you can quickly or easily refund. Utilize a little money at the beginning to avoid huge losses. The higher the amount of money you use for swing trading, the higher the number of losses that can come up due to the many risks that are involved in swing trading. Most traders boast around with a huge amount of cash for trading and, unfortunately, end up making huge losses. Also, do not trade with your school fees or rent, you will have issues with your school finance.

Being Emotional on the Money Lost

Catching feelings in trading is not advised for any swing traders. Some traders give up when losses occur and decide to quit. Do not be a faint-hearted trader; you need to be strong that the money lost will get refunded. Stand strong and wish yourself good luck.

Being Too Much Aggressive

Most unsuccessful swing traders failed to succeed because of their aggressive behavior. Being aggressive makes you lose a lot of money which leads to the failure of swing trading. This normally happens on a bullish type of market. Relax, and everything will work out.

Laziness and Being Irresponsible

All types of trading are tough. You need to put much effort into your swing trading in order to widen your knowledge. Failing to do much research will not keep you informed and updated. You need to go with the trend. Do not be left behind. Failing to go through different newsfeeds on swing trading will enable you to be outdated.

Irresponsible swing traders who lack trading plans and strategies get confused and finally decide to quit swing trading. You need to be responsible and make decisions even during the worst-case scenarios. Do not fail to work even on the small losses that occur during swing trading. Trade responsibly, taking into account all the risks involved in swing trading.

Ignoring Risk Management Trading Strategies

What do you expect when you fail to implement the few strategies needed for risk management? Swing traders who fail to implement the risk management strategies of course end up being involved with too many risks. You need to check on the different swing trading strategies that exist and choose the best that handles risks in swing trading. This will protect your trading capital and also the amount of profit accumulated. Failing to arm yourself well enough will bring failure to your trading.

Implementing Many Small Moves

This mistake is normally committed by novice traders who make moves on any small changes in the market. You find yourself making trades even on your weakest points. There are high chances of big losses during this time. You need to be extra cautious and only make sure moves when relevant changes occur in the market. Small moves contribute to huge losses. Trade at the right time according to your trading plan. Avoid this mistake in order to succeed in swing trading.

Being so Close to the Market

Traders who focus so much on the swing trading market end up living in worries all the time. You end up putting much effort even on small things that need less attention. Do something else other than trading. You can even do some cooking or even water flowers. Give yourself some time to catch a breath with a good mindset that everything will work out well. Do not be so close to the market—you will worry too much for nothing.

Lacking a Swing Trading Strategy

Strategies are like guidelines that exist in swing trading to help you when making decisions. Most of the swing traders forget to formulate the trading strategies when formulating the swing trading plan. Lacking swing trading strategies is a very bad idea. Strategies help you in managing risks and accumulating more profit. Always stick to your working strategies that are according to your trading plan.

Chapter 9: Forex Trading

GBP/USD	82%	1.54260	14:15 ▼	🕐 04:28
EUR/JPY	82%	135.365	14:15 ▼	🕐 04:28
GBP/JPY	81%	183.543	14:15 ▼	🕐 04:28
USD/JPY	79%	118.983	14:15 ▼	🕐 04:28
USD/CAD	79%	1.25174	14:15 ▼	🕐 04:28
USD/CHF	79%	0.94860	14:15 ▼	🕐 04:28
EUR/GBP	79%	0.73751	14:15 ▼	🕐 04:28
AUD/USD	79%	0.77601	14:15 ▼	🕐 04:28
AUD/NZD	79%	1.08661	14:15 ▼	🕐 04:28
NZD/USD	79%	0.75125	14:15 ▼	🕐 04:28

Forex is commonly known as foreign exchange or FX, and it involves the buying and selling of different currencies with the aim of making profits based on the changes in the value. The forex market is the largest market in the world; it is larger than the stock exchange market. Therefore, it attracts many traders. There is high liquidity in the foreign exchange market, and as such, this attracts both experienced and beginner traders. In fact, the forex trade market is so large that all the stock markets in the world cannot match its capacity. The foreign exchange market is decentralized across the globe; therefore, all the different currencies in the world are traded freely.

Currency Pairs

There are very many types of currencies across the world, and all of them have three-letter symbols; for example, the Euros are EUR, American Dollars are USD, British Pounds are GBP, Swiss Francs are CHF, etcetera. The currencies have been majorly divided into two major and minor currencies. The major currencies involve these derived from the powerful economies in the world that are; the USA, the UK, Japan, the Eurozone, Australia, Canada, New Zealand, and

Switzerland. These currencies create forex pairs with each other and with other minor currencies.

When one goes to a store to purchase some groceries or any other item, he/she needs to exchange one asset of value for another, for instance, milk for money. This applies to forex exchange too; buying and selling one currency for another. Every pair involves two currencies whereby one buys or sells the currencies against the other.

Forex pairs can be classified into three types, namely Major pairs, Exotic pairs, and Minor pairs. The major pairs always consist of the United States Dollar, and many people trade in them. The major pairs are USDCHF, USDJPY, EURUSD, AUDUSD, GBPUSD, NZDUSD, and USDCAD. The minor pairs involve all the currencies participating in the major pairs apart from the United States Dollar. They include CHFJPY, EURGBP, EURAUD, JPYAUD, NZDCAD et cetera. The exotic pairs involve one minor currency and one major currency, for instance, USDNOK, USDKSH, EURTRY, and so on.

How Does Forex Work?

Just like the stock markets, one can trade currencies depending on his/her prediction on the changes of value.

The greatest difference between stocks and currency trades is that forex can trade down and up very easily. If one thinks that a particular currency will have a value increase, he/she may buy it, and if he thinks that the currency will fall, he /she may sell it. The forex market is so large that finding a buyer or seller is too easy compared to other trade markets. Let's assume that a trader hears reports that a country such as China will devalue its currency with the intention of drawing more foreign investors into the country. If he/she thinks that the devaluing trend will continue, the trader may sell the currency of China against another, for example, the USD. The more the currency of China devalues against the United States dollar, the higher the trader's profit. However, if the currency gains value against the US dollar, then the trader will have increased losses and may want to leave the trade as soon as possible.

Summarily, Forex trading involves placing a bet on the value of one currency against the other. Remember that in a pair, the first currency is the base while the second currency is the secondary or the counter. For example, in the EUR/USD the EUR is the base while the USD is the counter. If a trader clicks buy or sell, he/she is buying or selling the base. This means that if a forex trader thinks that the EUR will increase in value in contrast with the United States dollar, he/she will buy the EURUSD. If the trader thinks that it will drop, he/she will sell the EURUSD. If, for instance, the asking price 0.7060 and the bid price is 0.7064, and then the spread price is 4 pips. Whether the value of the EUR rises or falls, the trader will make a profit or loss once he covers the spread price. The spread price is usually higher for minor currencies.

Basic Terms in Foreign Exchange

In foreign exchange, the term 'Position' refers to a trade that is in progress, and it is basically classified according to the expectation of traders. The term 'long position' refers to the trade where the trader has purchased a particular Currency (the first in a pair) with the expectation that the value will rise. When the trader sells back the currency to the market (expected to be a higher price than the purchase price), the trade is complete, and the long position is "closed." A short position refers to the trade where a trader sells a currency (the first in a pair) with the expectation that the value will fall, and then he/she buys it back at a lower price. When the trader buys the currency back ideally for less than he/she sold it the trade is complete, therefore "closed."

The pair that is mainly traded in the forex market is the American dollar versus the Euro or USDEUR. The currency identified on the left side is referred to as the base currency, while the one on the right is referred to as secondary currency. The base currency is the one a buyer or seller wishes to buy or sell, while the second currency is the one a trader uses to make the transaction. Each trade pair has two prices, the bid and the buy. The 'bid' is the selling price of the base currency, while the 'ask' is the buying price. The difference between the bid and the asking price is referred to as the spread, and it indicates the amount that brokers charge to keep the position open. The spreads become narrower when more currency is traded when a currency has high volatility. If a pair is very rare, the spread will be wider.

Usually, the quote prices are presented with 4 numbers after the dot. In the case of EURUSD for example, the price might be 1.2589 to mean that for every Euro that a trader wishes to buy, he/she will have to put in 1.2589 US dollars. Changes occurring in the value of the currency will be seen on the last figure after the dot. It is mainly referred to as a pip. The gains, the losses, and the spreads will normally be indicated in pips.

Another term commonly used in forex trading is going long, which means buying and going short means selling. A bullish trader normally predicts that the market will rise, while the bearish trader hopes that the market will fall to benefit. The term bull market indicates that the market will rise or increase, while the bear market indicates that the market will fall or decrease. Experienced traders normally base their decisions and strategies on market trends; therefore, they follow all the relevant events within the markets. The study of trends helps the traders to gain profit in the market.

Formally, traders had to call the brokers and inform them of the actions he/she should take in the market. However, technology has made it possible for many traders to transact directly using software referred to as a trading platform. There are many trading platforms available for the internet, computers and even phones. Every trader selects a platform that will work well with his/her trade strategy to reap maximum benefits.

Leveraged trading, also referred to as trading on the margin is a process that allows the traders to hold larger positions than they can with their own fortune only. In a large number of forex pairs, a trader can hold maximum leverage of 400:1, which means that for every $400 the trader will invest $1. Consequently, if he/she wishes to purchase 100000 EURUSD at the price of 1.2674, instead of paying $126,740 he/she will pay 25 percent for the amount. One should remember that the losses and profits usually depend on the size of the position, and as much as leveraging trade can magnify the profits, it can also enhance losses.

Example:

Let's say a trader wants to transact in the forex market. He/she logs onto the trading platform and checks the bid and ask price. Assuming that he/she finds that the asking price is 1.2356 and the bid price is 1.2359; the pip will be 1.2356-1.2359= 3 pips. The three pips will go to brokers. If for instance, that trader believes that the Euro will rise, he will put a 'buy' command. He will then select a particular number of units he/she wishes to buy for instance 10,000. The normal price for that would be $12356, and if the trader is relying on leverage trading, he will pay $30.89. If the markets move up as the trader had indicated, say to $1.2360, then he/she will make a profit.

Chapter 10: Conservative Strategy

for Forex Trading

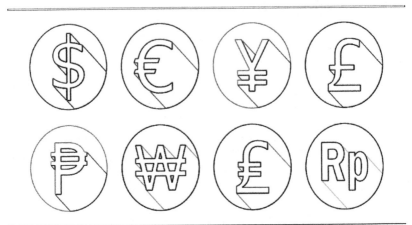

Analysis-Based Trading Strategies

Technical Analysis

As the name suggests, 'analysis,' this method focuses primarily on the evaluation of the market trends through charts as a means of predicting the to-be price trends of the market.

In this method, an evaluation of assets is done basing on statistics and past analysis of market actions like the then volumes and the past prices.

Technical analysis is not done with a primary objective of weighing the underlying value of assets; instead, charts with other measuring tools are used to define the patterns that are helpful in the future forecast in market actions.

It is believed that the market's future performance is easily determined by the past trends in its performance.

Trend Trading

In technical analysis, a trend is a very critical aspect. The tools used in this type of analysis, have a common motive which is simply to determine trends of the market.

Therefore, to trend is to move; in this context, it means the way the market is moving.

As we know, the fore market is a wavy and zigzag motion that represents the successive trails that define clearly troughs and peaks which are sometimes called lows and highs?

Depending on the available trends of the lows and highs, a trader can define the nature of the market type.

Other than the popular notion of the highs and lows, there is yet another format of the trends in Forex trading called: uptrend/downtrend and sideways trend.

Support and Resistance

It is quite imperative to know the meaning of the horizontal level before defining the support and resistance strategy. This is the level in the price signifying market support of the resistance. In technical analysis, resistance and support as used to refer to the lows or highs in prices in that order.

Support, in this case, refers to an area on a chart, which shows that the interest in buying is stronger than the selling force.

This is revealed through successive troughs. On the other hand, resistance level, as represented on the chart refers to an area where the buying force is outweighed by the selling concern.

Range Trading

It is also referred to as channel trading. This signifies the absence of market direction that may be associated with a lack of trends. It is used to identify the movement in the prices of currencies within the channels of which it is tasked to establish the range in the movements.

It can be achieved by linking sets of lows and highs to the horizontal-trend line. This is to say that the trader is tasked to establish the resistance and support levels with the area in the middle, which we refer to as the trading range.

Technical Indicators

When we talk of the technical indicators about Forex trade, we simply refer to the calculations that are inclined to the volume and the price of a given security.

When used, they are meant to corroborate quality and trend in the chart patterns as well as enable traders to identify sell and buy signals altogether. These indicators in technical analysis can create sell and buy signals via divergence as well as crossovers.

Whenever the prices go across the moving average, crossovers are seen however, divergence occurs only if the indicator and the price trends both move in different and opposite directions implying that there is a weakening in the price trend.

Forex Charts

In Technical analysis, we refer to a chart as a representation of the shifts in prices within a given time frame graphically. It reveals the movement in the security price over some time.

Different charts can be applied in search of diversified information and the skills and knowledge of the researcher.

Forex Volume

Forex volume indicates the total securities by number, traded in a certain time interval. The higher the volume, the higher the level of pressure; this is as indicated by chart specialists.

They can easily define the downward or the upward shifts in volume by observing the volume bars on the lower side of the charts. When a price movement is accompanied by a high volume, it becomes more valuable than if it is accompanied by low volumes.

Multiple Time-Frame Analysis

Security prices must be tracked over a period and in a unique time frame. This is so because a security price will tend to go through a series of time frames, and therefore, analysts need to review several time frames so that they establish the security's trade cycle.

Trading-Style Based Strategies

This is yet another technique, which offers a different way of classifying the trading styles. Through trading styles, trading strategies can be created, which could include but not limited to a buy-and-hold strategy, portfolio trading, trading algorithm, order and carry trades,

It is entirely dependent on your level of understanding, power, and weaknesses that determine the strategies that you will apply. Everyone needs a trading strategy, which best suits his desires according to his ability to apply it.

There is not a style of trading that you must use if you choose to trade, because what suits a person does not suit you and your needs.

Day Trading

This is the act of holding a position and disposing of it the same day. This implies that this type of person does not hold security for more than a day.

You have the right if only you have the ability to conducting more than one type of trade in a single day as long as you do not hold a position for more than one day. This means that before the closure of the market, you must have liquidated all your open positions.

There is a challenge in today's trading where if you hold onto a position for that long the chances of losing it are high. Based on whatever style you are using, the targets in the price may vary.

Scalping Strategy

This is characterized by short and quick operations and is applied mainly to achieve vast returns on small price variations. Scalpers can initiate over 200 trades per day with the intention of making good profits on small shifts in price levels.

Fading Strategy

In this case, fading refers to a trade that is initiated against the trend. When the trend moves up, faders sell in the hope that there will be a fall in prices; similarly, they may buy when prices rise.

They buy when the price is escalating and sell when the prices are coming down a notion called fading. It is very contrary to other trends and also to the nature of business.

The trade is usually against the usual trends with reasons such as the buyers at hand may be risking. The securities are usually over-purchased and the earlier may be set for profits.

Daily-Pivot Trading

Currencies are very volatile, and as such, traders may wish to capitalize on that to make profits. This is exactly the case with the pivot strategy.

A turning point, as well as the pivot, is a very critical and unique pointer obtained through the computation of the statistical average of the low, high, and closing prices of currency pairs.

The secret to this strategy lies in the aspect of purchasing securities at their lowest prices and selling them at their best prices in the course of the day.

Momentum Strategy

This is characterized by defining the strongest position that will end up trading the highest. In this case, the trader may drop the currency with signs of dropping in price and go for that currency that has positive signs of going up through the day.

A momentum trader has got several indicators, which help him detect the trends in the securities before he makes his decisions called 'momentum-oscillators.' Such a trader will tend to invest deeply in news feeds which he entirely depends on for price predetermination and decision making.

Buy & Hold Strategy

In this case, a position is bought and held for quite a long before being sold so that the prices escalate even if it takes longer. Whoever does this has no business with the short-term price changes as well as indications. However, this type of strategy best suits the stock traders.

In this case, technical analysis becomes invalid because the trader here is a passive investor who has no rush in determining the market trends of the stocks and securities.

Order-Types Trading Strategies

Trading in order will help the trader to join or move out of a position at the very right time by use of various orders, which include but not limited to market, pending limit, stop-loss, and stop as well as other orders.

At this particular moment, most advanced platforms are fitted with different kinds of orders for trading that are not the common buy/sell buttons. Every order type signifies a certain strategy. You must know how and perhaps when to handle orders before you can use them effectively.

The following are trader orders that can be applied by traders:

- Market order- is put to enable the trader to buy/ sell at a ripe price.
- Pending order-enable traders to buy/sell at previously set prices.
- Limit order guides the trader to buy/sell assets at specific price levels.
- Stop-loss order placed to lower a trade risk.

Algorithmic Based Strategy

This is as well-referred to as 'automated' Forex trade. There is software designed to help in the predetermination of times for purchasing and selling securities. This software operates on signals draw from the technical analysis.

To trade in this strategy, you need to issue instructions over the kind of signals that you would wish to search for and its subsequent interpretation. This is an example of a high trading platform, which comes with other supportive platforms for trading.

Examples of these kinds of trading platforms include meta-Trade 4 and Net-TradeX. However, Net-TradeX is a trading platform in which, in addition to its normal functionalities, it presents automated trading through its advisors.

This is referred to as a secondary platform that yields automatic trading and further sophisticates its processes through a language called: "Net-TradeX language."

It goes ahead to provide room for some trading operations traditionally, for example; to open and to close a position to place orders as well as the use of the technical tools for analysis purposes.

Meta-Trader 4 similarly is a trading platform, which makes it possible for the execution of algorithmic trade via an incorporated program-language "MQL4." In this type of platform, traders can come up with called-Advisors, trading–robots with indicators of their own. All acts of making advisors, which include: to debug, to test, to optimize and compiling the program, are all done and made active through the meta-Trader 4 editor.

Robots are made in this case to take away the emotional concept of the traders, which in most cases hinders the free and competent engagement in the trade across the platforms. Emotions have and supply a negative attitude to the traders, especially when there is hope for a loss.

Chapter 11: Advanced Strategy for

Forex Trading

How to Create Your Easy Strategies to Start and Make Money?

There are two different types of people who trade on foreign exchange. 1.) Those who have chosen to make a full-time career of it, and 2.) Those who prefer to dabble enough to make a tidy little passive income. The strategies listed here are for those part-time traders and are simple and practical enough to help you get started earning in a short amount of time. Here are the strategies that you may not have even thought about when it comes to trade, such as different currency pairs, the time of day you trade, and additional features you can take advantage of to help you on your way to success.

The Variables to Watch Out for

The new trader should always approach their first investments with caution. You should know the currencies you want to trade and the time of day you plan to make your transactions. We will talk about why this is important a little later. It is also good to develop a plan to make sure you are ready to trade simultaneously every day. Consistency is the key to success. By now, you should have at least a basic understanding of how to read market data and read the price action charts. If not, go back and study those again before you proceed. You should also have a good grasp of the market's function and the different currency pairs and know how to make the best use of the technology available to help you.

There may be many things to think about, but it is possible to make a nice steady income in the Forex Market as a part-time trader. However, as your income rises, it may be tempting to cast your day job aside for this type of income, but I advise you to wait for a while before making such a major decision.

Let's Talk About Time

There is a reason why timing is critical when you invest in foreign exchange. While the market is open 24-hours a day, the trade opportunities will change throughout. Find the time of day when most individuals will be making similar trades like the ones you plan to make. Keep in mind that if you plan to trade only on occasion, the opportunities to buy or sell a particular currency will be reduced. In a volatile market like Forex, rapid changes can frequently happen, so when you know the kind of trade you want and when it is most likely to be done, you can take great pains to be on point when the most activity is likely to happen.

Those who choose to trade at night may find that only certain types of currencies are available at the volume sizes you need. By learning how volume trades are made, you can choose from the currencies available when actively working on the market.

The foreign markets are open 24-hours a day because as the day passes through certain time zones, individual markets have definite open and close times. When the business day closes in a one-time zone, it will be open in another. It does not mean that all markets are open 24-hours a day. This is important to understand when choosing to trade currencies.

For example, the trading day starts in the Asian time zone at 8:00 AM (21:00 GMT). Later, the areas in Australia and Tokyo followed by Singapore. Some of these areas will be open simultaneously, at least for a few hours each day, as they move around the globe. As the one-time zone closes, another will open with a few zones overlapping each other throughout the day. It is this overlap that can create a lot of excitement in the market. As a trader, this can provide you with many great opportunities and many risks throughout the day.

One of the best strategies is to become very knowledgeable about the times and how each zone relates to the other. As you analyze the market, you will eventually be able to single out how other traders navigate these time changes and adapt their forms of trade accordingly.

Other Factors Related to Time

Other factors may not readily come to mind when it comes to trading on the Forex Market. Daylight Savings Time and other time factors can create whole new challenges for your trading practices. Holidays can cause changes in opening and closing times all around the globe. As you study the currencies and the things that affect their trade, you will also need to understand how these factors can impact the type of trades made and when they are made.

You can see how this can have an impact on your trading practices. For example, if you plan to trade the USD/JPY currency pair, you need to know what times those trades are available. A quick look at these markets' schedules to learn when the time zones overlap will tell you when you will make those trades. A Google search reveals these times for the US markets:

The New York Exchange is open from 8:00 AM – 5:00 PM EST.
The Tokyo Exchange is open from 7:00 PM – 4:00 AM EST.

As you can see, these times do not overlap anywhere on the clock. But since it is not enough to settle for a good time to trade, you want to find the optimum time to make the trade. In most cases, you would wait for the overlapping time to trade these two currencies, as this will be when a business is the most active. So, what can you do here?

The solution is simple. The currency pairs see a lot of activity around the clock. Almost every nation with currency in the system will be trading in these two currencies. The yen is actively traded globally, and so is the US dollar. Because they are both very stable currencies, you will see lots of activity for these two throughout the day. So, when considering the timing for this type of trade study, the market to find the most active trade times to make your purchase.

You can learn this by consulting the hourly volatility chart that shows exactly how many PIPs the USD/JPY moves per hour. The times to avoid trade will be straightforward to spot once you understand what you are looking for. As a general rule, the slower the currency movement, the less likely an investor will see a positive change.

Other currencies traded against the USD that could pose a time challenge are USD/EUR, EUR/GBP, EUR/CHF, and EUR/JPY. Of course, many other currency pairs can also present similar challenges, but these are the most highly traded, which increases your chances of making a profit. As you can see, Forex strategy starts with knowing how to take advantage of the time to maximize your profits. The secret is to trade during peak times, where high volumes are being traded to ensure liquidity. Since each currency pair has its own times of peak performance, getting in at the right time takes on a whole new meaning.

Chapter 12: Typical Beginner's

Errors in Forex Trading

Overtrading

Overtrading simply refers to a situation where you trade for longer hours than expected, or you invest more money than you should. We have already mentioned that Forex trading can be addictive, like most gambling games. If you get into Forex without having a clear understanding, you may end up making the mistake of overtrading. When can overtrading occur most likely?

When you are making too much money: It is common for traders to keep on investing in a trade as long as they are making money. The right time to stop trading is when you are making enough money. People who are addicted to trading do not get enough of the action. They continue trading even after reaching their profit target for the day, week, or month. For such people, profits do not mean the end of the business. They keep on investing and trying to earn more even if they have made enough profit, risking losing the money they have already made.

If you are on a winning streak, as we said before about the anti-martingale technique, it could be okay to increase your risk and continue investing. But, first of all, you must understand this technique. Then you must include it in your trading plan with written rules; you must test it, and above all, you must follow it also during losing streaks of trades. Most of the time, traders act this way not because they are following a trading plan, but because they are following their greed.

To ensure that you avoid overtrading, you need to set your trading hours. Forex is a 24-hour business. This means that you can trade at any time of the day at any place you are. To avoid the temptation to continue trading even when you are tired, set your trading hours. You should also ensure that your trading hours occur at a time when you are free. Most people who overtrade combine their trading with other activities. If you continue trading at a time when you should be busy doing another activity, you may find that the combination of multiple activities takes away your ability to trade properly due to the lack of focus.

When you are making losses: The other scenario where people get involved in overtrading is when they are making losses. Losses are very enticing. It is dangerous for a person to start making losses when there is still a lot of money in his or her trading account. For instance, if you funded your

USD with $10,000 and set your investment risk at 2%, you may think that your investments are insignificant. In this case, after losing the first $200, you may think that you can recoup your money. While it is okay to try to recover lost money, you should not rely on impulse and emotions when making such critical trade decisions. Your impulse will tell you to reinvest immediately. Most people invest huge sums of money in the hope that they can recoup their money in the shortest time possible. The more money you lose, the more confused you get. Your mind loses control, and you eventually start making choices that are not rational.

This overtrading mistake can be avoided if you take a break. After closing a trade, whether it leads to profit or loss, you should take some time away from the screen. This is a matter of discipline. You should make up your mind to ensure that you control your actions and make trade decisions that will positively impact your life. You must learn to accept and deal with losses since they are part of the business.

When you have too much time: The other reason why people engage in overtrading is that they have too much time on their hands. They say, "An idle mind is the devil's workshop." While Forex trading is a good and positive venture that can earn you a handsome amount of money, you should not spend your entire day thinking about the trade. As we have observed, Forex markets operate 24 hours a day. You may be fooled to think that trading around the clock is the best option for you. In reality, you should avoid trading for long hours. Even if you have plenty of time on your hands, you should try as much as possible to stick to your chosen trading hours. Engage in other activities after trading, even if it means playing games or watching movies. If you notice that you are getting addicted to your Forex trading apps, uninstall all trading apps on your mobile devices so that you may stay away from the trading platform when it is not the right time to trade.

When you lack self-discipline: The other reason why most traders get involved in overtrading is simply a lack of self-discipline. If you know you are a person who lacks self-control, try avoiding Forex as much as possible. Self-discipline simply means that you have patience and emotional control. You should be able to stop yourself from taking emotional actions. The only way to survive as a Forex trader is to ensure that you follow the rules you have outlined in your trading plan. There is no way you can expect to succeed if you cannot follow the rules, you have created yourself. People who lack self-control are quick to make decisions without considering the consequences. Forex trading is a game of numbers. In this trade, you must be sure that every action you take has the maximum potential of being a success. If you start making decisions that are not based on facts, you may end up losing a fortune in Forex. As you learn to trade, you eventually stop making errors that are associated with emotional instability. Your discipline will help you stop overtrading or making any other mistakes that you might have committed. To ensure that you stop overtrading, you must first answer the question of "How much trading is too much trading?" Once you know your limits, try to stop when you reach them.

Canceling the Stop Loss and Allow Losses to Run

This is a mistake that is made by both young and experienced traders. The stop-loss order is one of the most important tools that you can use to manage your risk in your trading activities. Unfortunately, the stop-loss order also limits your profits in some instances. You may feel that the price is just about to reach a resistance or support level, but the stop loss point has almost been surpassed. What most traders do is to cancel the stop-loss order and stay in, hoping that the trade may turn in their favor.

If you cancel the stop-loss order, you may result in two situations: you can make a lot of money or lose a lot of money. The fact that you can make a lot of money should never be a motivation for you to cancel the stop-loss order. Canceling the stop-loss order is a big mistake because if you follow a strategy with a statistical edge, probabilities are in favor of the stop loss, not vice versa. Any action you take in Forex should be geared towards protecting your capital and then providing an additional income. If you approach Forex with the mentality of getting rich quickly, you will likely lose all your money.

There are two main reasons why people end up canceling their stop-loss orders:

A chance to make more profits: As already mentioned above, Forex trading does not guarantee 100% success even if you follow all the outlined strategies in this book.

With an estimated success rate of 50%-60% based on analytical data, most traders try making a lot of money in a short time by choosing an alternative means of prediction. This means that most traders are more likely to use their instinct than follow a strategy with a statistical edge. While instinct trading can be beneficial, it is also very risky. If you keep on reading volatile news and blogs, you may fool yourself to think that you are ready for the Big Money. Those who encourage traders to make bold moves are experienced brokers. They encourage you to stop following your plan and take risks based on how you feel. Our first rule of thumb is always to ensure that emotions are not part of the business. If you spot an opportunity that you feel can lead to huge profits, avoid it as quickly as possible. What you feel does not matter when it comes to real numbers. If the charts are giving you a negative signal, it is because the odds are against your trade. Instead of trying to win against statistics, it is better to turn to more secure options. The best security option you have is the stop-loss order. With the stop-loss order, you can change the way you do your business and protect yourself from the risk of losing all your money.

Fear of Losing: The other reason why any person would cancel the stop-loss order is the fear of losing. If you are a wise trader, you understand that one position does not determine your final outcome. Trading is a probability game. What really counts is that on a large number of trades, the profits outweigh the losses. Losses are part of the game, and you have to learn to accept them. If one position turns out to be negative, you have the chance of trading in a new position and making more money. The main reason why people should protect their principal investment using the stop-loss order is that they can still engage in other trades and keep staying in business. Being in a position to continue trading even when things have gone against you is the best thing that can happen to any trader.

Not Following the Trading Plan

The other big mistake that is made by almost all traders is failing to follow the trading plan. The main reason why traders should follow the plan is that it helps avoid making mistakes. Mistakes are caused by bad choices, and bad choices cause losses. If you are in a moment of frustration, you are likely to make a mistake. However, if you stick to your trading plan, you do not give your emotions the chance to lead you to lose money. Some of the common errors that occur due to abandoning the trading plan include:

Changing your trading strategy: One of the most important factors outlined in your trading plan is the trading strategy. We have looked at multiple strategies. Each of the strategies has its positives and negatives. When you create a plan, you choose whether to use one strategy or use many. The choice to use a certain strategy is determined by your understanding of the market and your trial results. Before you settle on a trading strategy, it is advisable indeed to try it out and find if it is effective according to your market analysis and if it gives you a statistical edge. Changing your chosen trading strategy midway is the worst mistake you could make. This is not only a mistake because it may lead to losses, but it leads to questioning your full trading plan. The only reason you have a plan is so that you may follow it and utilize it to the end. If you believe in whatever you are doing, there are chances that you will make money from it. In case you choose to change the strategy, it should be because you have observed the market and analyzed it. Change your trading strategy only if you have the data to show that it is better to do so. You should have valid reasons, which can be verified by other traders.

Conclusion

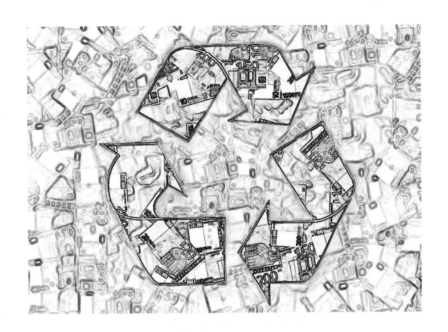

So, what do you think?

How long did you get through this little book? Was the duration enough to help you ease into your new life as a day trader?

If that is the case, then wonderful! Hopefully, the book has provided you with the assistance you need to navigate this new and challenging world.

While I was writing this, I sometimes talked to my friend Ron about how this was turning out to be an encapsulation of everything that I have learned in day trading. While I read textbooks, mingled in online forums, and attended little certification classes, it is a friend's guidance that got me through everything. I am very thankful that I have a friend in him.

But guess what? He likes being in the background, happy that he is successful, at least with the goals that he has set for himself. As for his mentee, yours truly, day trading has afforded me something that goes beyond the usual 9 to 5. I get the excitement of wins and the obvious benefits of earning extra money. It felt liberating to be outside my cubicle prison, at least in spirit. I had been able to extend my reach to something that could help me earn money without me toiling for hours a day.

So why did I say that success was earned, mainly because I had trading friends?

Well, think of it this way.

A stranger approaches you and tells you about this new way of earning money. He wants to have a nice chat over coffee. This stranger insists that you have to invest at least $25,000 so that you can trade with a reputable broker.

Nothing he said is wrong so far. Aren't those the facts that we have talked about?

But he is a stranger. The coffee invite sounds reminiscent of some scammers that you know of.

With Ron, it is different. He did not invite me at all. Instead, he just got engrossed in day trading. Then, his life changes followed. He left his 9 to 5 to set up his business. We got worried about him because he was a married man with kids. He could not just be leaving something that is so sure?

What about pension plans? Retirement? Security?

Suddenly, we saw that life had started to improve. We were the ones who asked questions, and he was ready to answer.

What I am trying to say here is that I hope I was able to answer your questions. I hope that you were able to consider me as your day trading guide, your Ron. Indeed, I am not physically present. However, I wish the contents of this book would have given you a sense of security to find a reputable broker to day trade with.

Are you still in your 9 to 5 cubicle? It does not matter. Nobody is rushing you to do anything right now. It is our decision to make. Right now, though, you have been equipped with everything that you need to succeed:

Chapter 22.   Knowledge

Chapter 23.   Opportunity

Chapter 24.   Assurance

You now know-how:

- To find the right broker
- To identify a good trading platform
- To read and understand the various parts of a trading platform

- To recognize market trends and patterns
- To apply risk management
- To make decisions with or without a mentor
- To play it safe while also being decisive
- To handle stress in the short-period trading format
- To see the science and logic of trading

When to use Day Trading?

Day trading is best for people who are comfortable taking a lot of risks. You need to be able to cope with high amounts of volatility and be able to trade during all hours since day trading is an active style of investing.

Day trading is best suited for short-term traders who follow the markets closely and can take advantage of intra-day price changes.

When to use Swing Trading?

Swing traders typically have more time on their hands than day traders, which means they can either wait hours or days for the market conditions that they want. Unlike day traders, who try to make a few quick trades every day, swing traders might hold their stocks for weeks or months at a time.

If you're interested in market timing, developing a good sense for when price levels will be low or high helps to have the time to wait for the conditions to develop.

Swing trading is best suited for long-term traders who follow the markets. Swing traders like to buy stocks and hold them for up to six months at a time, selling them only if they show signs of deteriorating performance.

When to use Forex Trading?

The world's currency markets are huge and can move dramatically. If you believe that moves in currency rates will significantly affect your portfolio value, you might want to try forex trading.

Forex trading requires more experience and knowledge than the other options on this list, so it's less suitable for people who only have a little bit of experience. If you choose the forex market, you'll need to be able to read charts and technical analysis to figure out trends and pounce on opportunities as soon as they appear.

Trading strategies are especially important in the forex market because it doesn't have an open-ended period of trading. For example, if you want to buy foreign currency at 1:00 today (when rates are high) and sell at 1:00 tomorrow (when rates are low), you stand to make a tidy profit if rates stay relatively flat between those two times.

The markets are open five days a week on average, with some high-volume currencies trading for 22 hours per day. Some currency pairs are only open for a few hours per day, so intraday opportunities might be limited.

Forex trading is best suited for people who have experience in other markets or in trading in general. If you want to trade forex, it's probably best to start developing your skills through practice accounts and classes. You might not be able to afford big losses (or profits) at first, but the more you trade, the better you'll get at it and the better your chances of success.

You are ready. You did not even have to leave the comfort of your home. This book has provided you with a path that will help you journey towards financial success.

Be wary, though. This book does not promise miracles. It only assures you that no matter how seemingly volatile the financial market is, you can make sense of patterns and trends to win at it.

For now, I wish you the best of luck. I hope you will make the most of the information that you have been given. Remember that your patience, strategy, and risk management are more crucial to success than high-tech monitors and computers.

CRYPTOCURRENCY INVESTING

CRYPTOCURRENCIES TRADING STRATEGIES FOR BEGINNERS.

HOW TO INVEST IN BITCOIN, NFT, CRYPTOART, ALTCOIN, AND ETHEREUM TO GET YOUR MONEY SAFE AND PROFIT FROM THE BLOCKCHAIN

Introduction

Thank you for choosing this guide.

If you have purchased this book, it is because you are looking for a simple clear and concise text that can train you carefully, using comprehensible language, and accompany you in the world of cryptocurrencies. Great, you are starting off on the right foot.

It is necessary to make a premise: investing is not a simple thing.

Before starting to put capital at stake, it is necessary to know very well the financial market, the trends, the forecasts provided by official sources and other materials of analysis. There are strong fluctuations in the world of financial markets and there always will be, no one can refrain from them, but on the other hand, it is also not as difficult as it seems. To be able to operate in the cryptocurrency market in fact, it is not necessary to have particular technical skills comparable to a Wall Street broker, but it is necessary to inform oneself and however to act with caution, to make weighted investments in relation to one's personal finances, especially in a digital currency market that is often subject to strong market fluctuations, sometimes bullish but sometimes very bearish.

To give you a sneak peek of the cryptocurrency market, let us take the queen of the market, namely Bitcoin (BTC), as a model and reference. Since its invention in 2009, this currency had undergone an amazing growth until 2017, when 1 bitcoin had reached the record amount of 20,000 US dollars. Over the next two years, the same coin had undergone a dizzying slump to reach a listing of around $8,000. As of today, early 2021, the coin has touched $50,000. Analysts speculate that the same coin could reach $100,000 by the end of 2021, but it is difficult to make concrete predictions.

Therefore, if you are not already an expert, in order to become a trader and an investor, you must at least be extremely aware of what you are doing. It is fundamental to avoid diving into the void and gambling of any kind to avoid getting caught up in easy enthusiasms. It is fine to have funds and energy and to invest large sums of money in a very profitable market but being aware that it is still uncertain. Vice versa, to be taken by panic and fear if there is a bearish trend. The psychological and emotional factor has always played an important role on the markets, but we must be stronger, have the right approach and act as much as possible with knowledge and competence.

What Are Cryptocurrencies and How Do They Work?

Let us start by saying that cryptocurrencies are virtual currencies that allow for financial transactions thanks to complex cryptography that allows for the secure and anonymous generation, storage, and trading of a specific digital token.

Initially, cryptocurrencies were not born to be considered currencies, but they have become so over time.

Satoshi Nakamoto, the one who considers himself the inventor of Bitcoins, simply wanted to develop a peer-to-peer electronic cash system for sharing files.

Unlike all his predecessors, Nakamoto managed to prove that it was possible to have a cryptocurrency without the need for a central authority.

In practice, thanks to the peer-to-peer system, when the transaction has taken place, it will have to be confirmed by the miners. Only miners can confirm transactions. As long as a transaction is not confirmed, it can be forged. Instead, when it is confirmed, the transaction is no longer editable and enters the historical transactions, the so-called blockchain.

When a transaction has been confirmed by a miner, each node must add it to its database.

Learn more as you read this book.

Chapter 1: The Blockchain

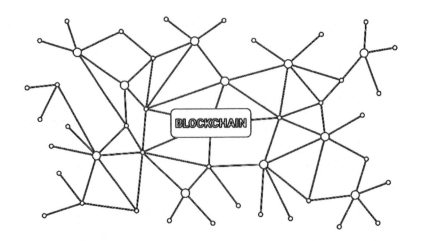

This will explain how blocks are used to unlock the blockchain's full potential by the time you've reached the end, you will have absorbed the key concepts of the blockchain and will understand how it functions within Bitcoin.

Blockchain – What Is It?

The blockchain is simply a public ledger that offers complete transparency to the Bitcoin system. It contains every Bitcoin transaction in its entirety since Bitcoin first began in 2009. All additional transactions are logged on the blockchain as they occur. The technology behind Bitcoin is easily capable of that much.

First, let's talk about what we mean by a block. If the blockchain were an accountant's ledger, it would be appropriate to view the original block as the ledger's first page.

Each new block on the network consists of a hash. A hash is a shorter, random mix of characters based on the earlier block. Ever since the first block appeared on the network, a continuous chain of transactions has occurred, a block at a time. You can trace each transaction that occurs all the way back to the genesis of the initial block. Because each new page contains a summary of the prior pages, it makes sense that the ledger size will increase, extending the length of the blockchain as more data appear.

The Bitcoin blockchain consists of an open ledger. This ledger records each transaction as it occurs. Basically, the blockchain is a bookkeeping tool that provides complete transparency, with all transactions visible to the financial world. This total transparency is what traditional financial institutions fear. They don't want to layout their numbers as openly as the blockchain.

Each node is a computer that runs the Bitcoin software. The software detects and validates new transactions. It also retains a copy of each transaction on the system. As transactions are added to the existing blockchain, the nodes retain a complete timeline of how Bitcoin has evolved financially.

Each new block is created in chronological order, containing the preceding block's hash. If there's an inconsistency between a block and its predecessor, the network will reject the transaction as incorrect.

Blockchain Analytics

In 2014 a new trend emerged in Bitcoin's blockchain technology. Blockchain analysis arrived, adding a whole new market to the Bitcoin system. This analysis is only possible because of Bitcoin's transparency. Whether it is advantageous or harmful remains to be seen.

One thing that has assisted Bitcoin in its growth as a mainstream payment method is being able to see how people are spending their bitcoin, not only by looking at the products and services bought and sold but also by seeing how long they are holding the bitcoin they receive in their wallets. You can pay out bitcoin in the same way you spend your cash. You can make a bitcoin payment at any time, any place. Now that we can analyze how long people hold onto their coins, we can target our marketing to stimulate the rest of the population to use their bitcoin.

Blockchain analysis adds to the legitimacy of the whole platform. Because Bitcoin is so young, we are facing plenty of unknowns. Blockchain analysis helps us get a handle on some of those unknowns, making investment less of a leap in the dark. It provides valuable information to industry experts that will help Blockchain mature and continue to flourish.

Thanks to blockchain analysis, we can start to discern how bitcoin hoarding impacts the entire market. We can track trends that will tell us how people are spending their bitcoin and where most new wallets are coming from.

Understandably, a small proportion of the oldest bitcoin recorded on the network has not traded in years. Some may belong to the founder, Satoshi Nakamoto, but they may also belong to early investors who have now forgotten about Bitcoin completely. It could be possible that private keys have been lost, rendering funds held in those wallets completely useless. However, blockchain analysis can give us insight into the rate of unclaimable bitcoin.

Beyond Transactions

You can use the blockchain for more than you could ever imagine. You can track packages in real-time, anywhere in the world. You can create copyright claims, fight online piracy and stop counterfeit products, just by using blockchain technology. Of course, the blockchain is used mostly for the financial side of things, to record transactions. Yet, I advise you to keep an open mind, remembering that blockchain technology is so much more than just a form of currency. The blockchain can go far beyond a financial transaction's ledger. Here are some projects currently underway that prove how superbly blockchain technology can adapt to a variety of needs.

Decentralized storage: Users are given tokens for components of the blockchain that they allow to be stored on their devices. Users can apply the tokens to store parts of their data on the blockchain, too. These are a few of the bona fide organizations involved in decentralized storage:

Chapter 1. Storj

Chapter 2. Maidsafe

Chapter 3. Nebulous

Chapter 4. Sia

Chapter 5. Filecoin

Extra blockchain layer - This adds an extra top layer to the blockchain that focuses on data storage, such as healthcare records. At the time of writing, some of the major players are:

Chapter 8. Factom

The transparency of blockchain technology offers endless technological uses. Developers are only beginning to explore the extent of its potential.

Blockchain Applications

The current focus of blockchain developers is primarily financial services. This is understandable as Bitcoin is focused on combining financial services for everyone across the globe. However, vast unexplored areas exist.

The idea at the heart of blockchain applications is similar to Bitcoin, restoring all power to the user and eliminating the need for centralized companies and services. Because of the transparency that blockchain provides, blockchain applications offer unparalleled technological advances.

Here is a sampling of the many ways blockchain-based applications can simplify your life:

Lower your electric bills. The app compares multiple rates and switches services rapidly to take advantage of savings.

Get deeper information about products. Blockchain-based information can provide details of where an item was manufactured and where the components came from. Developed by Provenance.

Ridesharing is vetted by the blockchain, without the middleman to take out a cut, developed by Arcade City.

Protect valuables with proof of ownership stored on a blockchain.

Ensure your charitable giving reaches the intended recipients. See BitGive.

Check the source of your meat or produce. Developed by Provenance for the UK grocery market.

Manage music royalties and ensure writers get paid for piece work. Apps developed by Smoogs and Revelator.

Store your identification documents and information in a secure location. Certificates of birth, death, and marriage can be stored where authorized persons can access them.

You can control what information you reveal to which people. For example, if you want to buy cigarettes, the clerk only needs to see proof that you are of age, so that's the extent of the information you provide, nothing else.

Store your will in a secure location accessible by your attorney or executor upon your death. See MyWish.

Become a Developer

Blockchain technology is a unique development. There's nothing else like it in the world, so you can count on a pretty steep learning curve at the start. However, any blockchain-related skills you can gain will be highly marketable in the foreseeable future. If you can learn to create blockchain applications, you'll most likely be in demand for a long time.

It can be very time-consuming to create and develop a blockchain-based application. There is a huge amount of code to be written and multiple outcomes to account for. These applications require a substantial amount of funding. Yet, venture capitalist investment continues to rise, regardless of bitcoin's volatile ups and downs.

The blockchain is all about creating communities that make choices more accessible to the average person. Much of the time, a group of people with the same idea will work together and share ways to improve it. The obvious example is the number of alternative digital currencies that have arisen since Bitcoin appeared on the scene. This results in the developing blockchain not being tied to one program. One of blockchain developers' greatest assets is diversification. Only time will reveal whether this community-style spirit will continue or if the process will become commercialized.

Bitcoin 2.0

For several services, ranging from capital controlling to investment vehicles and all things in between, Bitcoin has been considered a currency. However, people have started to realize that Bitcoin is far more than a payment method. Bitcoin 2.0 provides an application and a platform that reflects that reality.

Bitcoin and blockchain technology will be pivotal in providing further enhancements to the financial world. The financial sector has seen little to no change over the last 45 years, so I'd imagine ample opportunity remains for improving on the status quo.

Blockchains provide a perfect replacement for authentication processing on sites such as Twitter or Facebook. The potential has not gone unnoticed; many financial institutions are now looking into ways to use the blockchain in their businesses. Admittedly, even though some of these businesses can't see a future for Bitcoin in currency terms, they do want to make use of the blockchain, because it offers almost unlimited potential for applications that will provide real-world improvements.

Bitcoin 2.0 is attracting plenty of attention because it can broadcast blocks of data on the network. Instead of including information about transactions, Bitcoin blocks are able to transfer data of any kind to users and accomplish this openly. Engineers and developers are currently looking into the possibilities of using this technology to manage and store copyright claims, passport photos, real estate registrations, and other information.

Bitcoin 2.0 will vastly improve the current Bitcoin exchange. To this date, the majority of exchanges allow Bitcoin users to send, receive and store digital currency. Bitcoin 2.0 will introduce additional features like peer-to-peer lending, accounts that yield interest, and quite possibly the capacity to lend financial security without any assistance from a broker or bank.

Bitcoin 2.0 will also do away with the middleman when it comes to buying and selling. Technically, ownership of products could be tied to digital tokens, which can then be transferred to another blockchain user, together with a payment for the transaction. Realistically, there is vast potential for e-commerce transactions around the world to take place on the blockchain.

Another option for Bitcoin 2.0 employs blockchain technology to provide virtual identification cards that users can implement to complete verification processes. Instead of having to send sensitive information to third parties, who would then store them on a central server, the virtual ID card could be verified by the blockchain. This means the person who owns the identity card has total control of the data, while the seller is unable to store any of the information.

Bitcoin 2.0 is set to create a new type of decentralized market in the future since it becomes a new branch of innovative technology under current construction. However, let's not move away from the idea that blockchain technology relies on the support of the community for its existence. The main purpose of Bitcoin 2.0 is to create a decentralized service with applications that will encourage people to start their own businesses in whatever line of work they wish to pursue. It is only my opinion, but I feel there is little that Bitcoin 2.0 will not achieve once it becomes a part of mainstream life.

Chapter 2: Understand the Reasons to Invest in Cryptocurrencies

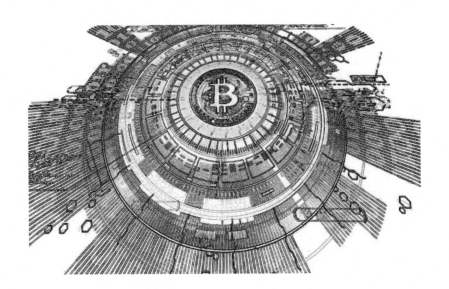

Alternatives have also been developed through cryptographic or encrypted opinions as a digital alternative to more conventional exchange methods such as cash or credit cards.

First, a think-tank sees cryptocurrencies as a financial platform for fraudsters, terrorists, and criminality – particularly given their participation in ransomware and trafficking on the Dark Web.

Instead, recent Bitcoin surges have created cryptocurrencies as a viable investment – and will have a positive effect on the accounts and trading habits of leading investors worldwide with the positive hype that blockchain technology is promoting.

In this document, the more optimistic features and benefits of blockchain will be addressed. The plus points will be considered an attractive alternative to more advanced modes of financial commerce.

Many people believe cryptocurrencies to be a primary store of money, but the concept is much more. Bitcoin is rooted in "capitalist revolt," not as a means of paying for the pizza. In a decentralized, accurate, irreversible recording and value transmission method, certain advantages are inferred. Global leaders in politics and economics are being noted, and you can therefore take notice.

Although you don't want to invest in cryptocurrency as something but a hedge, you would certainly enjoy learning how the future's financial and political climate is to be changed through cryptocurrency.

Our ability to share information has changed forever with the advent of the World Wide Web and the digital Internet. In the past, if we want details, we have to call someone, give them a fax, buy a library or borrow a book from a library or wait for days before somebody provides us with a brochure. It looks unimaginable now.

Now with currency trading, the same digital transition is taking place. Cryptocurrency exchange increases the way we send and receive capital and revolutionizes our willingness to exchange value assets with individuals worldwide. It would soon become as archaic to go to a physical bank or give someone a cash transfer that takes several business days to clear up the charges and deliver a paper via fax.

Although Internet connectivity enabled us to share knowledge on an individual basis globally and instantly via the simple clicking of a website, it was not possible to do the same with money before the emergence of Bitcoin and crypto-assets. In the middle of the deal, we wanted a third party because we did not trust a foreigner online and checked their identification. Instead of relying on one another, our dependence will be on a bank, a credit card company, or some other intermediary such as PayPal or a clearinghouse to avoid replication and guarantee the secure sending and receiving of our funds.

However, for 11 years before the Bitcoin White Paper had been written by the individual or individuals pseudonymously named Satoshi Takemoto, a new age of opportunities for global value sharing had been opened. Trading in crypto-currency means today that everyone else can open an account somewhere in the world and start trading anonymously and safely with anyone else—by swapping digital currencies—without any broker and any associated costs and charges. This is just the tip of the iceberg, though, and some other advantages of cryptocurrency trading can be seen below:

Transactions

The otherwise easy deal may be made costlier by conventional company contracts, traders, marketers, and legal representatives. Paperwork, brokerage fees, commissions, and any other special terms can apply.

One of the benefits of blockchain trading is that it is one-on-one, a peer-to-peer networking structure that traditional practices are "cutting the middle man off." This makes audit tracks simpler, less ambiguous on who is to pay whom, and more accountable since each of the two parties involved in a deal knows who they are.

Asset Transfers

One financial specialist defines the cryptocurrency blockchain as equivalent to a "massive property rights ledger," which can be used to introduce and implement contracts with two-party parties for commodity goods such as cars or property. However, the cryptocurrency ecosystem blockchain may also be used to promote professional transition processes.

Cryptocurrency contracts may, for example, be structured to complement third-party permissions, to mention external evidence, or to be settled in the future at some time or date defined. And because you, as the owners of cryptocurrency, rule your account entirely, this minimizes time and cost in allowing transactions of properties.

More Confidential Transactions

Each time you make an exchange for the cash/credit schemes, the entire transaction history will become a bank/ credit agency reference record. At the most straightforward stage, it can require checking your account's balance to make sure enough money is given. For more complex or business-critical transactions, a complete evaluation of the financial record may be sufficient.

Another critical benefit of cryptocurrencies is that any deal you do is a single exchange of terms and conditions between two parties. Furthermore, information sharing takes place "press" to relay specifically what you intend to give to the receiver – and nothing more.

This safeguards your financial past privacy and prohibits you from being revealed at some point in the transaction chain by a more considerable danger to account or identification amount in the conventional system.

Transaction Fees

You have read the monthly bank or credit card business account statements and have balked at the volume of the payment's charges levied for checks, moving cash, or breathing in the face of the banking firms concerned. Transaction charges can take a big bite from your savings— especially if you carry out several transactions in a month.

Benefits from crypto-currency networks typically do not extend because the data miners (remarkable and different computer systems) who crunch the number created by bitcoin earn compensation. Bitcoin and other cryptocurrencies

Use third-party maintenance providers to administer the cryptocurrency wallet. There might be individual external costs involved, but another drawback of cryptocurrency being that it is all expected to be far cheaper than the processing charges paid through conventional finance structures.

Greater Access to Credit

Cryptocurrencies are enabled by automated data transmission and the Internet. These services are also feasible for anybody who has a viable data connection, a specific knowledge of the provided crypto-currency networks, and ready access to their respective websites and portals.

There are figures that globally, 2,2 billion people now have internet or telephone connectivity but do not currently have access to conventional banking and exchange networks. This massive market of eager customers—if the appropriate infrastructure (digital and regulatory) is placed together—can a cryptocurrency ecosystem to allow wealth transactions and transaction processing available.

Easier International Trade

While currently largely unregulated as a legal tender at the national level, it is by their very existence that cryptocurrencies are not subject to a particular country's exchange rates, interest rates, transaction costs, and any extra fees.

Cross-border exchanges and transactions can be carried out without risks of currency volatility, etc., using the peer-to-peer system of blockchain technology.

Individual Ownership

You turn the administration of your finances over in a conventional bank or credit card scheme to a third party who conducts life or death over your money. Accounts can be suspended without warning for infringements of a financial company's terms of operation—forcing you as a manager of the store to leap through hoops to add to the scheme.

Maybe the main benefit in the case of cryptocurrencies is that you alone possess the associated private and public cryptocurrency keys to shape the identification or address of your cryptocurrency network unless you have assigned the control of your wallet to the third-party provider.

Adaptability

More than 1200 separate cryptocurrencies and altcoins are already in worldwide circulation. Many of them somewhat brief, but importantly, cryptocurrencies' versatility is demonstrated in real use cases.

There are, for example, "privacy coins" to cover up the identity on the blockchain and supply chain tokens to allow supply chain processes for different types of industries.

Strong Security

Since the sale of a cryptocurrency is accepted, it cannot be revoked, as in credit card companies' "chargeback" purchases. This is a precaution against theft, forcing the customer and vendor to agree on refunds in the case of an error or return policies.

The robust encryption methods used in the distributed ledger (blockchain) and transaction processes in cryptocurrencies secure against theft and account abuse and maintain customer confidentiality.

Better Payment Structure

You will want to explore crypto use if you have ever been angry waiting for a cash transfer from a bank account. Instant payments are less costly than services such as PayPal. The use of crypto also prevents illegitimate charges, and transfers cannot be reversed on a blockchain.

You can also transfer money anywhere you want using crypto without any broker checking your transaction history. This requires foreign beneficiaries who willingly stop the costly currency exchange costs of PayPal.

Another benefit when using blockchain is the idea of micropayment or on-demand payment structure. The embedded fees you pay with a credit card vanish with blockchain, making micropayments a fact every second or minute. Instead of paying a streaming video subscription fee, you can pay crypto-only if you watch a movie, for example. Streamium is also a video streaming service that does.

Growth Investment

Even if you are not an enormous crypto buff, you undoubtedly learned about Bitcoin's mania around Christmas 2017. Bitcoin soared in terms of valuation, hitting nearly $20,000 a penny. It was the most significant financial investment ever. Since then, Bitcoin's value compared to the dollar has decreased, but crypto bulls believe it can improve its performance in 2017 and take over the rest of the crypto market.

More than ever, investors—both individuals and institutions—have a kind of crypto. This includes very public skeptics such as Jamie Demon, JPMorgan Chase Chief Executive Officer. The Chicago Mercantile Exchange (CME) provides

Bitcoin's Futures options, giving the mainstream sustainability it had not had until its 2017 start. The crypto market is marked by robust potential investment in growth: increased visibility and sense, a relatively low market cap compared with the conventional asset classes, and a steady increase in utility.

Financial Stability

Most US investors consider crypto as an investment risky. The U.S. dollar can be the reserve currency globally and is also one of the planet's most reliable currencies. Crypto is potentially a more stable source of money for a nation such as Venezuela. This is more than just a fantasy or experiment —all of them have double their Bitcoin use year after year, Nigeria, Australia, Spain, and Canada.

The public uses Bitcoin to save their lives in countries like Venezuela. The government cannot regulate bitcoin just as much as it can control a fiat currency. Russia is finding its cryptography and criminalizing all such non-sanctioned rivals. Zimbabweans tend to cryptograph the government's gold-backed money.

Smart Contracts

Imagine that a prosecutor never needs to pay another lawyer. Dream of an immobilization contract without any escrow costs. This is a future where Ethereal advocates believe is real. The intelligent agreement built on the ethereal framework and quantified by the Cryptocurrency of Ether takes the unchangeable, fraud-less blockchain into the law sector. Smart contracts create a 100% safe route for a transaction to be reached without the judiciaries.

Ethereal was too well-received to surpass Bitcoin in terms of new users during the last year. The principle of smart contracts. Developers from ethereal say that ethereal is soon to beat Bitcoin in the number of developers, day-to-day exchanges, and purchases.

Decentralized Social Media

Recent tensions were raised between Facebook and Twitter due to their readiness to regulate their website. We fail according to who you ask. A shared social network is one of the intentional applications of cryptocurrencies. There is no overarching authority in this system to censor divisive content or not to censor them.

Chapter 3: Understanding the Technical and Fundamental Analysis in Crypto Trading

Technical Analysis

Technical analysis (sometimes abbreviated as TA) forecasts future cryptocurrency prices and market trends based on historical data. It anticipates whether the price trends will be up (bull) or down (bear). This is done through the use of technical indicators, which calculate the historical and current market price of an asset and analyze price trends.

Analyzing historical price charts and collected volume data determines whether the coin is undervalued or overvalued.

Assumptions of Technical Analysis

Technical analysis is based on the following assumptions.

The price movement follows certain trends. Bitcoin prices do not change randomly but tend to follow particular trends that last for either short or long periods. It uses past performance to predict future prices.

Bitcoin prices are determined by multiple variables. The price movement of the coin is due to past and future demand of the coin, current market prices, and regulations governing the cryptocurrency market.

History tends to repeat itself. What happened in the past is used to predict what will happen in the future. Past changes can easily predict future market changes. Traders tend to behave the same way when presented with a similar market condition.

Types of Technical Analysis

There are three components used in technical analysis:

Chapter 1. Chart lines: Chart lines are used to indicate the points where price changes. Using historical price data, current prices, and volume data, analysts can draw charting lines to show the exact points where the prices tend to change.

Chapter 2. Patterns: Chart patterns predict price movement. They show the price direction and extrapolate to show where prices are headed to.

Chapter 3. Indicator oscillators: This analysis tool uses statistical methods to determine the buy and sell signals.

Analysts and cryptocurrency investors rely on the charts, to get visual data on price trends and market momentum.

Technical Indicators

Technical indicators are investment analysis tools used to calculate and interpret market trends. Traders rely on these tools to determine the right time to invest in cryptocurrencies. Investors can receive alerts on any new investment opportunities and price changes.

Traders can know the price movement of cryptocurrency assets whether they move up, down, or sideways. The price movement is calculated using historical price data, current prices, and trade volume data.

Technical indicators are very important in analyzing cryptocurrency investments. They help investors to:

- Predict price movement and future price direction.
- Confirm market trends in the price movement of cryptocurrencies, such as Bitcoin.
- Alert investors to whether prices are going up, down, or sideways to allow traders to plan ahead for trade.

Cryptocurrency investors rely on these indicators to determine the short-term price movement. They also evaluate the asset's long-term price changes to determine when to enter or exit the market.

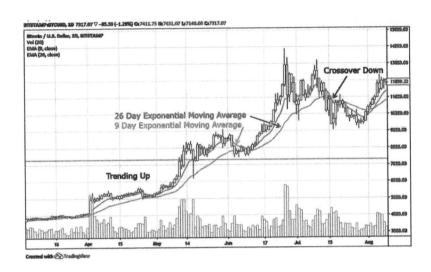

Some of the common technical indicators used include calculating Moving Averages (MA) and the Relative Strength Index (RSI). For example, you can plot a chart to show the Bitcoin price direction for 12 and 26 days, respectively.

There are several indicators to observe when analyzing a particular cryptocurrency asset. To choose the right indicator, you need to first understand how each indicator works and how each indicator will affect your investment strategy.

Because of the volatile nature of cryptocurrency assets, monitoring the price direction or a Bitcoin price chart will help the investor evaluate both high and low trading patterns. If the chart assumes an upward trend, this will indicate higher trend lines; a downward trend indicates a series of low trend lines.

Sometimes the cryptocurrency will move sideways. In such a case, it does not move in any particular vertical direction at all. Investors should be very careful when using only one indicator, such as trend lines, to predict future prices, since the trends can move in any direction. It is much better to use two or more indicators as confirmation of a move, up or down.

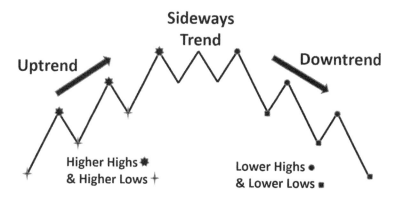

A technical analysis chart, drawn based on historical prices and trading volume data, represents the past decisions made by investors on the buying and selling of cryptocurrency assets. As investors, we use past data to predict future investments. For example, a typical investor who bought Bitcoin will monitor the price of Bitcoin. If the price falls in comparison to the initial buying price, the investor may wait until the price reaches the break-even point to sell the cryptocurrency. As savvy investors, we recognize this as Support/Resistance (explained later in this book) and can use this to our advantage.

Price movement is influenced by both internal and external constraints. Multiple forces including human emotions like fear, panic, greed, anxiety, hope, and hysteria affect the prices of cryptocurrency. These emotions lead to dramatic shifts in the prices of the cryptocurrency asset. Therefore, price movement is not only based on facts but also on expectations.

Trend Analysis

Trend analysis uses technical tools to determine price movements; it help traders know when to buy, sell, or hold a cryptocurrency asset.

This technique analyzes past cryptocurrency prices to predict future price movements. It determines an upward trend when asset prices continue to rise and detects a downward trend when prices keep decreasing over several consecutive days.

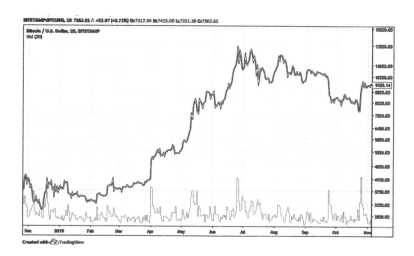

Trend lines, moving averages, and polarity analysis are the major tools used to determine price trends. We will focus on the use of trend lines.

Using trend lines is one of the most popular techniques used in technical analysis. They are used to show the consistent movement of prices either up, down, or sideways. Price movements vary based on the timeframe and whether the investor is observing on a daily, weekly, monthly or quarterly basis.

Drawing Trend Lines

Trend lines indicate the general direction of the price. Straight lines are drawn above and below the price line. Trend lines also show support and resistance areas, which can determine when to enter or exit a trade. Trend lines can show increased supply or demand.

Downward trend lines are drawn above the price of the plotted chart, while upward trend lines are drawn below the price. The upward trend line is used to estimate support, while the downward trendline is used to estimate resistance.

<u>Rules of Thumb for Trend Lines</u>

Chapter 25. There must be at least two highs or lows to have a valid trend line (3 points are preferred). The trend line is further validated if it intersects the price line a 3rd time. Bitcoin is so volatile, that it may be hard to find the 3rd point validation.

Chapter 26. Larger time frames result in better trend lines. Start with weekly or daily charts, and then check the smaller time frames to confirm.

Chapter 27. Sometimes trend lines cut through the low or high portion of a candle. Try not to cut through the body of the candle. If the trend line does not fit without being forced, it probably is not a valid trend.

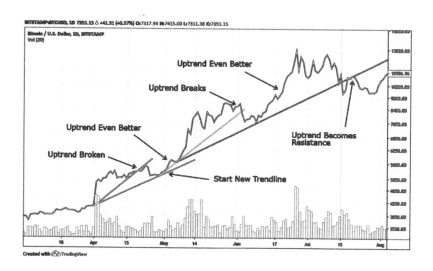

In the above chart, the prices touched the trend line at least two times in the given timeframe. The line represents the area of support, and it indicates when traders should be looking for buying opportunities. Sometimes the upward trendline can become a resistance line, as shown on the right side.

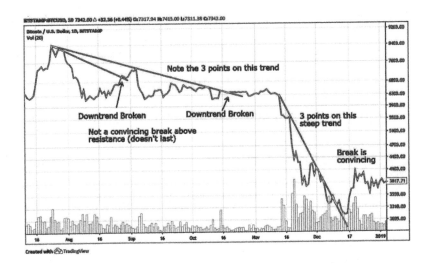

The downtrend touched the trend line three times in the given timeframe. The trend line in the graph represents resistance, and this indicates where the buyers are expected to slow down their buying. Traders use this, to sell their cryptocurrency near the top.

Fundamental Analysis

Fundamental analysis is also called the lifeblood of investment. The key to using it is to gather as much information and real facts as possible. It is based on the premise that the more you understand a particular cryptocurrency, the more likely you will be able to predict its price movement in the market. Hence, when you use fundamental analysis, you should follow the latest news.

The news has a powerful influence on the price of a cryptocurrency.

Just to give you an idea: when CNN featured just how high the price of Bitcoin was increasing at that time; it further pushed the price of Bitcoin upward. When China declared that it would close down all its cryptocurrency exchanges, the price of Bitcoin and other cryptocurrencies dropped. When Russia removed its ban on the use of Bitcoins and other cryptocurrencies, the price of Bitcoin experienced a significant increase in value. As you can see, by being aware of the latest news and analyzing its implications in the market, you can get a good idea of how the price of certain cryptocurrencies will most likely be affected. `

News is not the only source of information. You should also check the white paper released by the developer of a cryptocurrency. Although it may be hard to understand due to the technical terms, it will nonetheless provide you with useful information regarding the cryptocurrency.

You should also join related online groups and forums. Many developers are active in these places, and this will allow you to not only get information from the developers, and you can even contact them if you want. Needless to say, you can also learn from the other members of the cryptocurrency community. From time to time, you will surely come across interesting points of view, as well as useful strategies that you can use to make a profit in the cryptocurrency market.

This tool is important because it deals with the basics. If you do not understand the basics; how do you think you can make the right investment decision otherwise? Therefore, always do your research and analysis of the different cryptocurrencies in the market. Do not be lazy.

Fundamental analysis can be used with other tools. People usually use this tool together with technical analysis. If you consider yourself a true and professional cryptocurrency investor/trader, then it is a must that you use it, regardless of other tools that you may want to use. After all, if you do not know the fundamentals, it would be hard to think of yourself as a real investor/trader.

Chapter 4: How to Advanced Crypto Trading with Success

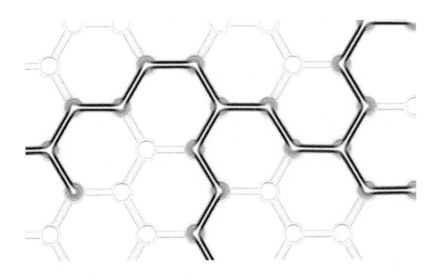

There's one more thing you need to know before you plunge into the cryptocurrency world: how to receive cryptocurrency.

In the cryptocurrency industry, there are many ways to make money. To begin, you should thoroughly familiarize yourself with them and select the one that best fits your lifestyle, financial situation, preferences, and other factors. You can also choose multiple coins and cleverly combine them. You would have a greater chance to diversify your risks and gain more in this situation.

In today's cryptocurrency industry, there are a variety of ways to profit:

- Long-term investment
- Trading
- Mining
- Participating in ICO
- Re-selling cryptocurrency.

Here's a short rundown on each of these approaches. After that, I'll go over each strategy in greater detail.

Long-Term Investment

If you choose this method of benefit, you should have the following:

- A one-to-two-year duration (invest a sum of money you can easily "freeze" for several years)
- A significant sum of money (if you can invest in parts only, this too can be viewed as a long-term investment) Preparedness for danger (which are higher than in the banking sector).

In the long run, you benefit from substantial capital gains.

Trading

If you prefer this method of benefit, you should have the following:

- The passage of time (not the time for waiting as with long-term investment, but the free time you can devote daily to trading)
- A modest sum of money
- Perseverance and diligence are required.
- Intelligence created by machines (as you have to work with numbers and charts)

It's possible to keep an eye on things and keep track of what's going on.

To potentially make money quickly and earn recurring profits, you beat the market and take risks (the higher the possible gain, the higher the risk).

Mining

Mining is the method of making new bitcoins or cryptocurrencies. If you're interested in making money with cryptocurrencies, you'll need to determine if you want to do it as a hobby or go into skilled mining.

You'll need the following items for hobbyist mining:

- Mechanical intelligence (or a mechanically intelligent friend or advisor)
- Support for new companies (usually up to six mining farms)
- Preparedness for technological issues and disruptions
- Equipment protection from external influences (pets, children, etc.).

In mining, you make money by making a small but consistent profit. You also have the option of not only trading but also managing the market.

If you want to go into technical mining, you'll need the following items:

- Mechanical intelligence (or a mechanically intelligent friend or advisor)
- Investments or startup money
- Locations
- a group
  - Availability to take on responsibility.

You will make a regular and consistent profit by running your own mining farm; you can also control the market rather than just trade in it. Furthermore, you will have the potential to own something concrete and sell your company in the future.

ICOS (Initial Coin Offering)

Many people have taken part in so-called initial coin offerings (ICOs) to date (Initial Coin Offering). In a nutshell, this is a different take on the crowdfunding model, close to an IPO. Participants contribute money to the construction of a project in exchange for potential benefits, although there are no guarantees.

An initial coin offering (ICO) is when a project issues vouchers or tokens that can be used to pay for site services with cryptocurrencies in the future.

A venture fund, i.e., an investment fund that works with creative businesses and ventures, has a lot in common with an ICO (startups). A venture fund invests in stocks or shares in high-risk or reasonably high-risk businesses with the expectation of exceptionally high income.

In general, 70 percent to 80 percent of such initiatives fail to pay off. The benefit from the remaining 20% -30%, on the other hand, covers all losses.

If you think you're courageous enough to fund a project with no promises, consider the following:

- Am I willing to take on additional risks?
- Is there a capital cushion for diversification in my portfolio?

You make money with an ICO by taking huge risks in exchange for a chance to make a lot of money.

Re-Selling Cryptocurrency

Trading and reselling cryptocurrencies have a lot in common. You can benefit from currency fluctuations here as well, but unlike trading, it's a game between wholesale and retail rates rather than the market or exchange rate.

If you're interested in making money this way, you should:

- Do not take risks
- Operate in small sums only
- Understand that income depends on your turnover.

So far, we've just scratched the surface of the simple ways to benefit from the cryptocurrency sector. Let's take a closer look at each approach now.

Making Long-Term Investments: A More In-Depth Look

You may remember Warren Buffett's first rule: never lose money. This is particularly true for long-term investments, where the goal is to retain the money rather than lose it.

Let's go over some of the foundations of making a long-term investment:

- Do not lose money; reduce risks
- Do not make a fuss

- Reap benefit in future

This is how you can set up your cryptocurrency portfolio for long-term investment.

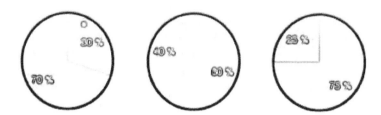

The blue color is used to denote positions that are more moderate and stable but maybe less lucrative. The green color denotes positions that are riskier but also more promising. Blue coins are the more stable currency at the moment.

Chapter 5: Create a Crypto Strategy that Matches Your Goals

Every new step requires proper planning to have smooth execution, and this holds true for cryptocurrency too. It is unwise to get into an area without any functional knowledge, especially when it is entirely new to you. The volatility in the price value and unexpected fluctuations in the market could turn your financial status topsy-turvy within seconds if you went with a blind approach. Therefore, it is crucial to have a strategic plan set up with a proper and systematic technique before you decide to make money using cryptocurrencies.

Your decision of choosing long-term or short-term goals becomes quick when you have a strategic plan in place.

Strategic Planning with Cryptocurrencies

When there is a defined strategy, the decision made is mostly right, thus helping in a smooth implementation process without any bottlenecks. The below-mentioned steps can be followed to devise a strategic plan for choosing the right cryptocurrency strategy to help achieve your financial target:

- Write down the goals.
- Identify if the goal benefits are short-term or long-term.
- Determine the objectives required to fulfill the goals.
- Sketch the plan outline.

- Compare the theoretical plan with practical possibilities, i.e., capital money, the period of waiting, expected profit, estimating the unavoidable losses, financial stability, etc.
- Categorize the possibilities.
- Choose the right cryptocurrency strategy based on the drafted plan.
  - Get ready to implement the devised plan.

Asking the following questions of yourself will help in choosing the right strategy to gain better profits with minimal risk:

- Have you already decided on the cryptocurrency you want to use to earn that extra money?
- Do you know which technology cryptocurrency works on and what is the concept behind the same?
- Will you want to make fast cash or are you going to wait for the right moment to enjoy long-term benefits?
- Do you want to go with the long-term investment strategy or short-term trading strategy (sell the coins whenever there is a price hike)?
- Have you decided on the 'capital amount' you will want to invest in the cryptocurrency?

- Is your wait-time decided (months or years you will be holding to the coin)?

- Do you have complete knowledge of the cryptocurrency exchanges available in the market and have you decided on the one you will want to go ahead with?

- Have you taken the necessary steps to store the purchased crypto coins in a secured manner by choosing the right cryptocurrency wallet (preferably offline or hardware wallet)?

If you have convincing answers to all the above-mentioned queries, then you are ready to get to the implementation phase.

Cryptocurrency Failure – An Example

A virus by the name 'WannaCry' attacked systems (computers) of key companies across 150 countries in May 2017. The computers that were under the attack of the virus had popup messages that said—"Oops! Your files have been encrypted." It was alarming as many vital files were compromised, and unfortunately, cryptocurrencies were one among them. Hackers had the upper hand, and they demanded 'big money' to open the encrypted files. They wanted $300 in Bitcoins from all the computer owners whose computers had been hacked. The owners were given three days to arrange the money, and in case they failed to do so, the locked files would be deleted. Since Bitcoin transactions are anonymous, it was impossible to track the cyber hackers.

Though it is not possible to predict such incidents, this won't have affected cryptocurrency owners if they had taken additional steps to keep their local system double-safe by installing the best anti-virus software onto their systems (preferably buying the best ones instead of using trial versions) especially when they had their crypto coins stored on the PC. When it comes to cryptocurrency strategy, the most important thing to be remembered is to ensure the purchased cryptocurrencies are stored in a secured manner (with a backup)

Importance of Strategic Planning

Having a proper strategic plan is essential to ensure the money flow is smooth with good profits and there are no major setbacks when withdrawing funds. When your objectives are clear with set priorities, the process is easy, thereby allowing you to achieve your moneymaking goals, as you desired.

The major uses of having a proper and calculated plan for your cryptocurrency strategies are as follows:

- The sole intention of attaining the objectives is fulfilled.
- Focusing on the idea becomes easier when the plan is appropriately devised.
- It permits the investor to make use of his money, resources and time in a precise manner based on the plan.
- When the entire plan outline is structured clearly with all the required details, implementation is never a difficult task.

When you choose a sensitive market such as cryptocurrency, it becomes your responsibility to make sure that you know the ins and outs of the chosen cryptocurrency, the underlying technology it uses, the financial benefits it offers, and the threats it can pose during the entire cycle.

Benefits of a smart strategic plan:

- When the framework is set, it is easy to choose the method which best suits you based on your set goals.
- You can quickly decide which cryptocurrency strategies you want to go ahead with from the available choices:
  - Investment
  - Trading
  - Mining, etc.
  - When the decision is made, you can have your concentration focused and start to travel towards a 'set' direction
  - Managing the risk will not be a tough task if you have already made the right plan (based on long-term or short-term goals)
  - Your decision-making skills will have also improved to a great extent as you are aware of the entire cycle thus allowing you to take the right decision spontaneously.

Things to Remember When Choosing Cryptocurrency Strategy

The below-mentioned points will definitely be of help to finalize the cryptocurrency strategy that suits based on your requirements and goals:

- o Understand the history behind cryptocurrencies and the reasons which led to the invention of the virtual currency

- o Be aware of the underlying technology that cryptocurrencies use –blockchain technology. (If you are someone who invested in crypto coins but have no clue about blockchain technology, then you are in the wrong place. It is important to know everything about the stock you are investing in.)

- o Be careful not to repeat the 'famous' mistakes again (Don't invest based on the price value. Don't be in a hurry to sell your crypto coin the moment you see a price hike. Don't invest in a crypto coin if you don't have plans to hold on to the coin for a minimum period – at least three years. Don't compare the characteristics of altcoins with Bitcoins and dream that it will become big the same way Bitcoin made it big.)

- Diversify your investment plans and don't get completely drawn into cryptocurrency day trading, as it can become a dangerous mistake.
- Last but not the least; ensure your crypto coins are stored in the right wallets in a secured manner. Have a backup of the private key and seed.

Chapter 6: Tools and Advice

Before you study a few "all-inclusive" technical indicators at the earliest opportunity and pick a well-known crypto-exchange (you can also utilize a troll box, but at the same time better without it), you should once become familiar with certain key principles of trading.

The list below is not comprehensive. However, for a beginning, these standards are sufficient because experience comes with time.

Begin Trading with Free Funds That You Are Not Afraid to Lose

It is smarter to store the main part of cryptocurrency savings not on a centralized trade but rather in a reliable wallet. These assets can be seen as a long-term investment.

Simultaneously, resources "frozen" on a crypto wallet can mean a lost short or medium-term benefit for a dealer since they are not involved in circulation. Thus, a portion of these assets can, in any case, be kept on a few cryptocurrency exchanges.

Try not to open a "full cutlet" position, and it will be very safe for beginners to practice little trades, every one of which can be restricted, state, 1–2% of the store. Slowly, with the acquisition of skills and self-assurance, this breaking point can be somewhat raised. If you can hardly wait to enter a higher percentage of the deposit, at that point, it is good to wait for the ideal moment for this—for instance, a good correction in the cost of a resource.

Try not to go to the bank for a loan than to purchase cryptocurrency and "play" on the exchange. Try not to tune in to different well-wishers advising how they figured out how to "make 1000%" and quickly settle with the bank!

It is greatly improved and more secure to deposit some of your free assets now and then. For instance, calculate your budget so that, state, 5–10% of your monthly payment would be spent purchasing cryptocurrency to top up a deposit on a crypto exchange. Over the long term, it will also be possible to expand the deposit because of the steady recapitalization of benefits.

Try Not to Be Afraid to Lose Free Assets

First, you have allocated a crucial segment of your reserve funds for exchanging, haven't you? Second, even the best and most experienced merchants at times make mistakes. Losses (and they can happen for different reasons: trade tricks, hacker attacks, token delisting, loss of private keys from a record on a decentralized site, and so forth) and delayed drawdowns should be seen as risks with a high probability. Also, they gain from their mistakes. If that achievement had not been replaced by failure, it most likely would not be so interesting.

As in the past, the cryptocurrency market is amazingly volatile and, one may even say, unpredictable. The capitalization of cryptocurrencies is exceptionally subject to different essential factors that immediately impact market members' feelings. Significant and not very informative on the crypto business can rapidly "duplicate by zero" even the specialized investigation formats from the most experienced participants. The effective market hypothesis is good, but you should also carefully investigate the central elements.

Be ready for the way that sometimes you will purchase an overvalued altcoin "on highs," and then you will wait for quite a long time until its value moves toward its former levels, to at any rate "break-even."

The same bitcoin doesn't develop indefinitely, and very deep drawdowns happen. For instance, following the breakdown of Mt. Gox, the first cryptocurrency went into a protracted correction, where it remained for around two years.

In the chart below, you can perceive how not long after arriving at values above $ 1000, the value started to fall quickly. At that point, after trading halted in February 2014, the value drops accelerated much more. The recession went on for around two years, with a strong recovery starting in 2016.

The individuals who ended up being more patient and stronger in the soul than the others benefited in an extremely effective 2017 for cryptocurrencies. The individuals who sold bitcoins toward the finish of a year ago for $ 19,000 and then bought them for $ 6,000 a couple of months after the fact are most likely satisfied with the consequences of their investment activities. Thus, at the hour of this writing, Bitcoin is trading at levels above $ 8000.

Similar circumstances happened with "digital silver"—the Litecoin cryptocurrency, and different resources.

Try Not to Keep Eggs in the Same Basket

This easy, effective, and simultaneous principle of risk management the board is called broadening. The risk distribution using different resources, wallets, and trading platforms balance out the benefit of the cryptocurrency portfolio and ensures against the deficiency of everything simultaneously.

Thus, you should not get hung up on any "too elegant" crypto-trade. Every one of them has its advantages and disadvantages, just as its arrangement of coins in the listing. For instance, Poloniex has a basic, intuitive interface and a genuinely rich collection of altcoins. Bitfinex has further developed investigation graphs from TradingView; however, associating with this trade can be hard for beginner brokers.

You need not get hung up on anybody's digital currency, whatever growth dynamics it might show. Remember: broadening decreases risk as well as increasing return on investment.

Purchase Less Expensive and Sell More

When people go to the regular food market, they try to purchase acceptable quality vegetables at a relatively modest cost. Most individuals don't accept the costliest items available, not focusing on their newness and quality.

Getting on the trade, numerous newcomers to trading do the inverse. At seeing a diagram of a quickly developing resource, many are trying to "jump into the last vehicle of the departing train," whatever the cost. Simultaneously, they frequently don't consider how there is consistently a downturn after development and the other way around. By and large, after purchasing "on the highs," a beginner merchant will be disappointed — the value starts to decline sharply. Quick development is full of a strong fall in the cost of a resource.

A special case for opening a trade can be if, for instance, a procedure includes exchanging on a level breakout. However, beginners should follow a simple rule from the start "bought cheaper, sold more costly." Regardless of whether you notice just this rule and stick to the elementary standards of risk management, you can get a pretty much stable benefit. It was not to no end that John Rockefeller once stated: "Purchase when blood is pouring in the city."

Numerous individuals purchase and sell by taking a look at the group and reading the trollbox. A successful trader should not follow the group, but against it, selling a resource when the main part of not very experienced players is euphoric and keep on purchasing. Purchasing is better when the hamsters are simply starting to feel excruciating annoyance. All in all, consistently purchase from pessimists and sell to optimists.

Choose Liquid Cryptocurrencies

Numerous financial specialists suggest putting aside a significant portion of the crypto portfolio for bitcoin. This isn't only a tribute for the main cryptocurrency, and there is some logic behind it. First, Bitcoin is the most un- unpredictable, consistently growing crypto resource. In other words, the first cryptocurrency normally has a higher Sharpe proportion compared with most altcoins. Besides, numerous altcoins frequently lose value over the long term (particularly about bitcoin).

At this point, the assertion that bitcoin has "crazy volatility" has lost a portion of its preceding relevance. Thus, toward the finish of a year ago, the daily volatility of bitcoin for quite a while was comparable to the range of fluctuations in oil costs and was lower than that of Twitter shares:

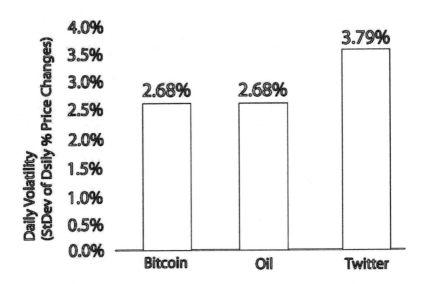

In the following graph, you can consider that to be the interest for bitcoin develops, infrastructure creates, and its value rises, the digital currency's volatility also reduces. It is presently much lower than it was a couple of years back, and it's 30-day normal rarely exceeds the 5% level:

To finally be convinced of the generally low instability of the bitcoin value, you can compare it and fluid altcoins, including Litecoin and Ethereum (ETH). Moreover, as per the top of the CME Group, Terry Duffy, the mix of cryptocurrencies with the traditional financial market will help decrease their instability.

Another argument for highly liquid cryptocurrencies is that they are less presented to the risk of scams. Thus, when in doubt, there is a serious development group behind the top altcoins. They are also more willingly remembered for the listing of the biggest cryptoexchanges, which pay, specifically, attention regarding capitalization, transaction volume, project reputation, and so on. Fluid altcoins draw in crypto investors from everywhere globally if simply because they are at the top of the ratings, for example, Coinmarketcap. Also, like this more frequently than other cryptocurrencies go over everybody's eyes.

Altcoins with high capitalization and high exchanging volume are considerably less susceptible to delisting risk and have moderately low instability. In addition to other things, such cryptocurrencies as Ethereum, DASH, Litecoin, and so on, uphold numerous multicurrency crypto wallets, which means that traders won't need to think for quite a while about where to withdraw benefit from trading (or "wrap up the fishing rods" in time in the event of a risk to the exchange scam).

It is much more improved and significantly more charming to exchange what you know something about and the achievement of which you least uncertainty. The coin of a task on which active and productive work is being done has less risk of a sharp dump.

Try Not to Trust Someone Who Says That $ 100 Is Sufficient to Get Rich on the Stock Exchange

The bigger the store, the more chances to actualize effective risk management. The less the deposit level falls on each different order, the less the risk of losing capital.

So, if you have at any rate two or three thousand dollars in your account, then you can put not 1–2, but rather twelve orders at once on different money pairs, without taking a chance with all methods. You can also place a few orders from various levels on a similar money pair.

You can figure the price movement of some coin that was purchased before for $ 100 at the exceptionally base. Then again, with a negative result of events and a sharp dump, the measure of $ 100 can rapidly evaporate. As referenced before, you shouldn't go all-in and bet everything on one "publicity" crypto resource. It is smarter to gradually capitalize benefits from little trades and develop a trading account. When the capital develops to a decent sum, then similar 1–2% of the store with a "traditionalist" 10–30% benefit from the transaction will bring substantial pay without fail.

In case you have just $ 100, don't hurry to begin trading, save a little more money, or just put it "for quite a while" in bitcoin. On the stock trade, try not only to increase "cash with cash" but also just to keep what you have.

More Trades — More Benefit

This point covers the past from various perspectives. Try not to bet everything on one coin, exchange numerous crypto resources. If the benefit is imperceptible on little orders, don't stress; think of it as valuable training.

If you truly need to motivate yourself with the first tolerable benefit from trading, trade a few sets, attempting to make small but profitable trades all the more regularly. Along these lines, with a small capital, you will build the turnover of funds, which will positively affect financial outcomes. The development of capital is, in some cases, more significant than its size.

Chapter 7: Exchange

Cryptocurrencies

You have to be in the right place at the right time. Bitcoin was worth almost nothing in 2009, but could you imagine how much it would fetch today? Exchanges like Coinbase let you buy and sell cryptocurrencies for US dollars and other major currencies. Not only does this make for a quick exchange, but it also ensures that whatever you bought can be used anywhere else in the world.

How to Exchange Cryptocurrencies?

Exchanging cryptocurrencies is an easy process. In order for it to work, your cryptocurrency must first be exchanged for another type of cryptocurrency.

Bitcoin can be exchanged for other cryptocurrencies such as Ethereum by using a bitcoin exchange. You can make a trade from USD or EUR and get 1 Ethereum for every 500 (or whatever) Bitcoin you have. This has become popular with the number of ICOs now raising funds in Ethereum than they would in Bitcoin or fiat currency like USD. Jaxx is a good example of this.

Market makers buy or sell cryptocurrency to maintain the price in line with demand and supply. They are typically a few investors who keep track of the market, and when they see demand outpacing supply, they buy or sell to manipulate the price. Some exchanges make market makers users of their platform; others do not.

There is one more way to exchange cryptocurrencies:

Exchanges are websites that let you buy and sell cryptocurrencies for cash. Many run through peer-to-peer trading (P2P) servers from all over the world and can accept anyone as a trader regardless of age, location or identity. They work like online marketplaces, matching buyers and sellers, and then handling the transactions themselves. To make this possible, exchanges use escrow services, just like when buying a house. This means that money is held in an account on your behalf until the exchange between cryptocurrency and cash is complete. Once you have made a trade it's important to withdraw your money into your bank account or wallet as quickly as possible.

Credit/Debit cards

Many cryptocurrencies' exchanges work through major credit cards like Visa and MasterCard, and you can buy Bitcoin or other cryptocurrencies with these cards. The advantage of using a credit/debit card is that it allows for easier access to funds when making an investment decision right in the middle of a rally or dip.

Instead of using a credit/debit card to buy cryptocurrencies, you can buy them with PayPal or a bank transfer. These are more secure than using a credit/debit card and will usually let you withdraw your funds any time if you don't want to hold them.

Withdrawing your funds is easy. You can use the wallet software on your smartphone, tablet or PC to send it from the exchange directly to your personal wallet. Usually, there is no extra fee and it can be done at any time within 24 hours of receiving the funds. In some cases, there are also withdrawal limits or fees for a different currency like USD (although this is rare).

Common Issues with Exchanges

Not all exchanges are equal, and some have a lower reputation than others. Therefore, it is important to understand the common issues that occur with these websites in order to avoid being scammed or hacked into giving up your cryptocurrency without your consent.

Exchange Transaction Rate

The cryptocurrency exchange rate does not change much. Therefore, most exchanges match buyers with sellers based on their deals. This means that when you want to buy a 1 ETH for 500 BTC, the seller will have given you an address (an identifier) where he wants to receive his 500 Bitcoin. He then sends the 1 Ethereum to this address, and once it is there, the seller can now claim his funds.

The main issue with exchanges is that sellers often overpay for their orders, so they are taking a loss on the trade. This leads to an imbalance in the marketplace and causes users to lose out. Accordingly, some exchanges (like Coinbase) have lower trade rates than others. As with any type of trading, you should always check the rate before making a purchase, as it could be lower than what you expected.

Exchange Blockchains

Most cryptocurrency exchanges use blockchains (distributed ledgers) that record all trades made inside their system from buyers to sellers as well as transactions between two entities. This ensures that there is no double-spending, which is one of the main benefits of cryptocurrencies. However, the major issue with exchanges is that they are sometimes hacked by cybercriminals that want to steal user funds.

In some cases, this can be prevented by using two-factor authentication (2FA) on both your exchange account and your personal email address. This prevents hackers from accessing your accounts without first providing a private key or a code that you use to access your account.

Chapter 8: Market Perspectives

Future Visions – 2022

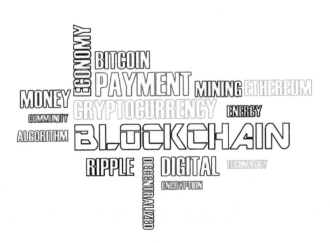

Although the recent bearish cycle has, over the last 12 months, burned a large part of the increases received by the entire sector, the prospects for the world of cryptocurrencies in 2022 and for the following years appear to be decidedly rosy. Contrary to what some might argue, there are already numerous use cases for this technology; the benefits for the community are indisputable, and it would be simply crazy to think that all this can return to the magician's cylinder and simply disappear into nothingness.

On the other hand, the banks themselves are making no secret of wanting to explore the potential offered by the blockchain, as it is becoming increasingly clear that the crypto market is here to stay. Paradoxically, not even a couple of days ago, I was reading yet another article in a well-known economic newspaper in which yet another observer on duty compared for the umpteenth time cryptocurrencies to the famous tulip bubble of 1636; all this appears ridiculous, and it is not enough to superimpose a couple of graphs to get out of the embarrassment that making such an absurd statement inevitably entails.

The bubbles, properly called, form in a reasonably short period of time, explode just as quickly, and then never reform again. We can notice such behavior in coins like BTC (or others, among those with the largest market capitalization) only if we accept to isolate what has happened in the last 15 months and ignore everything else.

If the market, on the other hand, were to prove to be capable of reacting as it did in the past, not only the major currencies appear destined to recover the losses accumulated in 2018, but it even seems plausible that they could reach new historical highs. What we really need to ask ourselves when we decide that we might be interested in investing in cryptocurrencies is whether we think that blockchain technology can gain more and more space in the coming years or not. If we stop for a moment to think about what the world will be like in 10, 15, or 20 years, then it becomes difficult to assume that blockchain and DLT technologies can simply disappear from circulation. These innovations already have all the characteristics necessary to make us understand that they are not destined to disappear at all, but that they will finally establish themselves in the long term. If we think of other technologies of the past that have ended up revolutionizing our present, we realize how much time plays a crucial role when we talk about these topics; the inventor of 3D printers, for example, initially struggled to find someone interested in that technology since it seemed to all cost too much and had few practical applications

Today, however, 3D printers have greatly revolutionized the world of industrial production. The same electric cars that have long been branded as a whim for the rich, commonly considered for many years too expensive and difficult to recharge for them to spread on the market, today are pointed to by everyone as the future of transportation.

All this seems destined to repeat itself with cryptocurrencies, a technology widely snubbed by many "experts" on duty who do not seem able to fully understand the revolutionary scope that a technology such as a blockchain carries with it. Therefore, speaking with the detractor of the moment, what we will notice is that our dear friend will inevitably "stick" to the graphs to demonstrate that the price drop is so important that it automatically decrees the death of the market; they will not hear reasons, they will not accept explanations, they will show with absolute certainty all the most disturbing features of the BTC chart, highlighting even the smallest bearish signal to take it right.

What these people have not understood is that normally, those who operate with cryptocurrencies do not care for the price in a moment X. There was a moment, for example, when BTC plunged to $2 after hitting $32. I challenge anyone today not to wish they had bought even a dozen coins for the price of $32; certainly, those who bought on that peak had very stressful months later, during which they accumulated painful losses, but those who accepted to play the game in a long-term perspective were able to subsequently take off great satisfaction.

The price, when we talk about cryptocurrencies, is not considered relevant compared to the price we will see in three years. Since what makes the difference with cryptocurrencies is first of all adoption; that is, it all depends on how many people agree to use this technology. The question we should ask ourselves before any other is if in five years the number of people using BTC will be increased or decreased. The answer to this question, based on what we have seen in the last ten years, clearly appears to be that the number of users is destined to increase. Many of the people I know myself could very well start using this technology in the next ten years.

All this does not mean, of course, that there will be no new collapses, with coins that today have an important capitalization and that could instead in a few years completely disappear from the market. But it is baseless to think that the whole market will disappear. If we look at the number of users, what we understand is that the race in recent years, which has made BTC fly up in price, appears to be a small appetizer in consideration of the still small number of people who use this technology.

A new year, a fresh perspective, and the most important step to any successful cryptocurrency investment strategy: knowing how the market will change in five years.

So, what is in store for Cryptocurrency Investing for the year 2022?

Top Cryptocurrencies (Other Than Bitcoin) Keep Rising

Cryptocurrencies that are not based upon the principles of blockchain technology will soon ditch their blockchain to join the cryptocurrency revolution. Some of these include Ethereum Classic, NEO coin, and IOTA coin.

The valuable role of decentralization is taken seriously by many developers who are currently developing decentralized applications on blockchain platforms. It's a new business model that has yet to flourish but will continue to grow over the next five years.

The demand for crypto-miners also continues to rise especially in business industries where they need computing power at their disposals such as the gaming industry and resource-limited economies such as Venezuela, Iran, Russia, China, etc.

Regulation Will Start to Tighten

The debate on regulation vs. self-regulation is not over yet. Some countries may still have their hearts and minds set on working with the United Nations to create a global framework for regulation in cryptocurrencies. The U.S government, on the other hand, will continue to be opposed to cryptocurrency regulations despite the cryptocurrency market value touching $800 billion in 2017 and $300 billion for most of 2018.

Regulation is expected to be implemented globally in the following years but it will make it difficult for blockchain startups that are not located in regulated jurisdictions such as Hong Kong, Switzerland, Singapore and Japan which attract talent from Europe, North America and China.

Bitcoin mining will continue to be difficult for hobby miners in the U.S. and Europe where energy costs are high due to higher taxes on energy production.

Bitcoin and Ethereum Move Away from Their Past Image

Bitcoin's past image of a currency that was used for criminal activities may be fading away especially among business owners who want a competitive advantage in their market by promoting bitcoin use. The new perception of bitcoin is as the new internet currency which is faster, more private and anonymous than any other digital payment service thus making it a better choice in the future.

Moreover, Ethereum which started as one of the most promising smart contract blockchain platforms will continue to experience challenges in scalability and decentralization. As a result, more of these business-ready blockchain platforms such as EOS, Cardano and NEO will emerge.

Retail Investors Continue to Explore Cryptocurrencies

Cryptocurrency investors are anticipated to be highly educated in a financial community based on social media where they can read cryptocurrency news and reviews by other investors. Cryptocurrencies are expected to be used by retailers to sell their products and services online including Amazon and eBay up until 2022 when the market is fully mature.

Blockchain Developers Remain in High Demand

Although developers are much more in demand as the blockchain market grows, the competition will also grow. Developers who have experience with C++, Java and Go will continue to be sought after despite the high level of competition for their skills.

Cryptocurrency Payment Acceptance and Adoption Will Increase

Retailers such as Dell and Microsoft which accepted bitcoin as a valid payment method since 2014 are still pioneers in cryptocurrency payment adoption among all other major online retail service providers including Amazon, eBay and Stripe. The rest of the retailers will follow suit this year up until 2022 until Bitcoin is universally accepted as one of many viable digital payment methods for goods or services purchased online.

Cryptocurrencies Will Be Regulated in Most Countries

A lot of cryptocurrencies including bitcoin and Ethereum are not regulation-free worldwide since they are centralized in a particular country. As the blockchain ecosystem matures this year, more regulations will come into force to ensure that every cryptocurrency is safe, secure and reliable for consumers who may not have much knowledge about how cryptocurrencies operate.

Cryptocurrency Exchanges Will Experience Exponential Growth

In 2017, the cryptocurrency market experienced massive exchange growth amidst the price surge of Bitcoin from $1,000 to $19,000. Bitcoin exchanges, which provide sufficient liquidity, helped bitcoin enthusiasts trade in the cryptocurrency using fiat currencies such as USD and other cryptocurrencies for the convenience of doing so. Bitcoin exchanges such as Bitfinex, Kraken and Bitstamp have received a lot of attention from bitcoin enthusiasts in 2017.

Cryptocurrency exchange businesses will experience a very significant increase this year as more bitcoins are mined by miners utilizing ASIC chips, especially those with high hashpower such as Antminer S9s.

Bitcoin Price Will Be Set to Reach $100,000 By 2022

Bitcoin has been touted as the currency that will become stable enough to grow by mining the maximum number of transactions and increase transaction speed at a faster rate than any other cryptocurrency.

In fact, when you buy Bitcoin (BTC) above $9,750, you should be alert of the possibility of the price rising up to $100,000 within 10 years.

However, if the Bitcoin price falls down too much, it will become difficult for mining and investment as the number of unconfirmed BTC transactions on the network will decrease.

Thus, when Bitcoin (BTC) reaches $100,000 in 2022, it is likely that the BTC price may drop back down to $1 or below by 2025 because there will be less transactions with more confirmed BTC transactions.

Here are some experts in cryptocurrency trading and their predictions and suggestions for 2022:

Ronnie Moas

Ronnie Moas is an independent analyst and founder of Standpoint Research which was set up in 2014 to provide investors with research reports to assist them with their cryptocurrency investments. He predicted that BTC will reach $28,000 by 2022 based on his assumptions that bitcoin will become a global store of value similar to gold in the long run.

Sam Doctor

Sam Doctor is the CEO and founder of Satoshi Studios which is a blockchain technology company that provides a consumer-friendly mobile cryptocurrency wallet app for bitcoin and Ethereum. He believes that Bitcoin price will reach $250,000 by 2022 because of the mass adoption of bitcoin as a payment method in retail stores worldwide.

Tim Draper

Tim Draper has been predicting the Bitcoin price to reach $250,000 by 2022 so he will be hopeful for these 5 years to come. He has also predicted that BTC may drop to $100 within 7 years after reaching over $250,000.

Anthony Pompliano

Anthony Pompliano is an American venture capital investor and founder of Morgan Creek Digital Assets, which has a $40 million cryptocurrency investment portfolio. He believes that Bitcoin's price will reach $50,000 by 2022 because BTC is currently being used as a store of value and as a digital gold standard in the cryptocurrency market.

Kyle Samani

Kyle Samani is the co-founder of Multicoin Capital cryptocurrency hedge fund firm which has $25 million in assets under management. He predicts that the price of BTC will reach $100,000 or more by 2022 due to its potential to be an alternative store of value in countries with weak fiat currencies such as Zimbabwe.

Ari Paul

Ari Paul is the co-founder of the hedge fund BlockTower Capital which has over $100 million in assets under management. He predicts that BTC will reach $100,000 by

2022 because it can be used to purchase goods and services online at a cheaper cost while transferring money cheaply without any third-party involvement.

Tom Lee

JPMorgan Chase's former chief equity strategist Tom Lee has predicted that Bitcoin will reach $25,000 by 2022 due to its exceptional performance in the cryptocurrency market. He said "The way I see bitcoin playing out is kind of simulating a digital version of gold. That's why I call it 'digital gold.'"

Rakesh Agrawal

Rakesh Agrawal is the co-founder of DCG, which has over $900 million in digital assets under management. He predicts that BTC will reach $250,000 by 2022 because it can be used to invest in ICO tokens at a very low cost, and more ICO token startups will be launched this year which provide a legitimate investment opportunity for investors.

Mike Novogratz

Mike Novogratz is a former hedge fund manager and founder of Galaxy Digital Capital Management which has over $200 million in assets under management. He believes that Bitcoin price will reach $50,000 by 2022 because it can be used to invest in ICO tokens at a very low cost, and more ICO token startups will be launched this year which provide a legitimate investment opportunity for investors.

John McAfee

John McAfee predicted that BTC would reach $1 million by 2020 but he is not the only person who thinks that way. Many people like him think that Bitcoin price will continue to grow despite the recent pullback from $19,500 at the time of writing.

Chapter 9: Main Characteristic of Bitcoin

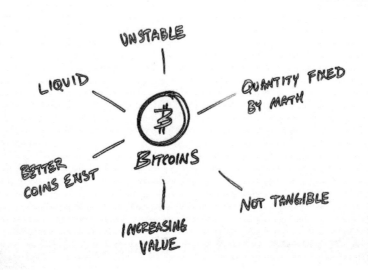

UNSTABLE

LIQUID

QUANTITY FIXED
BY MATH

BETTER
COINS EXIST

Bitcoins

NOT TANGIBLE

INCREASING
VALUE

While most of the mainstream has become familiar with Bitcoin due to its rising price, the most sought-after cryptocurrency to date has a history that extends far beyond financial value.

Bitcoin was first created in 2008 when a pseudonymous known as "Satoshi Nakamoto" released a white paper entitled "Bitcoin: A Peer-to-Peer Electronic Cash System."

The white paper's abstract notes that Bitcoin would enable a peer-to-peer version of electronic cash that would allow online payments to be sent directly between parties without third-party intermediaries. As such, the Bitcoin white paper was not focused on the value of bitcoin as a currency or investment, but rather on the potential of an entirely new financial system reliant on traditional institutions.

This new financial system would be powered by blockchain technology, a concept that was not mentioned in the Bitcoin white paper, yet serves as the underlying distributed digital ledger where all Bitcoin transactions are publicly processed and recorded.

Keep in mind, "Bitcoin" and "blockchain" are two separate things. Classifying Bitcoin and blockchain as the same is actually a common mistake made by those unfamiliar with cryptocurrency. Understanding that a blockchain network is a digital ledger that powers Bitcoin is extremely important. It's also worth noting that "Bitcoin" written with a capital "B" is used to describe the concept of Bitcoin or its network. One would refer to "bitcoin" as a unit of account with a lowercase "b."

Specifically speaking, the Bitcoin blockchain is an example of an open, permissionless blockchain network. This means that all Bitcoin transactions are transparent and traceable. A user's Bitcoin address is generated by complex cryptographic code that provides a high level of anonymity, adding a degree of privacy to bitcoin transactions. In other words, a Bitcoin address is a randomly generated string of letters and numbers.

Bitcoin as a Store of Value

Given Bitcoin's background, it's important to understand Bitcoin as a store of value, or an asset capable of retaining value over time, like gold.

Although Bitcoin came into existence in 2008, the digital asset was officially implemented the following year when Satoshi Nakamoto open-sourced the code, making it publicly available.

Bitcoin—or "BTC," which is the ticker symbol for bitcoin—initially had very little value. According to BTC Margin Trading, bitcoin's first price increase occurred during July 2010, when the valuation of a single Bitcoin went from $0.0008 to $0.08.

As of writing this book, the price of one bitcoin has reached new all-time highs, or "ATHs," exceeding $57,000. Silicon Valley venture capitalist Tim Draper has predicted that the price of bitcoin will continue to increase in the coming years, reaching an all-time high of $250,000 or more.

Yet while Bitcoin has certainly come a long way since 2009, it's clear that BTC is a very volatile asset. The BTC Margin Trading website notes that bitcoin's lowest volatility took place between September and October 2016, when the price of BTC fluctuated 0.81% in just 30 days. A Forbes article from December 2020 explains that bitcoin volatility reached 68.64% on November 30th, 2020, which was the most since June 5th, 2020.

Given this information, some of you may be wondering why bitcoin makes a great store of value. After all, Bitcoin is backed by mathematical computations. While this may be, there is a finite supply of bitcoin in circulation. Unlike fiat money, for example, the U.S. dollar, only 21 million units of bitcoin will ever be produced. This is why some crypto enthusiasts refer to bitcoin as "digital gold."

It's also important to explain how bitcoin is created in a basic sense. Each new bitcoin comes into existence through a process known as "mining." Some of you might have heard that mining a bitcoin requires a lot of energy, as energy is needed to confirm transactions.

This means that a bitcoin "miner" works to verify 1 megabyte (MB) worth of bitcoin transactions, also known as a "block." Once this block size has been confirmed, miners are rewarded in bitcoin.

The 1 MB limit was set by Satoshi Nakamoto, yet some miners have argued that the block size should be increased to accommodate more data so that the Bitcoin network can process and verify transactions faster. Bitcoin transactions currently take on average anywhere from 10 minutes to an hour to complete.

As time passes, mining rewards diminish due to events referred to as "halvings." A Bitcoin halving takes place every four years or so, occurring when 210,000 blocks have been mined. Once 210,000 blocks have been achieved, the reward given to a bitcoin miner is cut in half. For example, during the first halving event, this number was reduced to 25 BTC. The next halving cut that down to 12.5 BTC. As of writing this book, the most recent May 2020 Bitcoin halving reduced the circulation down to 6.25 BTC.

This process will continue for another 100 years or so until the final fraction of a coin has made its way into circulation.

Chapter 10: Risk Management Strategies for Bitcoin

When it comes to Bitcoin, security is going to be extremely important and something that you are always going to want to think about when you are using Bitcoin.

The banking system is going to be like a garden that has been walled in. there is not going to be much that is going to happen to the money other than you are using it each day. Your bank is going to be responsible for making sure that the money is safe whenever you put it in their institution. So, if something goes wrong, your bank is going to have a number that you are going to be able to contact so that you can get the issue fixed or a chargeback initiated. You will not need to worry about any special procedures or backups when it comes to how your money is going to be handled. The only thing that you are going to have to worry about is spending your money on what it needs to be spent on.

But this is going to be different when you are using Bitcoin. The biggest issue you are going to that a vast majority of consumers will not be used to the big shift that is going to occur when the responsibility for their money is shifted to them. This causes people to lose a lot of money even though they do not do it on purpose. It often happens because of simple mistakes that you are not going to know about until it happens. Plus, you are not going to be able to contact anyone once this error has been made so that your error can be fixed. When it comes to Bitcoin, you are going to be your own bank, and it will be on you to make sure you are taking care of the security of your Bitcoins.

Basic Rules

It is not hard to go to your local newspaper and find a story about someone losing Bitcoin because of human error, technical error, or someone steals them. But there are a lot of mistakes that you are going to be able to prevent by following some basic rules.

When you are using an online service such as the Bitcoin trade, you are going to need to be using two-factor authentication. If you are not using a two-factor authentication, then anyone is going to be able to gain access to your account and steal your coins. The only thing that they are going to need is your account password. The scary thing is that this happens a lot. Attackers are going to get your password through a wide variety of techniques that hackers use. It could take the hacker a minute to get your password, but they will eventually get it. You need to check your account management settings for the account that you are using so that you can turn on the two-factor authentication.

Tip: when you are going through and setting up your authentication, you will receive a secret key that will be tied to a QR code that you will be able to scan with your phone through a QR scanner. You are going to need to print out your code so that it is on a piece of paper that you can keep in a safe place that only you have access to. This is going to make it to where you can make sure that you are the only one who can get into your account even if you lose your phone.

Ensure that you have direct control of your Bitcoins. If you do not have a private key, then you are not going to have control of your coins. Being that coins are stored in a wallet, that wallet is also going to have a private and public key. A public key will be the address that you can give out to people so that they can send you coins. If you do not have your coins to the address which you have control of directly, then they are not going to be in your control.

When that happens, you are going to end up losing the coins forever.

You should keep regular backups of your wallet. You should not have to be told to keep backups of your wallet, but there are going to be some people out there that do not think to back up their wallet. You should make backups with any critical data that you are working with, especially when that data is going to be dealing with money. It is an innovative idea that you have a safety net that is going to allow you to place your data on a hard drive just in case you lose your computer to a natural disaster or it crashes. Once your coins are gone, they are gone forever. No one else is going to get those coins; they are going to vanish into a space that no one is going to have access to.

Tip: you are going to need to look up a hierarchical deterministic wallet that is going to enable you to perform a single-time backup. This backup is going to make it to where there are twelve to twenty-four simple human words that you are going to have to write down and place in a safe place so you can access it later. This will make it to where you are not going to be required to do regular backups.

Security Challenges with Bitcoin

There are financial regulators that are figuring out that Bitcoin is going to have some significant financial losses when it comes to the financial stability of the programs. Some of these liabilities include:

The distribution of the ledger system, which is not regulated at the moment by any financial regulator. For example, some systems are going to be more vulnerable to fraud caused by the collision of network participants.

An increase in trading delays. It has been clocked that most negotiations are going to take around forty-three minutes to complete.

There is the concern that Bitcoin could become a currency that is used by terrorists and cybercriminals, which could lead to the government shutting down Bitcoin.

There are some negotiations that have not been able to be completed, which causes them to remain unverified forever.

Chapter 11: Bitcoin versus Other Cryptocurrencies

Bitcoin has been touted as the future of currency, but a closer look at other cryptocurrencies reveals they are also promising. But which is better? Bitcoin or another cryptocurrency? Here, I will compare and contrast them to demonstrate why bitcoin might be the best option for you.

In this day and age, knowing which cryptocurrency to invest in can be a challenge for novice investors. There are so many options available and new ones coming out daily that it may seem overwhelming to know where to start. That is why it is important for investors to know how each cryptocurrency differs from one another in terms of what they offer their users. Here, I will fill you in on what is new and exciting with other cryptocurrencies and why they are worth considering to add to your investment portfolio.

As bitcoin continues its upward surge, many investors have looked for alternative ways to invest their money. Some people may have had a hard time getting into bitcoin because it can be more complicated than other forms of investment, but they don't want to miss out on the opportunity that bitcoin presents. That is why so many investors are looking at alternative cryptocurrencies that they can invest in without having to take as much risk as they would with an untested currency like bitcoin. Cryptocurrencies other than bitcoin can also be easier to buy and sell. Most of these are already accepted by multiple online marketplaces, making it easy for them to trade on the open market.

Similarities with Other Cryptocurrencies

One of the main draws of investing in an alternative cryptocurrency (altcoin) is that they have a lot in common with bitcoin. They are built on a blockchain network, meaning they are decentralized, and they are all based on open-source software. This means that anyone can see how the currency works and look through the code to see how it operates. Most of these alternative currencies use proof of work to ensure that the currency is not created without any effort by users. Proof of work requires the user to perform computational tasks in order to verify transactions occurring across the network. With proof of work, we also see another similarity between these altcoins and bitcoin: They use mining software running on dedicated computers to process transactions across their networks and keep them secure.

Algorithms Used in Other Cryptocurrencies

Another similarity these alternative cryptocurrencies share is the algorithms they use to secure their networks. Proof of work is used in both bitcoin and alternative cryptocurrencies, and it is considered one of the most difficult ways to mine a cryptocurrency. Because this method of securing the network is so difficult, it produces a fair amount of hash power which means there are more people able to mine some currencies than others. Other algorithms used by altcoins include proof of stake and proof of service.

Proof of stake does not actually require users to do any computational tasks when verifying transactions across the network, but it does require them to hold a certain amount of currency at all times for their currency network to operate.

Differences with Other Cryptocurrencies

One of the biggest differences between these alternative currencies and bitcoin is mining. Altcoins don't have the same computational power as bitcoin, and they can be more difficult to mine. Since there are not many miners working to secure these networks, there is often a lot of extra processing time devoted to confirming transactions. This can cause delays in transaction times, which means day-to-day commerce may not be feasible on a large scale with these altcoins.

Another difference between these altcoins and bitcoin is the amount of currency being created each year. Bitcoin has a hard cap for the number of bitcoins that will ever be created, meaning there will never be more than 21 million bitcoins available. With alternative cryptocurrencies, there is no hard cap and every year, more currency is created than the earlier year. For example, in 2017, there were 4.2 billion bitcoins in existence, but in 2020, this number will only be 3.6 billion.

Chapter 12: Identify Top-Performing Cryptocurrencies

Since bitcoin has been introduced, numerous advanced monetary forms enter the market. Various elective cryptographic types of cash or altcoins have been dispatched – following the accomplishment of Bitcoin, and they have formed into 700 in number. Some are being sold more affordable than Bitcoin, while some will overall be more open than Bitcoin. In this piece of the book – 12 of the most standard cryptographic types of cash will be told. Maybe you recently found out about Bitcoin and have some mysterious things on how its capacities, yet this time you will enter the universe of Cryptocurrency and appreciate what are the enthusiastic financial norms inside cryptographic cash.

Bitcoin

Bitcoin is the first and most standard cryptographic cash on earth, some don't think about its world yet it truly stays as a general portion system. Bitcoin has no bank; honestly, it relies upon mathematical affirmations. Similarly, with the development of email, no one has control over the Bitcoin plan. Undoubtedly, even the get-together and individual behind it really stay a secret, simply the pen name Nakamoto is has been familiar with the general population.

Bitcoin can be used in purchasing stock, sending money, travel setting up for the web, and buying automated things – by this, trades are made with no centerman, which implies no banks are needed in any way, shape or form.

Ethereum

In 2011 a computer programmer named Vitalik Buterin from Toronto initially built up an interest in Bitcoin. Buterin, a 19-year-old at the time, helped establish the online news website Bitcoin Magazine and created some articles on the world of cryptocurrencies. In the year 2013 Buterin have conveyed the white paper. Which depicts an elective stage planned for any decentralized application a designer needs to fabricate. The structure was then called Ethereum, similarly, like Bitcoin, Ethereum is in like manner a scattered public blockchain network. Even though there is some specific differentiation between the two cryptographic cash because, in Ethereum, backhoes work to secure Ether instead of mining. Ether is a digit of code that allows the program or application to run—no one has Ethereum, nonetheless, its structure supporting its ability isn't free. Not at all like Bitcoin, Ether doesn't have a cap limit, in fact, 13 million Ether are mined each year.

To buy an Ether, you need to find it on the web or a person who has it and at the same time needs to trade it for cash. There is also another decision in case you need to have an Ether accessible, some endeavor to purchase a bitcoin first from trusted bitcoin exchangers by then trade it for Ethereum.

Litecoin

This computerized money is similarly delivered by mining; it was made by Google's past planner Charles Lee in October 2011. Litecoin is made to improve the speed of mining from the confined season of 10 minutes to 2.5 minutes while delivering a square. The said online money has faster trade than bitcoin because it uses "content computation," which favors a colossal proportion of quick RAM that is the explanation content is being known as the 'memory troublesome issue'. Similarly, like Bitcoin, Litecoin has moreover its limitation of 84 million coins and a market cap of $ 540, 274,528.26.

- Litecoin can manage a high volume of trades
- Reduces twofold spending attack
- Fast confirmation especially for merchants

Ripple

What is Ripple? Is Ripple equivalent to Bitcoin? Taking everything into account, it's a significant NO. Wave is a cash exchange and repayment network that uses a run-of-the-mill record supervised by an association and is endorsed by free laborers. The Ripple Labs, an overall money trade firm that is past OpenCoin, was assisted with building up by CEO Chris Larsen and CTO Jed McCaleb who is a lot of ground in mechanized cash. Jed McCaleb is at present managing the prevailing piece of Bitcoin trades on the planet. While Larsen used to be the excellent ally of the cash-related association E-LOAN—the rest of the Ripple designs moreover think about Bitcoin. Wave relies upon a shared public database—a significant differentiation with Bitcoin that is made by energy and handling raised proof of work. Wave is doesn't use blockchain advancement, the association's goal is to keep the money streaming openly.

Dash

Run was first dispatched as Xcoin, by then changed its name into Darkcoin, and in 2015 the Darkcoin has been rebranded into Dash, which is as of now the 6th most prominent Cryptocurrency on earth. Run is a dispersed Cryptocurrency that was forked out from Bitcoin bringing into faster and more private trades. Run is the first to have a decentralized blockchain organization system, similarly as various computerized types of cash Dash is moreover endeavoring to comprehend a part of Bitcoin's weights. It gives speedier trades and more obscure help to its customers. Run trades are made inside 4 seconds, far from the trade pattern of Bitcoin, which regularly requires 10 minutes to wrap up. Run is moreover acquired by mining, similarly to Bitcoin.

Monero

Monero is advanced money that has the most mystery when it goes to its trades made. It is a secured and untraceable money system that uses an exceptional kind of cryptography for a 100% unlikeable trade. Monero gets a critical degree of unmistakable quality on account of its security orchestrated features after it was dispatched in 2014. The mining cycle used by Monero relies upon Egalitarian thought.

IOTA

The cryptographic cash IOTA is a ton not exactly equivalent to the predominant part of online financial guidelines—it's planned for machine yet can't be mined. Molecule signifies 'Web of Things Application, it keeps an eye on the adaptability issues of blockchain and the trade expenses at the same time by discarding the square and chain. The specialists are to simply check two past trades, to submit them to the IOTA record. The total adaptability of these coins is fixed into 2,779,530,283,277,761 coins. Tractors don't have to control the association, and there is no central record for this advanced money.

Zcash

Money is dispatched by Roger Ver, Barry Seibert, and the Pantera Capital on October 28, 2016. Zcash is a decentralized and open-source computerized cash, it uses a remarkable ensured about an association called 'zk-snark.' This outstanding component allows the association to keep up and secure the record without uncovering the entireties in each trade.

Stellar

Jed McCaleb the superb ally of Ripple is the creator of this Stellar Cryptocurrency, which is similarly a portion development. Wonderful is almost comparable to the following portion developments – a decentralized laborer runs the association with a spread record that is invigorated every 2-5 seconds. It doesn't simply depend upon diggers, rather it uses Federated Byzantine Agreement (FBA) Algorithm, which helps for a speedier trade.

NEM

NEM is dispatched on March 31, 2015, as a common Cryptocurrency and blockchain stage, written in Java and C++ programming language. NEM signifies 'New Economy Movement', not at all like most advanced monetary standards NEM has its own arrangement figuring. This can hinder attacks against the association and all the exchanges made. NEM intends to make a sharp asset blockchain, which can perform significant excess jobs that needs to be done.

NEO

NEO is the principal decentralized and open-source Cryptocurrency in China, which was set up by Da Hongfei. Neo is a Cryptocurrency and blockchain stage at the same time; it was dispatched in 2014 as 'Antshares' and debranded last June 2017 as 'NEO'. Neo can maintain 10,000 trades for each second—using the Byzantine Fault Tolerance (Daft) arrangement framework.

TRON

This cryptographic cash was first present on September 9, 2017, and was set up by the TRON Foundation—a non-advantage relationship from Singapore. Tron is in like manner a decentralized, freely delivered advanced money, anyway has a component of an application. Tron's development is a storeroom that grants customers access to content taking all things together in parts of the world, with no assistance from Google Play Store. It furthermore allows content creators to obtain from sharing their substance.

Chapter 13: NFT

Non-Fungible Token

A non-fungible token, also as NFT, is a basic unit of information on a record-holding called a blockchain. Where each NFT can be addressed as a one-of-a-kind advanced thing, and subsequently, they may not be exchangeable. NFTs can also be advanced address documents like sound, video, workmanship, and type varying incentive work.

While the computerized records themselves are endlessly reproducible, the NFTs addressing them are followed on their fundamental blockchains and furnish purchasers with evidence of ownership.

The normal blockchains, for example, Ethereum, Bit-coin Cash, Flow, and so on each have their symbolic guidelines to characterize their utilization of NFTs.

NFTs can be utilized to commodity computerized manifestations, like advanced workmanship, computer game things, and music documents. Admittance to any duplicate of the first document, nonetheless, isn't limited to the proprietor of the token.

The primary NFTs were Ethereum-based and showed up around 2015. Expanded revenue on the lookout for NFTs has brought about an expanded hypothesis, as similar financial backers who had recently estimated on digital currencies started exchanging NFTs at incredibly expanding volumes.

NFTs generally run on a proof-of-work blockchain, which is less energy proficient than a proof-of-stake blockchain, which has brought about some analysis of the carbon impression for NFT exchanges.

In 2014, the Counterparty convention was delivered as an extra "shaded coin" layer on top of the Bitcoin blockchain, utilizing metadata in the Bit-coin record to make another record. In November 2014, Rob Myers delivered 100 (fungible) units of non-distinct cash named MY SOUL on both Counterparties and Doge party (a Counterparty clone based on top of Dogecoin), which could be viewed as creative expression.

It gives the idea that, at dispatch, the Counterparty convention spec empowered the printing of a hued coin with a solitary, non-detachable unit. A particularly single-unit coin could be freely characterized as a pointer NFT to some off-chain resource and would have hypothetically been traded tradable too, however, no proof that this printing happened in this period has yet surfaced.

The originally referred to genuine NFTs were delivered as a feature of Ethereal, a 33-by-33 3D guide of 457 available and tradable hexagonal tiles whereupon little constructions can be worked with Lego-like blocks. Adaptation 1.0, with inward exchanging instruments that may have things that include the remark of earning non-useful, was sent to the Ethereum fundamental net on October 21st, 2015. Form 1.1, delivered on Oct 29th, rejected these inner exchanging capacities altogether for a two-line "pet owner" work executable exclusively by the current tile owner. This change empowered outside exchanging and subsequently made the tiles trade tradable however trades didn't yet exist. After two days on October 31st, Ethereal variant 1.2 was sent with bug fixes, for example, keeping cash from being gulped when an exchange endeavor to purchase a generally possessed tile from the agreement. This adaptation was introduced at Devcon 1, the Ethereum Foundation's first completely open gathering, by Etheria's maker Cyrus Adkisson on November 13, 2015, in London, which includes the main tradable blockchain client-produced content and is considered "official" by the maker.

While the Etheria project was noticed by the local area designer in his shipment, virtually all tiles were not purchased for over 5 years, until 2021, when a strong interest in NFTs began a local area-wide search for notable NFTs.

On March 13, 2021, the excess 359 tiles of the "official" Ethereal 1.2 agreement were bought from the blockchain. The following day, the inquiry drove purchasers to Version, and all its leftover 409 tiles were likewise gobbled up by purchasers theorizing that it addresses the first-historically speaking trade tradable NFT shrewd contract, regardless of its maker's demand that v1.2 is "official."

NFT Projects

In June 2017, Crypto Punks were delivered on the Ethereum blockchain by American studio Larva Labs, a two-man group comprising Matt Hall and John Watkinson. Then, Moon Cat Rescue turned into the third non-fungible symbolic undertaking, which flew under the radar, yet in the long run took off on March 12, 2021.

At the end of 2017, another task called Crypto Kitties was delivered and went viral and in this line raised an investment of $12.5 million.

In 2018, Rare Bits, an NFT commercial center, and trade raised a $6 million investment. [39] Gnome dex, a collectible cards game stage made conceivable by NFTs, raised an $800,000 seed round. Decentraland, a blockchain-based virtual world, brought $26 million up in an underlying currency offering and had a $20 million inward economy as of September 2018.

Starting in 2019, Nike holds a patent for its blockchain-based NFT-shoes called 'Crypto Kicks'.

Smart Labs built up the Flow confirmation of-stake blockchain. Using it, in association with the NBA, they dispatched a beta form of their NBA Top Shot collectible and tradable NFT-based application in the main portion of 2020, which they had been chipping away at since 2018 it sells tokens in packs that they say contain media and information crushed together

01-October, 2020, it was finally declared that who want to lefts the beta and want to open all fans. As of Feb 28, 2021, an announcement was made by Dapper Lab that more NBA Top shot collectibles and NFTs are tradable. Which based on the main portion of that of 2020? Which, they chipping away had been since 2018. The token sales in packs that say media contain and together information was crushed.

What Is NFT, and Why It Is Important in the Crypto World

Like actual cash, cryptocurrency forms of money are fungible, i.e., they can be exchanged or traded, one for another. For instance, one Bit-coin is consistently equivalent in worth to another Bit-coin. Essentially, a solitary unit of Ether is consistently equivalent to another unit. This fungibility trademark makes cryptocurrency forms of money reasonable for use as a protected vehicle of exchange in the advanced economy.

NFTs move the crypto worldview by making every symbolic special and indispensable, consequently making it unthinkable for one non-fungible token to be equivalent to another. They are computerized portrayals of resources and have been compared to advance international IDs because every token contains a remarkable, non-adaptable character to recognize it from different tokens.

They are additionally extensible, which means you can join one NFT with another to "breed" a third, one-of-a-kind NFT.

Very much like Bit-coin, NFTs additionally contain possession subtleties for simply distinguishing proof and move between token holders. Owners can also add metadata or asset-identifying features to NFTs.

For example, tokens referring to coffee beans can be called a sensible trade. Alternatively, professionals can be login to their machine-made art with their publication in the metadata.

NFTs advanced from the ERC-721 norm. Created by a portion of similar individuals answerable for the ERC-20 brilliant agreement, ERC-721 characterizes the base interface —possession subtleties, security, and metadata— needed for the trade and circulation of gaming tokens. The ERC-1155 standard takes the idea further by lessening the exchange and capacity costs needed for NFTs and bunching numerous kinds of non-fungible tokens into a solitary agreement.

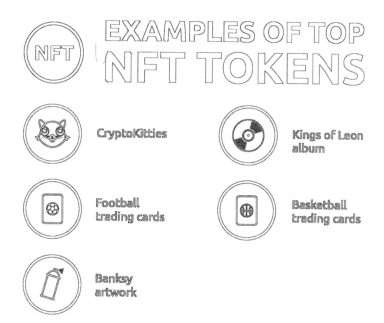

Maybe the most well-known use case for NFTs is that of CryptoKitties. Dispatched in November 2017, CryptoKitties are computerized portrayals of felines with novel IDs on Ethereum's blockchain. Every kitty is interesting and has a cost in ether.

They replicate among themselves and produce new posterity, which has various credits and valuations when contrasted with their folks. Inside a couple of brief a long time of being dispatched, CryptoKitties piled up a fan base that burned through $20 million worth of ether buying, taking care of, and sustaining them. A few aficionados even spent upwards of $100,000 on the exertion.

While the CryptoKitties use case may sound minor, succeeding ones have more genuine business suggestions. For instance, NFTs have been utilized in private value exchanges just as land bargains. One of the ramifications of empowering various sorts of tokens in an agreement is the capacity to give escrow to various kinds of NFTs, from fine art to land, into a solitary monetary exchange.

Non-fungible tokens, or NFTs, are more smoking than a grill in May at this moment. This is what they are, and why the world has gone NFT-psycho in the preceding month.

NFTs, From Fine Art to Land

Fungible (descriptive word): Replaceable by another indistinguishable thing; commonly exchangeable.

For every one of their disparities, that Rs 100 note in your pocket and a solitary bit-coin token offer something significant. They are the same as some other Rs 100 note or bit-coin. They were planned, as all monetary standards are, to be commonly compatible.

NFTs, then again, is a class of digital currency resources wherein everything, or token is exceptional. This makes them futile as money, yet very valuable for different things.

For example, indeed, making computerized workmanship, for one.

And because this is sparkling innovation, and we're individuals, and this is the web, NFTs originally went standard as—you got it—felines.

Created in October 2017, Crypto Kitties is a virtual game that permits players to embrace, raise and exchange virtual felines.

From its site: "Crypto Kitties is one of the world's first blockchain games. 'Blockchain' is the innovation that makes things like bit-coin conceivable. While Crypto Kitties is not computerized cash, it offers similar security: each Crypto Kitty is stand-out and 100% claimed by you. It can't be recreated, removed, or annihilated."

So that is it? Virtual felines? Not exactly. A ton has occurred since, particularly in the earlier month, during which NFTs have abandoned the nicest of specialty pursuits into a straight-up worldwide fixation.

The Big Bang: On Feb. 15, 2021, the revered Christies, established in 1766, turned into the principal significant sales management firm to report intends to sell a simply advanced piece of workmanship—an NFT made by computerized craftsman Mike Winkelmann, also known as Beeple.

Called every day-The First 5000, it includes, as the name proposes.

NFT Financial Traders Using Crypto

Sales of NFTs, or non-fungible tokens, have detonated lately, yet numerous purchasers and dealers aren't likely mindful of duty rules overseeing these exchanges.

Those who use digital currency to purchase NFTs could confront capital increase charges.

The IRS expresses that "on the off chance that you trade virtual money held as a capital resource for other property, including for products or virtual cash, you will perceive a capital addition or misfortune."

Sales of NFTs, or non-fungible tokens, have detonated as of late, besting $500 million every 2021. Alongside the offer of the $69 million Belle NFT named "Every day's: The First 5,000 Days" at Christie's last week, and the $3 million NFT tennis shoes, NFTs of everything from NBA feature recordings to Jack Dorsey tweets have made an immense new market of blockchain-based advanced resources for the purchase and sell.

Yet, specialists of cryptocurrency say about purchasers and vendors are not likely mindful of revenue internal services decided to charge that might because of issues down the road for them. The cost for them is a major lump of the benefits that they received. It may include the precarious possibility duty on any individual who wants to utilize their profoundly esteemed digital currency to buy the NFTs, which specialists say is most deals in NFTs.

"People's information on this assessment in the U.S. is poor," said Shehan Chandrasekera, head of expense technique at Coin Tracker, a stage for following crypto portfolios and duties. "I simply don't think individuals think about it."

At issue is ongoing IRS direction on utilizing digital currencies to purchase a resource, including an NFT. As a component of its guideline known as "demeanor of resources," the IRS expresses that "if you trade virtual money held as a capital resource for other property, including for merchandise or another virtual cash, you will perceive a capital increase or misfortune."

Chandrasekera said this has significant ramifications for the NFT furor, which is to a great extent being powered by gatherers utilizing bit-coin or ether to purchase NFTs. For example, if someone were to buy a unit of ether for $ 100 in 2018, it would currently be worth around $ 1,700. If you have any chance of using that unit of ether to buy a $ 1,700 NFT, they might agree not to pay tax on the ether as they basically use it to buy a decent or administrative service.

But under the IRS controls, the ether is a capital resource, not cash. So, the holder would need to pay the charge on the addition of $1,600 as a component of the NFT buy since the demonstration of trading it for another resource considers a deal or "attitude." So, they would owe the IRS — expecting a top capital increase pace of 20%—an expense of $320. They may likewise owe state charges since numerous states like New York and California charge capital additions as pay. (The standards around extra deal charges in each state for NFTs are less clear.)

"You're not spending money, you're spending a valued resource," Chandrasekera said. "So, spending it makes an available occasion."

Chapter 14: Cryptoart

What is Cryptoart?

Cryptoart refers to the process of creating a permanent and exclusive digital signature on a digital file of an artwork (tokenizing) and then transferring it to a virtual block to preserve the artwork's scarcity.

As the token holder, you have the option of keeping, selling or gifting your artworks to other potential buyers, but the original file of your artwork remains yours, safely helmed within your block.

Cryptoart can address issues in the digital art environment by using this newly developed technology: by using blockchain, artists can ensure the scarcity of the artwork they tokenize, preventing art theft and forgeries; the technology can also allow faster and more secure transactions between clients and creators.

The world's understanding of visual art is evolving. It's no wonder that as the world becomes more digital, the way we make, consume, and collect art has changed as well.

The emergence of rare digital art, also known as cryptoart, which combines technology and art to create a new market and medium, has exemplified this paradigm shift in the art world.

The unusual digital art market has sold over $7 million in sales since its launch in 2017 (give or take), with explosive growth in recent months. This movement has spawned online galleries and marketplaces, such as our MakersPlace, that use blockchain technology to secure, authenticate and apply scarcity to digital artworks, which was precedingly impossible.

Art's Progress

Since the beginning of time, human beings have valued beauty and visual stimulation. Indeed, paleoanthropologists claim that our aesthetic instincts were a core characteristic of humanism in our forefathers, dating back well before the Homo sapiens species we now belong to.

For millennia, our universal culture has been characterized by a love of beauty, also known as art. In all of its forms, art has inspired and represented religion, politics, and much more in culture. Across cultures, many scholars attribute the roots of art collecting to religion.

Visual art commissions were most often undertaken by religious figures and organizations in the (relatively) early days of human civilization, with "art collections" mostly housed in places of worship. Visual arts gradually spread through all facets of human culture, giving rise to the "art patron," who gathered purely for the love of art (or the hope of later profit).

The vast majority of the world's population now engages in some kind of art patronage, whether it's personal collecting or viewing the collections of various art institutions worldwide. The world we live in today is nothing like it was a few decades ago. Technology has a tremendous influence on every aspect of our lives.

It would be illogical to leave art out of this evolution. Our ever-evolving encounters with art have culminated in a paradigm shift that has ushered in the next phase of art consumption: the rare digital art revolution, which brings with it a slew of new possibilities for artists and art lovers.

Principles and Terminology of Cryptoart

We assume that one of the internet's most valuable industries will be fueled by boundary-pushing and verifiably scarce digital works over the next decade. Cryptoart is a natural progression from the age-old question, "What is art?"

On the other hand, art takes on a more expansive role in a natively interactive medium, intersecting with decentralized finance, virtual worlds, and social experience.

To grasp the potential of cryptoart, it's necessary to place it in the sense of earlier art movements. Legacy art movements can be seen as responses to (1) earlier art movements, and (2) related cultural phenomena across history.

In the mid-nineteenth century, if you asked "what is art," you would answer realism: the more accurate and practical the art, the better. However, this movement evolved into impressionism.

Artists responded to accuracy by experimenting with conceptual concepts and expressionism and abstract expressionism. Artists manipulated their work for effect, concentrating more on emotional intensity than a literal depiction. (Please note that we are condensing 20,000 Ph.D.

dissertations into sixty terms and we recognize that art history is much more complex and nuanced.)

The type of art piece may also be ephemeral and intangible, depending on the cultural context and the artist's viewpoint of street art or performance art.

Although it's impossible to pinpoint an art movement's period while it's occurring, we do know that in modern history, technological developments have had a greater impact on artistic speech.

The artistic work we create and share with the world has become increasingly digitized as our lives have become increasingly digitized. Although "digital" art has been around for nearly four decades, many artists have not reaped the same financial rewards as those who create physical works.

One of the reasons is that most monetization capacity around artistic expression has been predicated on the physical scarcity that moves with art throughout history. A one-time live performance artwork cannot be purchased and resold in the same way Cézanne's The Card Players or

Damien Hirst's formaldehyde shark can be purchased and resold for $250 million and $12 million, respectively.

The limitations of temporary art production have also afflicted the digital world. Still, for the opposite reason: the features of a digital original can be perfectly replicated and exchanged. Digital GIFs and MP3s are quickly copied without attribution or reference to the author. There hasn't been a native way to build and monitor digital scarcity that moves with innovative digital property outside legal compliance.

Bitcoin has shown that digital scarcity is possible in the field of money over the last decade. BTC has developed into a commodity money store of value, with a market capitalization of over $100 billion as of this writing.

Ethereum took the idea of digital scarcity beyond commodity currency, allowing any digital good (music, 3D objects files, GIFs, memes) to be made scarce programmatically. These objects are also one-of-a-kind or non-fungible in nature. CoinFund's Jake Brukhman wrote an excellent piece about this concept earlier this week.

ERC 721 is an Ethereum standard interface for non-fungible tokens (i.e., tokens with a unique identifier). We can see any address where it has ever been stored, bid on, or moved, to put it another way, flawless provenance.

We must not confuse an object's reproductive capabilities with its underlying rights regarding blockchain-based art today. The developer of a digital work will imbue it with programmatic scarcity, which is a first step toward demonstrating authenticity.

Property lawyers (including IP lawyers) also think of property rights as a "bundle of rights," similar to how a bundle of sticks is thought of. For a property's lifecycle, all of the different sticks in the package (e.g., use rights, leasing rights, publishing rights, film rights, distribution rights, and so on) may be owned by one person, many people in various combinations.

The first building block for digital artists to begin enjoying property rights and transferring those different rights for their sovereign digital creations is a token's verifiable scarcity over standards like ERC 721. ERC 1155 is based on this concept, allowing owners to establish licenses and model each exclusive right granted by the Copyright Act. Teams like Open Law are expected to continue to innovate in this field.

As a result, cryptoart would be as subversive to conventional art as Bitcoin has been to traditional finance. BTC and cryptoart are more similar than dissimilar, as we'll see below.

Art is a common means of storing value in today's society. Sales of traditional fine art hit $64 billion in 2019 and the overall value of traditional fine art is estimated to be over $3 trillion, but these estimates just scratch the surface.

The wealthiest segment of society powers a significant portion of the existing art market. Still, as cryptoart merges with the markets for collectibles, games, and investments, it promises to introduce a new wave of market investors into art.

Measuring the demand for cryptoart using only data from passengers on private jets is close to measuring the aggregate market for air travel using only data from passengers on private jets.

Chapter 15: Altcoin

Altcoins are the "not-bitcoins" and the "I have to prove myself that I am worth the attention" kind of coins or tokens. But you must have known that already.

How much do you think life will bring to your table when you are already doubtful?

There are so many people who still believe that some things do not count, it does not matter to them because they are not in that line of business or something, and thereby giving "why exactly should I care?" kind of attitude to every other thing.

Your environment includes the activities that are going on online or offline too. The talks about the cryptocurrencies good enough to invest in are part of the tiny details of all the activities in your environment.

I am not saying that, if you do not invest in a digital asset such as a cryptocurrency or even cryptocurrencies, you cannot be in a better investment. There are other things going on that you can pick from and then invest in.

But a digital asset like a cryptocurrency is a good investment that you can be sure that you are definitely getting your high returns from it. You can actually save for your retirement, reach any financial goal you have set for yourself, support others, or even expand your business as you are earning your high returns from your Cryptocurrency investment. If you invest in not just any cryptocurrency but "the cryptocurrencies," you are absolutely not wasting your money but, you are grooming your money through "the cryptocurrencies."

Listen, I am not telling you or anybody else that it is a must to start investing in cryptocurrencies neither am I saying that if you do not invest in it, you cannot reach your financial goal or have financial stability, expand your business, save towards retirement and so on. I am a preacher of paths, and when I see potentials in any path, I call the people's attention to such a path. Now, it is a digital path. I have seen much potentials that will be even more as we proceed more into the year.

I know that there is a saying in the Bible that "do not join multitude," but sometimes, multitudes are the ones to bring you into what can help you stand financially. Whenever you see the multitude going one-way, pay attention first and critically observe that way or place, they are going and let the Spirit tell you if the multitude going that way is a sign or not. I know one thing for sure, you cannot see people running and you will not become suddenly cautious of the situation at hand that will surely make you ask that "what is going on?"

I speak not against anything; I have to clear the air on that again. It is a very sensitive period to not care about the people's beliefs. I meant not even the slightest disregard or disrespect.

Having said all that, I will make a list of the cryptocurrencies that worth your investments. In addition to this, from an economist's angle or view, an investment happens then that is said to be an investment. But, whenever a loss is encountered, then people tend to call or term or tag it as a bad investment.

So, what about its meaning when it comes to finance?

Without further talk about it, things or something that can give or make the future production in the economy is the summary of it all.

Investment does not just come into play for man, it came as a result of man's desire to be successful in life. He needs to grow his wealth and also having an additional income.

He knows that the only way out is to invest to protect and add more to his present and future long-term financial security. You should have in mind that any money generated or gotten from your investments can guarantee you financial security and income if managed well.

Now I am suggesting a place you can actually put your money and get your high returns as an investor. The high market capitalization alone should give you a sense of confidence.

In an attempt to help you know the particular digital assets (cryptocurrency) that are so sure to make you have the kind of income you want to be getting, I have put it upon myself to help you know them and you can then decide to go with anyone or two or more of them.

I want you to know that at this particular junction, I am only talking about the top altcoins that you can put your money in.

And, I have explained the meaning of an altcoin, but if you do not know where the value of the altcoin stand, I will tell you that where they stand is where we are going to pick our favorites from as per the market capitalization and trading volume.

It is either you want to invest in it or you want to trade with it, either way, you will be in the system and the game already started from there. The goal is to do either of the two to increase what you put in it.

The altcoins are doing pretty well in the market but you know things will always be better than another one. The same goes for these digital assets too, as some are performing far too well than others.

It is now based on how to tell which particular ones will be outstanding and really

Without wasting time anymore, let us go into the list of the altcoins that have placed themselves at the top and have gained a lot of attention from people all around the world.

Chapter 16: Ethereum

Ethereum has become the most prominent and popular name within the long list of altcoins and is behind the only bitcoin in the size of its market cap. Unlike bitcoin, though, there are two sides to Ethereum. There's the startup firm that's building a business around blockchain technology. There's also ether, the token that's used to conduct business within the Ethereum network and the currency you purchase when buying into the name.

Ethereum's Origin

Ethereum is the brainchild of Vitalik Buterin and was developed as a tool to provide developers with a way to create decentralized applications on the blockchain, launching in 2015. To pay for services, such as creating an agreement with a developer to build such an application, others are used.

Buterin's primary breakthrough was the development of smart contracts. These allow two parties to agree to terms, without the requirement of a third party to confirm the results. Conditions are set by both parties on the blockchain, which allows the payer to track the efforts of the payee, without having to fund services that the developer doesn't provide. Once both parties agree to a set of services, the blockchain checks each box as the developer reaches each benchmark. It doesn't require a third party to watch over the transaction and the developer doesn't have to be concerned that the client might stiff them on pay, once the work is completed. It's beneficial to both parties because it removes the need for trust within the arrangement. Remember, when Satoshi Nakamoto developed his blockchain thesis, it hinged on removing the need for this trust from the financial agreement, which allowed bitcoin to become viable. Buterin advanced the theory, providing a way to remove trust from the contractual portion of an arrangement as well.

For reasons that may be obvious to you, this smart contract has immense potential in the business world. Ethereum is the platform that developers can use to build applications while also using these smart contract concepts.

Business Interest Blossoms

Unlike most other crypto names on the market, companies have moved quickly in developing their understanding and building potential use cases for Ethereum's technology. The

Enterprise Ethereum Alliance launched in 2017 so companies could come together to deliberate the possibilities of the technology and develop best practices for conducting business on the platform. It's filled with heavy-hitters, including representatives on the board from Microsoft, Accenture, Intel, and J.P. Morgan.

Ethereum's appeal stretches to the largest corporate entities because this blockchain contract could have an immense impact on compliance efforts. Imagine if a company could simply place within the blockchain all the rules and checkpoints a transaction must go through, from a compliance standpoint, trusting the technology to handle the checking and confirmation. It has the potential to reduce the complexity of the compliance needs, from manpower to the paper required to assuage government and accounting oversight.

How It's Used Now

Startups and legacy organizations are starting to adopt the Ethereum blockchain for a number of different reasons, both for business and consumer purposes. It has served as a platform for startups to launch new services. These adaptations by startups include developing a predictions market, which allows you to earn money by betting on the results of future events, including the fluctuations of individual stocks. JAAK wants to use the Ethereum platform to provide music rights holders with a fluid and decentralized way that will allow consumers and businesses to play and have access to music without a need for a label to coordinate the sale. And there's Transactive Grid, which allows energy contract holders to sell energy rights to third parties.

Then What's Ether?

Ether is what Ethereum built to conduct transactions on the blockchain and to raise ICO funds. When referring to the cryptocurrency, you will hear experts and analysts use ether and Ethereum interchangeably; Ethereum the company has become synonymous with ether the cryptocurrency. But by owning ether, you're not in some way owning the company that is operating smart contract technology. You're linked since what improves the adoption of Ethereum will also improve the transaction rates of ether.

What Makes Ether Unique?

In order for the cryptocurrency market to become a standard, one of two scenarios must play out. Either one cryptocurrency becomes the ultimate cryptocurrency, ensuring all other iterations or designs are obsolete. In this scenario, many cryptocurrency investors could find themselves disappointed with their investments, unless it's clear early on in this hypothetical coin's rise that it will become the preeminent name in the space or if it's like bitcoin, where there's already millions invested in the name.

The other scenario is that while one coin rises to become prominent—kind of like bitcoin today—there's a whole plethora of other names that are used for specific purposes and needs. It's in this scenario where ether really shines (unless it would somehow become that crypto to thwart all cryptos in the future). The reason it has proven to function well under these circumstances is that the company behind the crypto has shown itself to offer real value to businesses. This provides Ethereum with a layer of protection against the normal concerns that face startups, such as not enough demand for the product. Instead, you have a coin that has become the second largest name in the space because its use is growing through the improvement of the company. This means there's a legitimate demand for the coin (even if it remains small) that can help justify the rise it has seen over the past two years, even with the struggles in 2018.

A Corporate Darling

Cryptos don't just benefit from blockchain adoption. There are plenty of companies, like Walmart for example, that have built internal blockchains to help them track movements of supplies. They don't require a cryptocurrency to use this sort of blockchain. Instead, for cryptos to flourish, adoption of the blockchain would also require the use of the blockchain's crypto that the companies have developed. It means actual financial transactions are required on the blockchain to make it worthwhile, from an investor's perspective. And the larger the transactions, the stronger the crypto will become.

That's the sweet spot that Ethereum currently sits in. It has become the blockchain for business-to-business transactions, which creates a layer of security when evaluating the safety of the coin. As long as businesses see a need for the platform, they will continue to use it. And the stronger the businesses that enter the platform, the more reliable those transactions and rates will become. All of this will help the value of ether, since it would see incremental increases in its transaction rate, as the price rises. That's allowing for a legitimate upward movement in demand, which creates a reliable price increase.

Despite ether's early popularity, it hasn't reached that level of reliability. When companies like Microsoft and J.P. Morgan see a use for the blockchain, though, it's a positive sign that they also see potential in the currency used to transact on that chain.

The Value within the Internet of Things

An industry that has seen significant value in Ethereum's blockchain in the early days of development is within the Internet of Things (IOT). Since more devices have become connected via the Internet, using the Ethereum platform has proven a powerful way to ensure they remain functioning in unison.

As researchers at the Heider College of Business at Creighton University point out in a working paper on the values of bitcoin and Ethereum, a house connected to the

Ethereum network could unlock doors for an apartment the moment it's rented by a new tenant. "Ethereum has a better technological foundation than Bitcoin does to take advantage of these [IOT] needs," write the authors Julianne Harm, Josh Obregon, and Josh Stubbendick.

Its Contracts Were First

There's nothing like being the first to market with an idea like Ethereum was in the creation of smart contracts. The ability for it to join the blockchain movement, by reshaping the movement as it did, creates armor for the company. Since the founder of smart contracts, Buterin, remains at the company, it also gives businesses comfort that the mind behind the firm is engaged in the business.

Now other blockchain firms are offering smart contracts similar to Ethereum's offerings. With that comes a layer of competition. But because Ethereum introduced the concept and provided the initial framework, it prevents it from getting lost in the shuffle, at least for now. Of course, another tool could come along, blowing away Ethereum's offerings and therefore rendering ether obsolete. But that isn't likely in the short term, and, therefore, allows for some runway in the ether investment.

It's Easier to Mine Blocks

Unlike bitcoin, new ether blocks don't have nearly the hurdle to mine new coins. It's this way in order to encourage miners to validate the contracts that take place on the blockchain more quickly. Each one of Ethereum's blocks holds five ethers, and a set of blocks are expected to be uncovered every nineteen seconds. For bitcoin, that rate is every ten minutes. This allows for speedier transactions and improves the buying or selling of ethers. It also reduces the fees for those buying and selling coins, since there isn't the need to pay up to have a quick result.

The Ethereum Fundamentals

What you'll find as you look further into the ether is that as volatile as bitcoin, ether can be even more so. This is because there's so much potential for the Ethereum blockchain, but as a corporate entity, it also has the potential to become obsolete. This results in a nauseating ride that will pump up sharply when there are new businesses that sign onto the Ethereum blockchain. It could also drop dramatically if those businesses don't conduct the number of transactions as hoped when they signed onto the platform or when other players offering competing services join the market and start to show signs of momentum. You don't want your entire portfolio in the Ethereum space, but you also don't want to ignore the opportunity either.

Ethereum's Rise

While the layman investor will be wowed by bitcoin's height in total value, in many people's eyes, it's actually ether that saw the most remarkable increase in 2017. Since it ICOed in 2015, it's six years younger than bitcoin. At the time, 60 million ethers were released into the market. This meant that it had far less momentum heading into the penultimate year for cryptos and there's a much larger supply. Theoretically, this would suppress large forward movements, since there would be plenty of supply to match the increase in demand. That's not what happened in 2017. Heading into the year, one ether cost $8.30. By the end of the year, that price had risen to $722, resulting in an 8,600 percent increase in price.

But ether's rise comes with significant falls. By the middle of January 2018, ether had surpassed $1,347 only to see it lose 72 percent of its value by early April, as the entire crypto marketplace saw significant losses when investors tried to cash in on their unexpected gains and the exuberance in the market waned.

It's a symbol of cryptos' unique volatility, but also what you can expect from the ether at this point in Ethereum's history. There can be significant highs, but they come with those potential lows.

There's No Coin Limit

Unlike bitcoin, Ethereum didn't set a limit on the number of potential coins that could come onto the market. Bitcoin has a 21-million-coin ceiling (if you don't include its forks) while Ethereum hasn't set such a strict standard. This could potentially mess with the supply side of the coin, especially if too many coins come to market. Since ether launched with an initial coin offering, providing about 60 million ethers to the marketplace, it has added 18 million ethers a year. The code does limit the amount of ether that can be added on a yearly basis, leveling it at that 18 million mark.

However, there's no upside limit, although even Ethereum's cofounder Buterin has argued one should be set.

Transaction Volume Rises

If you were to sync up the transaction volume of Ethereum with the price of the coins, the two graphs would look almost identical. In early 2017, transaction volumes were near 40,000 per day before exploding in usage, surpassing nearly a million transactions by the end of the year. Much of this, though, was due to the increase in speculation surrounding the coin as new crypto users entered the market, hearing that Ethereum had become a crypto darling.

This trend also highlights that ether's price moves more on perceived value than bitcoin. If a large company decides to enter the Ethereum platform—and transactions jump—it could provide hard data to support ether's continued price improvement. But you want that transactional data to serve as an early indicator of price movements, not one that moves hand-in-hand with the price of the coin.

The rise of transactions also speaks to the benefit of becoming a tool for business purposes. As more businesses adopt the platform, however, you'll expect to see greater increases in the size of transaction volume.

Conclusion

I hope you have noticed that in this book, I have not only offered you a simple strategy to start trading in the cryptocurrency market, but we have been building this strategy together, step by step and from scratch. During the different tasks proposed in the book, you have had to put a lot of effort, you have had to do your part, but that makes you really understand how it works. You have understood how the frequency of operations you want to perform will determine the time you dedicate to investing, and this, in turn, will determine a lot the strategy you define. You have also understood the basis of the cryptocurrency market and a key concept right now: its high price variability. This feature offers incredible profit potential but is a double-edged sword: it also increases the risk of loss considerably. That is why we have spent some time talking about risk control tools and techniques and have seen how to use them in a trading strategy.

I hope you have understood the importance of this. You have also learned how to use the most basic and powerful indicators, but most importantly, you have learned how to include them in a trading strategy. There are indicators that give signals more often than others, and this feature is key to using one or the other in your trading strategy. You have understood how to combine different indicators to adjust the entry or exit for a trade. And we have also made a small introduction to the different techniques and tools you will find on your way.

I could have just given you the strategy, but there is much more value in explaining how to build a strategy. Your strategy is alive. First, you must learn to control your emotions, your reptilian brain, and we have designed together a strategy that will allow you to perform enough operations and with a size small enough to learn to control your emotions in record time. Without a goal and an adapted strategy, you would lose a lot of time and money until you reach that point. But now you have these two things. Once you master your emotions and your initial strategy, you can start making modifications, evolving your strategy, but only at that point. Remember that the cryptocurrency market is a young market that is constantly evolving, and in a few years, it may be better to adjust this strategy for a market with less volatility, i.e., a market with less risk and lower profit potential per unit of time. It is also quite possible that you will evolve yourself over time as a trader and investor.

You may find that you want to reduce the number of trades you make per year. When you make changes to your strategy, you will have plenty of data on your files. That's why it's so important and why I've been insisting throughout the book that you keep your lists and notes up to date. Keeping an updated list of projects and pairs is key. You will have your notes on what cycle they are in, whether they are near a cycle change or whether they are near an entry or exit signal. This will allow you to make an analysis of each pair in record time. You will only need a few minutes a day, and depending on the general market situation, you may not need to do anything for many days.

Keeping your trading history well detailed and always with notes and screenshots is also very important. This will allow you to assess and correct errors, but it will also serve as a database for modifying your strategy if you wish to do so in the future. At that time, you will have the tools and knowledge necessary to do so, and you can always revisit this guide if you feel it is appropriate. For that reason, you have made an effort to understand and practice all the tasks in this book. Knowledge and experience are something much more valuable than a strategy.

You have reached the end of this guide. Congratulations! But this is only the end of the first step in your journey to learn how to invest in the cryptocurrency market. Now you must put your knowledge at work, be constant and strict, take notes, and above all, control your emotions at key moments. With what you know now, and only with a little perseverance and discipline, I am sure you will manage to control your reptilian brain, get incredible gains, and most importantly, get to know yourself a little better.

Made in the USA
Monee, IL
25 March 2022

93540830R00384